IFIP Advances in Information and Communication Technology 589

Editor-in-Chief

Kai Rannenberg, Goethe University Frankfurt, Germany

IFIP – The International Federation for Information Processing

IFIP was founded in 1960 under the auspices of UNESCO, following the first World Computer Congress held in Paris the previous year. A federation for societies working in information processing, IFIP's aim is two-fold: to support information processing in the countries of its members and to encourage technology transfer to developing nations. As its mission statement clearly states:

IFIP is the global non-profit federation of societies of ICT professionals that aims at achieving a worldwide professional and socially responsible development and application of information and communication technologies.

IFIP is a non-profit-making organization, run almost solely by 2500 volunteers. It operates through a number of technical committees and working groups, which organize events and publications. IFIP's events range from large international open conferences to working conferences and local seminars.

The flagship event is the IFIP World Computer Congress, at which both invited and contributed papers are presented. Contributed papers are rigorously refereed and the rejection rate is high.

As with the Congress, participation in the open conferences is open to all and papers may be invited or submitted. Again, submitted papers are stringently refereed.

The working conferences are structured differently. They are usually run by a working group and attendance is generally smaller and occasionally by invitation only. Their purpose is to create an atmosphere conducive to innovation and development. Refereeing is also rigorous and papers are subjected to extensive group discussion.

Publications arising from IFIP events vary. The papers presented at the IFIP World Computer Congress and at open conferences are published as conference proceedings, while the results of the working conferences are often published as collections of selected and edited papers.

IFIP distinguishes three types of institutional membership: Country Representative Members, Members at Large, and Associate Members. The type of organization that can apply for membership is a wide variety and includes national or international societies of individual computer scientists/ICT professionals, associations or federations of such societies, government institutions/government related organizations, national or international research institutes or consortia, universities, academies of sciences, companies, national or international associations or federations of companies.

More information about this series at http://www.springer.com/series/6102

Gilbert Peterson · Sujeet Shenoi (Eds.)

Advances in Digital Forensics XVI

16th IFIP WG 11.9 International Conference
New Delhi, India, January 6–8, 2020
Revised Selected Papers

 Springer

Editors
Gilbert Peterson
Department of Electrical
and Computer Engineering
Air Force Institute of Technology
Wright-Patterson AFB, OH, USA

Sujeet Shenoi
Tandy School of Computer Science
University of Tulsa
Tulsa, OK, USA

ISSN 1868-4238   ISSN 1868-422X (electronic)
IFIP Advances in Information and Communication Technology
ISBN 978-3-030-56225-0   ISBN 978-3-030-56223-6 (eBook)
https://doi.org/10.1007/978-3-030-56223-6

This Springer imprint is published by the registered company Springer Nature Switzerland AG
The registered company address is: Gewerbestrasse 11, 6330 Cham, Switzerland

Contents

Contributing Authors

Nikolai Adderley recently received his M.S. degree in Cyber Operations from the Air Force Institute of Technology, Wright-Patterson Air Force Base, Ohio. His research interests include digital forensic analysis and investigation, digital forensic visualization and computer forensic time analysis.

Harald Baier is a Professor of Internet Security at Darmstadt University of Applied Sciences, Darmstadt, Germany; and a Principal Investigator at the National Research Center for Applied Cybersecurity, Darmstadt, Germany. His research interests include digital forensics, network anomaly detection and security protocols.

Naman Banati received a B.Tech. degree in Computer Science and Engineering from Netaji Subhas University of Technology, New Delhi, India. His research interests include security in machine learning applications, image processing and computer vision.

Nitesh Bharadwaj is a Ph.D. student in Computer Science and Engineering at the Defence Institute of Advanced Technology, Pune, India. His research interests include digital forensics and machine learning.

Jin Cao is a Computer Science Researcher at Tianjin University, Tianjin, China. His research interests are in the area of digital forensics.

Jiuming Chen is a Ph.D. student in Cyber Security at the Institute of Information Engineering, Chinese Academy of Sciences, Beijing, China. His research interests include digital forensics, data mining and machine learning.

Yao Chen is an M.S. student in Computer Science at Tianjin University, Tianjin, China. His research interests are in the area of data privacy.

Saheb Chhabra is a Ph.D. student in Computer Science and Engineering at Indraprastha Institute of Information Technology, New Delhi, India. His research interests include image processing and computer vision, and their applications to document fraud detection.

Kam-Pui Chow, Chair, IFIP WG 11.9 on Digital Forensics, is an Associate Professor of Computer Science at the University of Hong Kong, Hong Kong, China. His research interests include information security, digital forensics, live system forensics and digital surveillance.

Thomas Göbel is a Ph.D. student in Computer Science at Darmstadt University of Applied Sciences, Darmstadt, Germany; and a Researcher at the National Research Center for Applied Cybersecurity, Darmstadt, Germany. His research interests include network security, network forensics and anti-forensics.

Mahesh Govil is a Professor of Computer Science and Engineering at Malaviya National Institute of Technology, Jaipur, India; and the Director of National Institute of Technology Sikkim, Ravangla, India. His research interests include real-time systems, parallel and distributed systems, fault-tolerant systems and cloud computing.

Garima Gupta is a Postdoctoral Researcher in Computer Science and Engineering at Indraprastha Institute of Information Technology, New Delhi, India. Her research interests include image processing and computer vision, and their applications to document fraud detection.

Gaurav Gupta, Vice Chair, IFIP WG 11.9 on Digital Forensics, is a Scientist E in the Ministry of Electronics and Information Technology, New Delhi, India. His research interests include mobile device security, digital forensics, web application security, Internet of Things security and security in emerging technologies.

Julien Hachenberger is a Researcher at the Fraunhofer Institute for Secure Information Technology, Darmstadt, Germany. His research focuses on security in the manufacturing industry, especially in the context of Industrie 4.0.

Weiqing Huang is a Professor of Cyber Security at the Institute of Information Engineering, Chinese Academy of Sciences, Beijing, China. His research interests include signal processing theory and technology, electromagnetic acoustic-optic detection and protection, and information security.

Chenggang Jia is a Ph.D. student in Cyber Security at the Institute of Information Engineering, Chinese Academy of Sciences, Beijing, China. His research interests include digital forensics and information security.

Yongheng Jia is an M.S. student in Computer Science at Tianjin University, Tianjin, China. His research interests include malware detection and classification.

Jianguo Jiang is a Professor of Cyber Security at the Institute of Information Engineering, Chinese Academy of Sciences, Beijing, China. His research interests include network security, threat intelligence and data security.

James Jones is an Associate Professor of Digital Forensics at George Mason University, Fairfax, Virginia. His research interests include digital artifact persistence, extraction, analysis and manipulation.

Xiangui Kang is a Professor of Computer Science and Cyber Security in the School of Data and Computer Science at Sun Yat-Sen University, Guangzhou, China. His research interests include information forensics, watermarking, and multimedia communications and security.

Nhien-An Le-Khac is a Lecturer of Computer Science and the Director of the Forensic Computing and Cybercrime Investigation Program at University College Dublin, Dublin, Ireland. His research interests include digital forensics, cyber security and artificial intelligence.

Xiang Li is an M.E. student in Information and Communications Engineering at Hainan University, Haikou, China. His research interests include machine learning, computer vision and image processing.

Yuze Li is an M.S. student in Computer Science at Tianjin University, Tianjin, China. His research interests include digital forensics and deep learning.

Myeong Lim is a Ph.D. student in Information Technology at George Mason University, Fairfax, Virginia. His research interests include digital forensics, big data analysis and drive similarity.

Changwei Liu is a Principal Technology R&D Associate with Accenture in Arlington, Virginia. Her research interests include trustworthy artificial intelligence, cloud security and digital forensics.

Chao Liu is a Professor of Cyber Security at the Institute of Information Engineering, Chinese Academy of Sciences, Beijing, China. His research interests include mobile Internet security and network security evaluation.

Jingcheng Liu is an M.S. student in Computer Science at Tianjin University, Tianjin, China. His research interests include data privacy and intrusion detection.

Michael Losavio is an Assistant Professor of Criminal Justice at the University of Louisville, Louisville, Kentucky. His research interests include legal and social issues related to computing and digital crime.

Yonghao Mai is a Professor of Information Technology at Hubei Police University, Wuhan, China. His research interests include digital forensics, cyber security, data warehousing and data mining.

Maoyu Mao is an M.E. student in Cyber Security at Sun Yat-sen University, Guangzhou, China. Her research interests include audio forensics and machine learning.

Anand Kumar Mishra is a Ph.D. student in Computer Science and Engineering at Malaviya National Institute of Technology, Jaipur, India. His research interests include digital forensics and cyber security, especially related to cloud computing and container technology.

Martin Olivier is a Professor of Computer Science at the University of Pretoria, Pretoria, South Africa. His research focuses on digital forensics – in particular, the science of digital forensics and database forensics.

Gilbert Peterson is a Professor of Computer Science at the Air Force Institute of Technology, Wright-Patterson Air Force Base, Ohio. His research interests include digital forensics, artificial intelligence and statistical machine learning.

Emmanuel Pilli is an Associate Professor and Head of the Department of Computer Science and Engineering at Malaviya National Institute of Technology, Jaipur, India. His research interests include cyber security, digital forensics, cloud computing, big data, blockchains and the Internet of Things.

Thomas Schäfer is a Researcher at the National Research Center for Applied Cybersecurity, Darmstadt, Germany. His research interests include network forensics and automobile forensics.

Upasna Singh is an Assistant Professor of Computer Science and Engineering at the Defence Institute of Advanced Technology, Pune, India. Her research interests include digital forensics, machine learning and social network analysis.

Anoop Singhal is a Senior Computer Scientist and Program Manager in the Computer Security Division at the National Institute of Standards and Technology, Gaithersburg, Maryland. His research interests include network security, network forensics, cloud security and data mining.

Ranul Thantilage is a Ph.D. student in Computer Science at University College Dublin, Dublin, Ireland. His research interests include digital forensics, cyber security and big data analytics.

Jan Türr is an M.Sc. student in Computer Science at Technical University Darmstadt, Darmstadt, Germany. His research interests include digital forensics, network forensics and anti-forensics.

Yichen Wei is a Ph.D. student in Computer Science at the University of Hong Kong, Hong Kong, China. Her research interests include information security, digital forensics and artificial intelligence.

Duminda Wijesekera is a Professor of Computer Science at George Mason University, Fairfax, Virginia. His research interests include systems security, digital forensics and transportation systems.

Wencan Wu is an M.S. student in Computer Science at the University of Hong Kong, Hong Kong, China. His research interests include digital forensics and cyber security.

Liang Xiao is a Professor of Communications Engineering and Cyber Security in the School of Communications Engineering at Xiamen University, Fujian, China. Her research interests include wireless security, privacy protection and wireless communications.

Zhongcheng Xiao is an M.E. student in Software Engineering at Sun Yat-sen University, Guangzhou, China. His research interests include audio forensics and reinforcement learning.

Ken Yau is a Ph.D. student in Computer Science at the University of Hong Kong, Hong Kong, China. His research interests are in the area of digital forensics, with an emphasis on industrial control system forensics.

Siu-Ming Yiu is a Professor of Computer Science at the University of Hong Kong, Hong Kong, China. His research interests include security, cryptography, digital forensics and bioinformatics.

Min Yu is an Assistant Professor of Cyber Security at the Institute of Information Engineering, Chinese Academy of Sciences, Beijing, China. His research interests include malicious document detection, document content security and document security design and evaluation.

Jun Zhang is a Professor of Information Technology at Hubei Police University, Wuhan, China. His research interests include digital forensics, cryptography and cyber security.

Yaping Zhang is an Assistant Professor of Computer Science at Tianjin University, Tianjin, China. His research interests include network security, data mining and digital forensics.

Preface

Digital forensics deals with the acquisition, preservation, examination, analysis and presentation of electronic evidence. Computer networks, cloud computing, smartphones, embedded devices and the Internet of Things have expanded the role of digital forensics beyond traditional computer crime investigations. Practically every crime now involves some aspect of digital evidence; digital forensics provides the techniques and tools to articulate this evidence in legal proceedings. Digital forensics also has myriad intelligence applications; furthermore, it has a vital role in cyber security – investigations of security breaches yield valuable information that can be used to design more secure and resilient systems.

This book, *Advances in Digital Forensics XVI*, is the sixteenth volume in the annual series produced by the IFIP Working Group 11.9 on Digital Forensics, an international community of scientists, engineers and practitioners dedicated to advancing the state of the art of research and practice in digital forensics. The book presents original research results and innovative applications in digital forensics. Also, it highlights some of the major technical and legal issues related to digital evidence and electronic crime investigations.

This volume contains sixteen revised and edited chapters based on papers presented at the Sixteenth IFIP WG 11.9 International Conference on Digital Forensics, held in New Delhi, India on January 6-8, 2020. The papers were refereed by members of IFIP Working Group 11.9 and other internationally-recognized experts in digital forensics. The post-conference manuscripts submitted by the authors were rewritten to accommodate the suggestions provided by the conference attendees. They were subsequently revised by the editors to produce the final chapters published in this volume.

The chapters are organized into seven sections: Themes and Issues, Forensic Techniques, Filesystem Forensics, Cloud Forensics, Social Media Forensics, Multimedia Forensics and Novel Applications. The coverage of topics highlights the richness and vitality of the discipline, and offers promising avenues for future research in digital forensics.

This book is the result of the combined efforts of several individuals. In particular, we thank Gaurav Gupta for his tireless work on behalf of IFIP Working Group 11.9 on Digital Forensics. We also acknowledge the conference sponsors, Cellebrite, Magnet Forensics and Lab Systems, as well as the support provided by the Ministry of Electronics and Information Technology of the Government of India, U.S. National Science Foundation, U.S. National Security Agency and U.S. Secret Service.

GILBERT PETERSON AND SUJEET SHENOI

I

THEMES AND ISSUES

Chapter 1

DIGITAL FORENSICS AND THE BIG DATA DELUGE – SOME CONCERNS BASED ON RAMSEY THEORY

Martin Olivier

Abstract   Constructions of science that slowly change over time are deemed to be the basis of the reliability with which scientific knowledge is regarded. A potential paradigm shift based on big data is looming – many researchers believe that massive volumes of data have enough substance to capture knowledge without the theories needed in earlier epochs. Patterns in big data are deemed to be sufficient to make predictions about the future, as well as about the past as a form of understanding. This chapter uses an argument developed by Calude and Longo [6] to critically examine the belief system of the proponents of data-driven knowledge, especially as it applies to digital forensic science.

From Ramsey theory it follows that, if data is large enough, knowledge is imbued in the domain represented by the data purely based on the size of the data. The chapter concludes that it is generally impossible to distinguish between true domain knowledge and knowledge inferred from spurious patterns that must exist purely as a function of data size. In addition, what is deemed a significant pattern may be refuted by a pattern that has yet to be found. Hence, evidence based on patterns found in big data is tenuous at best. Digital forensics should therefore proceed with caution if it wants to embrace big data and the paradigms that evolve from and around big data.

Keywords: Digital forensic science, big data, Ramsey theory, epistemology

1.   Introduction

"Today, machine learning programs do a pretty good job most of the time, but they don't always work. People don't understand why they work or don't work. If I'm working on a problem and need to understand exactly why an algorithm works, I'm not going to apply machine learning."

                    Barbara Liskov, 2008 A.M. Turing Award Laureate [9]

© IFIP International Federation for Information Processing 2020
Published by Springer Nature Switzerland AG 2020
G. Peterson and S. Shenoi (Eds.): Advances in Digital Forensics XVI, IFIP AICT 589, pp. 3–23, 2020.
https://doi.org/10.1007/978-3-030-56223-6_1

"Deep learning and current AI, if you are really honest, has a lot of limitations. We are very very far from human intelligence, and there are some criticisms that are valid: It can propagate human biases, it's not easy to explain, it doesn't have common sense, it's more on the level of pattern matching than robust semantic understanding."

Jerome Pesenti, Vice President of Artificial Intelligence, Facebook [13]

From ancient times, science has operated on the basis of observation of interesting patterns. Patterns observed in the movement of celestial bodies, interactions between physical objects and even human behavior simplified prediction and, eventually, culminated in scientific understanding.

In 1782, John Smeaton, a British engineer, offered his scientific knowledge of sea currents as evidence in a case involving the silting of the harbor at Wells-next-the-Sea in Norfolk [22]. At that time, evidence relying on, say Newton's work, would have been classified as hearsay evidence unless Newton was called to confirm it – a challenge because Newton passed away in 1727. Since 1782, science and expert witnesses have become entrenched in legal proceedings.

We are currently at another watershed moment in history. With the advent of big data, data science and deep learning, patterns are being uncovered at an increasing rate and are used to predict future events. In forensic science, pressure is increasing to use these technologies to predict the past to provide a scientific basis for finding facts that may be useful in legal proceedings.

Numerous calls have been made to engage intelligent techniques:

"[Artificial Intelligence] in digital forensics ... does have a lot to offer the digital forensics community. In the short term it is likely that it can be immediately effective by the use of more complex pattern recognition and data mining techniques" [16].

"[M]achine learning could play an important role in advancing these [code attribution and automated reverse engineering] research areas" [16].

"Artificial Intelligence (AI) is an area of computer science that has concentrated on pattern recognition and ... we highlighted some of the main themes in AI and their appropriateness for use in a security and digital forensics context" [17].

"AI is the perfect tool to aggregate information from the specifications for cyber security ... This use of AI will lift the burden of classification of these data for the cyber analyst and provide a faster and more effective result for determining who is to blame and how to respond" [23].

However, from Ramsey theory, it is known that any dataset that is large enough will contain a multitude of regular patterns. The patterns stem from the size of the dataset, rather than anything represented by the data; the patterns are guaranteed to exist even in random data. A finding derived from big data may, therefore, have more to do with the size of the data than with the case being litigated. Such spurious patterns could lead to a spurious system of (in)justice.

This chapter follows the logic of a generic argument by Calude and Longo [6] – based on Ramsey theory and ergodic theory – to reflect on the role that big data and related technologies ought to play in forensic science, with a specific focus on digital forensic science.

This chapter also discusses some aspects of patterns and repetitions with specific reference to inferences based on the patterns. This is illustrated using court cases where short patterns played a significant role. The chapter explores the guaranteed presence of (often spurious) patterns in large datasets. Finally, it illustrates the inherent dangers that arise if digital forensic findings are based on inferences from patterns in big data.

2.   Patterns and Repetition

It is all too human to expect chaos in nature and then to interpret a pattern in the chaos as something of special significance. Conversely, many aspects of nature (such as the coming and going of seasons) produce expectations of a regular pattern, and any deviation from the pattern is often deemed significant. In games of chance, some events, such as throwing a pair of dice and getting a double is deemed lucky, and a series of such doubles may be deemed a lucky streak. However, the streak cannot continue for long before one begins to doubt the integrity of the dice. Conversely, one does not expect that the same person will win a lottery on a fairly regular basis – if this were to happen, one would doubt the integrity of the lottery system. In such sequences of events, there are often sequences that would seem normal and sequences that would seem to be anomalous.

On purely statistical grounds, if the probability of encountering some phenomenon is $p = 10^{-6}$, then one would expect to encounter the phenomenon, on average, once in a million inspected cases. If it is the probability of being born with an unusual medical condition, then the usual absence of the condition would in all likelihood be labelled as normal, and when a child is born with the condition, it would be deemed to be abnormal or, in the language used below, an anomaly.

In the examples above, the probabilities of the anomalies can be calculated rather accurately using basic probability theory and encountering them (on average) once in given periods of time or volumes are expected. More regular occurrences would, with very high probabilities, be indicative of anomalies.

However, as the chapter will explain, in a large dataset, data clusters that exhibit certain traits have to occur with mathematical certainty. The sizes and prevalence of the clusters are functions of data size and may be totally unrelated to what the data are purported to represent. It seems natural to denote the more prevalent clusters as normal and the less prevalent clusters as anomalies.

Such differentiation between normality and anomaly is often the basis of intrusion detection in computer networks and it is increasingly being applied in digital forensics. This claim will be substantiated below. However, if the occurrences of normal data and anomalies are due to the size of the data, rather than some justifiable theory, then the distinction between normality and anomaly is very tenuous at best (and would be wrong in many cases). If this is the case, such differences should not serve as the basis of scientific findings in forensic science.

To make matters more concrete, consider a web server request that contains an extremely long URL. Often this is indicative of an attempt to exploit a buffer overflow vulnerability in the server. Normal requests are typically relatively short compared with anomalous requests. In addition, if lengthy requests can be linked to known vulnerabilities in servers, then the odds would increase that they are indeed malicious requests.

Another common pattern in intrusion detection involves a port scan. Methods for hiding port scans often interfere with some of the regular features in typical port scans. A port scan is often an indication of nefarious intention, unless the port scan was performed as part of an official security assessment.

Correlating anomalous events such as unusual web requests and port scans with reported computing incidents may be useful. However, it is important to remember that causality may also work in the other direction, where the incident causes the anomaly. A computer system that has lost connectivity typically makes an unusually large number of attempts to re-establish connectivity. More importantly for the purposes of this chapter, anomalous patterns may be entirely unrelated to incidents to which they apparently correlate and deriving any significance from the patterns would be incorrect. Making this case convincingly has to be postponed. Understanding the belief in patterns begins at a much simpler point – where a small correlation is just too significant to ignore.

2.1   Small Correlations

Unexpected patterns are often deemed significant even in small data-sets. To the best of this author's knowledge, the interpretation of patterns in a cyber-related court case has not led to significant scrutiny of the presented evidence. Therefore, a well-known and widely discussed matter is used to reflect on the use of patterns as evidence in court.

Consider the infamous, now discredited, Meadow's law, which is based on patterns: "One sudden infant death is a tragedy, two is suspicious and three is murder, until proved otherwise" [15].

Meadow's law formed the basis of expert evidence in a number of cases. Arguably, the most prominent case was Regina v. Sally Clark [10]. Sally Clark's first son, Charles, died in December 1996, aged 11 weeks. The pathologist found that the death was due to natural causes.

Sally Clark's second son, Harry, died in January 1998, aged 8 weeks. The pathologist ruled Harry's death to be unnatural and revised his finding about Charles, whose death he also deemed to be unnatural.

Sir Samuel Roy Meadow (of Meadow's law fame) was an expert witness in the ensuing murder trial. His evidence was based on the law carrying his name, although the law was not mentioned explicitly during his testimony.

Sally Clark was found guilty and sentenced to life. However, she was released from jail in 2003 after a successful second appeal [11].

The pattern played a major role in Sally Clark's conviction and in the failure of her first appeal [10]. The judgment in the second appeal provides interesting insights into how the pattern was construed by the prosecution and jurors. This is discussed in more detail below.

2.2   Patterns and/or Knowledge

The previous paragraph illustrates that a potentially strong belief may be formed even when a very short pattern is considered. Court arguments turned on many facets of the Sally Clark case and the notion of probability was deemed of minor importance; rather, medical knowledge was deemed paramount in the original trial and in both appeals.

In contrast, machine learning, especially in the context of big data, has tended to ignore underlying knowledge and focus on patterns. Langley [14] describes the development as follows: "During the 1990s, a number of factors led to decreased interest in the role of knowledge. One was the growing use of statistical and pattern recognition approaches, which improved performance but which did not produce knowledge in any generally recognized form."

During earlier periods of artificial intelligence, underlying knowledge about problem domains was significant. Knowledge representation was at the core of expert systems and domain-specific heuristics improved the speed of machine learning. However, as machine learning developed, the focus shifted to an "increasing reliance on experimental evaluation that revolved around performance metrics [which] meant there was no evolutionary pressure to study knowledge-generating mechanisms" [14].

In a similar vein, Anderson [1] published an article in *Wired* with the provocative title borrowed from an earlier claim by a George Box – *The end of theory: The data deluge makes the scientific method obsolete.* In this article, Anderson declares:

> *"Out with every theory of human behavior, from linguistics to sociology. Forget taxonomy, ontology and psychology. Who knows why people do what they do? The point is they do it, and we can track and measure it with unprecedented fidelity. With enough data, the numbers speak for themselves."*

2.3 Big Data

Big data has been a concern in the context of digital forensics ever since it emerged as an academic discipline [2]. Some of the earliest concerns were about finding the proverbial needles in haystacks as the sizes of the haystacks increased [18]. Dramatic increases in the amount of storage associated with computers have made comprehensive forensic imaging very difficult. The emergence of the cloud has only exacerbated the problem.

However, in parallel with these concerns, a new field of study developed under the big data rubric. The principle underlying this field is that the universe and aspects of it behave according to some patterns. If enough data is available, the analysis of the data can reveal the patterns. Once the patterns are known, behavior becomes predictable. This knowledge can be monetized or other benefits may be derived from it. Meanwhile, the name of the field has changed over time – data mining, data analytics, data science. Machine learning and deep learning are closely associated with the field. This chapter uses the term big data unless specific differentiation is required.

Given the popularity of big data, it was only natural that researchers would posit the use of big data methods in digital forensics.

3. What Constitutes Correlation?

The Sally Clark case illustrates pattern recognition and correlation in a small dataset.

In the second appeal [11], the court pointed out that the previous courts (erroneously) accepted that the deaths of her two children were related (or correlated) on the following grounds (quoted verbatim):

(i) *Christopher and Harry were about the same age at death namely 11 weeks and 8 weeks.*

(ii) *They were both discovered unconscious by Mrs. Clark in the bedroom, allegedly both in a bouncy chair.*

(iii) *Both were found at about 9.30 in the evening, shortly after having taken a successful feed.*

(iv) *Mrs. Clark had been alone with each child when he was discovered lifeless.*

(v) *In each case Mr. Clark was either away or about to go away from home in connection with his work.*

(vi) *In each case there was evidence consistent with previous abuse.*

(vii) *In each case there was evidence consistent with recently inflicted deliberate injury.*

The appeal ruling considered each of these points systematically and rejected every point. It should be noted that these points were raised by the prosecution rather than the expert witnesses, and the court was, in principle, equipped to deal with such arguments. However, the incorrect reasoning in the original trial and the first appeal was only rectified by the second appeal [11].

In contrast, when an expert witness uses such methods, the court is ill equipped to deal with them, unless they are rebutted by other experts. The closest that any expert witness came to including anything similar in expert testimony was Meadow's testimony on the rarity of two infant deaths in one family. Meadow cited from a work that the prevalence of Sudden Infant Death Syndrome (SIDS) was one in 8,543 cases. Some claim that Meadow obtained this incidence from a 1995 article in *Lancet* [3]. Hence, with the probability p of a SIDS case estimated to be $p = \frac{1}{8543}$, Meadow determined the probability of repeated cases by multiplying the estimated probability p by the number of cases, assuming that the occurrences of SIDS were independent.

In the Sally Clark case, Meadow concluded that the probability of two SIDS deaths would be p^2 – or about one in 73 million. He proceeded to illustrate the rarity of two SIDS deaths using a sports betting analogy. Although the judge downplayed the importance of this number in his instructions to the jury, its effect arguably stuck. Of course, two deaths

in a family may not be independent – they may have been due to the
genetic makeup of the children – and hence, squaring the probability
(without showing independence) was incorrect. This was one of the
issues raised in a press release by the Royal Statistical Society [21] after
the denial of the first appeal [10].

The second aspect raised by the Royal Statistical Society [21] was the
emphasis on the small probability of a specific outcome. The probability
of SIDS is indeed small, but so is the probability (or relative prevalence)
of parents murdering multiple children. One cannot focus on the small
probability of a sequence of events S and proceed to conclude that another unlikely sequence of events B is the logical inference.

As a second example, consider the case of Australian, Kathleen Folbigg. Four of her children died very young: the first in 1989 at age
19 days, the second in 1991 at eight months, the third in 1993 at ten
months and the fourth in 1999 at 19 months. While experts used the
same calculations as Meadow during pretrial hearings, by the time Folbigg's trial started in March 2003, the British Court of Appeals had
already discredited Meadow's law and calculations.

Meadow's law was excluded by the court, but his ideas nevertheless
featured during the trial. A Professor Berry testified that "[t]he sudden and unexpected death of three children in the same family without
evidence of a natural cause is extraordinary. I am unable to rule out
that Caleb, Patrick, Sarah and possibly Laura Folbigg were suffocated
by the person who found them lifeless, and I believe that it is probable
that this was the case." On the other hand, a Professor Herdson deemed
the events to be too different to correspond to a pattern in which SIDS
deaths would occur, and used the absence of a specific pattern (amongst
others) to be indicative of unnatural causes of death.

In the Sally Clark and Kathleen Folbigg cases other evidence was in-
fluential in the eventual findings of the various courts. In fact, this other
evidence was eventually more important than the presence or absence of
patterns.

In the Sally Clark case, microbiological test results for Harry were
not available to the defense and were only discovered by them after
the first appeal. The second appellate court found that the availability
of these results, along with expert testimony, could have impacted the
jury's decision and concluded that the guilty verdict was unsafe. On
its own, the guilty verdict regarding Christopher's death was unsafe.
The prosecution did not apply for a re-trial and the convictions were set
aside.

In the Kathleen Folbigg case, diaries that she maintained played a
significant role in the proceedings and the outcome of the trial. Public

interest eventually led to a judicial inquiry by Reginald Blanch, former Chief Judge of the New South Wales District Court, who reviewed the case and heard new evidence. In his July 2019 report, Reginald Blanch concluded that "the Inquiry does not cause me to have any reasonable doubt as to the guilt of Kathleen Megan Folbigg for the offences of which she was convicted. Indeed, as indicated, the evidence which has emerged at the Inquiry, particularly her own explanations and behavior in respect of her diaries, makes her guilt of these offences even more certain." In addition, "there is no reasonable doubt as to any matter that may have affected the nature or severity of Ms. Folbigg's sentence" [4].

4.   Correlation in Big Data

Many papers express concern about or reject the notion that data can speak for itself without the need for a theory. One only has to look through the many papers that cite Anderson's claim [1] to find such critiques.

Calude and Longo [6] make a critique that should be taken seriously in digital forensics. They "prove that very large databases have to contain arbitrary correlations. These correlations appear only due to the size, not the nature, of data. They can be found in 'random' generated, large enough databases, which ... implies that *most correlations are spurious*" [emphasis by Calude and Longo].

Calude and Longo use a number of theorems from Ramsey theory and ergodic theory that are relevant in the current context. This chapter only focuses on the final claim made by Calude and Longo that is based on Ramsey theory, but a different exposition is provided.

5.   Ramsey Theory

Ramsey theory studies the number of objects that should be present in a collection for order to emerge. Perhaps the best-known example involves a scenario where people attend a party. Any two people at the party will either have met previously or be mutual strangers. If colors are used to represent the relationships between pairs of people, the case where they have previously met may be represented by the color green while the case where they are mutual strangers may be represented by the color red.

The fundamental question in Ramsey theory is: What is the minimum number of people who need to be at the party to have at least c cases of the same color (or, stated differently, to have c monochromatic cases).

If, for example, c is chosen to be one, it is easy to show that $n = 2$. Specifically, the relationship between two attendees a and b can be represented graphically as an edge between vertices a and b; the edge is green if they know each other and red if they are mutual strangers.

Furthermore, if $c = 2$ then $n = 3$. Specifically, attendees a, b and c can be depicted graphically as a triangle with vertices a, b and c, and edges (a, b), (a, c) and (b, c) whose colors represent the relationships. Since there are two colors (red and green) and three edges, at least two edges must have the same color.

The notation $R(s, t)$ is used to depict the so-called Ramsey numbers. $R(s, t)$ is the minimum number of objects in a set such that some relationship holds among at least s members of the set, or does not hold among at least t members of the set.

As illustrated by the party problem, it is natural to think about Ramsey theory in terms of graphs. In graph theory, a complete graph is one where every vertex is connected to every other vertex. For n vertices, the corresponding complete graph is denoted by K_n. A clique is a subgraph that is complete – where all the vertices are connected. In this context, the task is to color a complete graph using two colors. One color (say green) is used to color an edge if the relationship holds between the vertices connected by the edge; the other color (say red) is used to color an edge if the relationship does not hold between the two connected vertices. Then, the Ramsey number $R(s, t)$ is the smallest n such that graph K_n must either contain a clique of s (or larger) with green edges or a clique of size t (or larger) with red edges. Note that, instead of saying that a subgraph consists of, say, green edges, it is more appropriate to say that a subgraph is induced by red edges. The former term is used here for reasons of simplicity.

In general, the binary relationship used above – that some relationship holds or does not hold – is too restrictive. It is useful to talk about any set of relationships that form a partition of the possible relationships that may hold between the vertices. If the vertices represent events that occurred in a computer system under investigation, then the time between the events may for some reason be deemed to be a possibly relevant relationship. As an arbitrary example, events that occurred hours apart, minutes apart and seconds (or less) apart form such a partition – assuming a definition of time exists for events that occurred multiple times. Obviously, a more precise notion of the informal concepts of hours, minutes and seconds would also be required.

A cautionary note is required at this stage. The Ramsey theory introduced here (following the exposition by Calude and Longo [6]) is based on undirected graphs, where the relationships between objects or events are symmetric. An appropriate example is the time between events. However, the question of whether an event preceded another event, coincided with it or followed it is asymmetric and is, therefore, not covered by the current discussion. In any case, the exclusion of asymmetric relationships is not material in this chapter.

5.1   Finite Ramsey Theorem

In 1930, Ramsey [20] proved the following theorem that is the foundation of the theory carrying his name:

> *Given any r, n and μ, we can find an m_0 such that, if $m \geq m_0$ and the r-combinations of any Γ_m are divided in any manner into μ mutually exclusive classes C_i ($i = 1, 2, \ldots, \mu$), then Γ_m must contain a sub-class Δ_n such that all the r-combinations of members of Δ_n belong to the same C_i."*

An r-combination is a set of r elements that occur in a dataset. If the dataset contains the values $\{a, b, c, d\}$, then the 3-combinations present are: $\{a, b, c\}$, $\{a, b, d\}$, $\{a, c, d\}$ and $\{b, c, d\}$. Every 3-combination is assigned to one of μ classes (or colors, as used previously).

An analogy with the training phase of supervised machine learning can provide insights into the theorem. In supervised learning, a number of inputs are provided to a classifier along with the class associated with the inputs. Let r inputs be used for each instance to be classified and let every instance be assigned to one of the μ classes. Let n be some number that is chosen. Then, using only μ and n, a number m_0 can be determined such that any selection of m_0 instances in the training data will have at least n instances that belong to the same class. Note that this analogy says nothing about the learning that may occur. It merely says that having at least n instances of the same class in the training data is unavoidable.

More formally, what the Finite Ramsey theorem does predict (and guarantee) is that there is some (finite) number m_0 such that after classifying m_0 of the r-combinations, n of the r-combinations will have been assigned to one of the classes. The theorem says nothing about the first class that will reach this n threshold. It just says that the threshold will have been reached. The point m_0 at which a class is guaranteed to reach the n threshold can sometimes be calculated precisely. Upper bounds can be determined for cases where it cannot (yet) be calculated precisely.

The fact that a certain relationship between members of some set holds relatively often in a dataset may be of interest in unravelling an incident. Ramsey's theorem warns us to proceed with care. However, it seems much more likely that an activity of interest in a digital forensic investigation would consist of several actions that together constitute an anomalous (or otherwise useful) indication of what transpired (or is otherwise useful).

For example, in a case involving network communications, a message may be deemed to be significant in terms of the hosts involved in sending the message and the ports used. Hence, tuples consisting of these four values may be deemed useful and classified in some manner. Whether these values would be sufficient (or even relevant) cannot be answered without more context.

As a more concrete example, consider the problem of authorship attribution, which often uses contiguous sequences of linguistic elements called n-grams. These elements may be letters, words, word pairs, phonemes or other entities that experimentally turn out to be useful. In a 2018 authorship attribution competition [12], "n-grams were the most popular type of features to represent texts in" one of the primary tasks in the competition. "More specifically, character and word n-grams [were] used by the majority of the participants."

Although the Finite Ramsey theorem does not play a significant role in the remainder of this chapter, it sets the stage for the Van der Waerden theorem of 1927, which is part of Ramsey theory. Once again, the logic of Calude and Longo [6] is employed.

5.2   Van der Waerden's Theorem

The Finite Ramsey theorem provides a threshold beyond which a certain number of relationships among the members of a set is guaranteed. In contrast, Van der Waerden's theorem considers regular occurrences of some value in a sequence of values. It provides a threshold for the length of the sequence. Once the sequence is as long as or longer than the computed threshold, it is mathematically guaranteed that some value will occur regularly at least k times in the sequence for any given k. Formally, Van der Waerden's theorem states that the repeated value will appear in an arithmetic progression. More informally, these k (or more) identical values will have the same number of values separating them. This pattern is referred to as a periodic pattern, in the sense that, once the pattern starts, every p^{th} value in the sequence is the same for at least k occurrences. The threshold (or minimum sequence length) from which point the repetitions are guaranteed is known as the Van der Waerden number. The Van der Waerden number depends only on two values: (i) number of distinct values that occur in the sequence; and (ii) number of repetitions k that are desired. The sequence may correspond to a series of process states, where a process is in the ready queue (R), executing

(E), blocked (B), suspended (S) or terminating (T). Its execution history may correspond to the process sequence:

R E B R E S E T

where the process states are listed using the first letters of their names.

In this example, the alphabet has five values. To have a guaranteed periodic repetition that repeats, say $k = 100$ times, it is only needed to determine the Van der Waerden value for an alphabet of size five and a pattern of length 100.

Again using concepts from graph theory, the alphabet can be a set of colors and, rather than talking about the size of the alphabet, it is more convenient to simply refer to the number of colors in the sequence. Of course, the colors may represent relationships between elements of some set (as it did in the Ramsey theory above). The sequence to which Van der Waerden's theorem is used may, in the case of digital forensics, be the sequence of changes in relationships between entities deemed to be of interest in an examination.

The Van der Waerden number for $k = 3$ repetitions based on two colors is 9. Assume that the two colors are red (R) and green (G). Then, it is possible to construct a sequence of eight colors that have no periodic repetition of length $k = 3$.

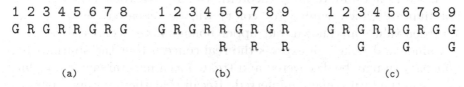

(a)   (b)   (c)

Figure 1. Van der Waerden example.

Consider the string in Figure 1(a) where the positions of the colors R and G are indicated above each color. The sequence has no periodic repetitions.

To extend the sequence, the next item in the sequence has to be R or G. Since the Van der Waerden number is 9, a repeating pattern is guaranteed. If R is added, R occurs at positions 5, 7 and 9, as shown in Figure 1(b). In the language used above, from position 5 onwards, every second color is R and this is true for $k = 3$. In contrast, if G is added as the ninth color, the G occurs in positions 3, 6 and 9. Every third character (starting at position 3) is G and it repeats $k = 3$ times as shown in Figure 1(c).

An important aspect of Van der Waerden's theorem is illustrated by the example above. Specifically, the theorem does not predict which value will recur and it does not predict the distance between the recurring values. However, it guarantees that a periodic pattern of the required length will be present in the sequence.

To present the work using more formal notation, assume that each member of a sequence of integers $\{1, 2, 3, \ldots, N\}$ is mapped to one of a finite number of colors c. Given a number k, a value w exists such that the numbers $\{1, 2, 3, \ldots, w\}$ contain at least k integers of the same color that are equidistant from each other.

Let Σ be an alphabet with c symbols. Let $s_1 s_2 s_3 \ldots s_n$ be a string on Σ. Then, for any value k, a value w exists such that the same symbol would be repeated at least k times at equidistant positions in the string. Stated differently, for any string of length w, there would be values j and p such that:

$$s_j = s_{j+p} = s_{j+2p} = \cdots = s_{j+(k-1)p}$$

The smallest number for which every string produced has at least k periodic repetitions given an alphabet of size c is the Van der Waerden number, which is denoted as $W(c, k)$. The value of $W(2, 3)$ is used to demonstrate the concept. It is easy to show that $W(2, 3) > 8$ because it is simple to produce a string using two symbols such that the same symbol does not occur at equidistant positions.

As with the Finite Ramsey theorem, Van der Waerden's theorem does not indicate which symbol (or color) will be repeated. Few Van der Waerden values are known, but upper bounds have been established.

Calude and Longo [6] express the real concern that the spurious regular pattern may be discovered and treated as a natural law from which events in the future may be inferred. Recall that the minimum length k of the regular pattern can be determined arbitrarily and that any machine learning application that needs k inputs for learning and testing, will learn the pattern and make highly accurate predictions within the repeated pattern. Forensics may indeed use such a law, but often data analysis in digital forensics is retrospective.

Consider a case where an incident occurs at time t. An investigator would collect as much data as possible leading up to the incident. Assume that data is available from time t_0. From the Van der Waerden theorem it is known that some regular pattern of at least length k exists in the data, with the value k limited only by the size of the available data.

A viable approach is to search the data for anomalies by working from time t backwards until an anomaly has been found or no anomaly is found if the start of the data has been reached. Assume that the search for an anomaly stops at time $t' < t$ without excluding the possibility that $t' = t_0$. Also, assume that the repeating pattern occurs from time t_a to time t_b. Note that this does not suggest that all the available data should be sorted according to time; however, in many cases, data about events would have an associated time or, at least, be ordered relatively.

At this point, it is instructive to consider strategies for visualizing the data. The options include: (i) data may be sorted as one long (linear) sequence of events; (ii) data from various logs may be placed in parallel lines so that the times of the various recorded events line up; (iii) data may be sorted according to event type (whether in one long line or in parallel lines); (iv) data may be subdivided into more lines with one line per user on whose authority the event occurs; (v) data may be stratified per node and/or per instance when multiprocessors or cloud computing are used; or (vi) data may be ordered in some other way. Patterns may occur on a given time line, across time lines at some specific time or involve various time lines in some systematic manner. None of these matters as far as the conclusion is concerned. However, thinking about such cases may make it simpler for a digital forensic practitioner to intuitively accept that a pattern may indeed be discovered. Van der Waerden' theorem guarantees that a pattern will be present.

Given the ever increasing size of available data, it is possible to assume that in the general case that warrants a thorough investigation, sufficient data will be available to guarantee a pattern of length k, where k exceeds the maximum sequences typically used in machine learning. In any case, if a longer k is required, more data would be needed and the availability of this data would not be a problem. In days gone by, logs were destroyed because storage space was limited, but storage capacities have increased significantly while storage costs have decreased, eliminating the need to delete logged data. Moreover, the growth of big data has disincentivized data deletion merely because the data is old.

5.3 Logic of Inference

Suppose a spurious pattern is discovered – a pattern for which no causal reason exists.

As a temporal example, assume that evidence is available from time t_0 up to time t_1. Assume that the incident occurred at time t with $t_0 \leq t \leq t_1$.

In order to simplify the discussion, two brackets are used to indicate a recurring pattern. A square bracket indicates that the pattern started at exactly the time written before or after it whereas a round bracket indicates that some time has elapsed. Thus, $t_0[)t$ would indicate that the recurring pattern was present at the time of the available evidence was collected, but stopped some time before the incident. Similarly, $t[)t_1$ would indicate that the pattern started exactly when the incident occurred, but did not continue until the end of the period during which the evidence was collected. The notation remains readable without expressly mentioning t_0 and t_1, so the simplified expression of when the incident occurred will be used. Of course, if the incident occurred repeatedly, the exposition would become more complex, but a single occurrence will suffice for the current discussion.

Any pattern that coincides with the incident would likely be deemed significant. Hence, $(]t, t[)$ and $t[]$ are likely to be seen as traces of cause or effect, with $(]$ possibly seen as causal traces and $t[)$ and $t[]$ seen as traces of effect. Note that such cause and effect interpretations would most probably be wrong, but would appear to be rather convincing. Similarly, a pattern that covers the incident (t) may incorrectly be seen as traces of some enabling condition.

More generally, the investigator may observe the pattern and attempt to determine why the pattern disappeared (or began in the first place) in the hope that it might shed light on the case. If machine learning is deployed on the dataset, it may learn from the pattern what is deemed to be normal and flag subsequent values as anomalies.

The discussion above assumed that a spurious pattern was discovered and used for analysis. However, the starting point of the discussion was that the pattern was spurious. Therefore, by definition, it is useless in the analysis of the case.

One possible defense for the use of patterns is that they may be useful as starting points to search for causality. As noted in this chapter, this is indeed true – many laws of nature were first observed as patterns and later understood in causal terms. However, the underlying question in the current scenario is whether the search for patterns is, at least, useful as a mechanism to reduce the search space for causality.

The short answer is that there are too many patterns in a big dataset. Finding all the patterns and testing them for significance would be too time consuming.

For a more formal discussion, assume that the relationships between data points are expressed as colors. Neither the arity of the relationships nor the number of possible categories (or colors) into which the relationships can be classified are important in the current discussion. They merely have an effect on whether there is enough data to enable the application of Van der Waerden's theorem. While a more precise calculation is possible for a specific case, the assumption is that the big data context implies that sufficient data is available.

To be more concrete, assume that a bag of colored relationships emerges and that the elements of the bag are arranged in a sequence S. The sequence is the result of the pre-processing mentioned earlier. It may be a temporal sequence of events with information of little significance eliminated or some other mechanism would be used to arrange the relationships.

Assume that a pattern of length n is deemed significant, where the value of n may depend on the machine learning technique to be used or any some other prerequisite for significance. Let s be the number of elements in a sequence. Let w_n be the Van der Waerden number that guarantees a pattern of length n. As implied earlier, it is assumed that $s \geq W_n$ in the context of big data.

Before continuing, it is important to reflect on the classification of a specific collection of data points into a particular class (or, in the language of graph theory, a particular color that it shares with other collections of data points). Some classifications are straightforward. For example, in the TCP/IP networking context, the expected port ranges for requests or responses, directions of requests or responses, and many other attributes can be classified as normal or anomalous without much debate. However, the question whether this particular classification scheme would be useful (or lead to the best possible evidence) is far from clear. In the big scheme of things, it is known that the corpora from which machine learning occurs often encode irrational categories. See, for example, recent papers that illustrate how racism may be – and has been – learned through artificial intelligence [5, 8, 19]. Indeed, confusion between patterns in criminal behavior and patterns of criminal behavior is just one example that may impact corpora used to characterize crime.

The point is that classifications of training sets often engage irrational assumptions that are propagated when machines learn the biases as factually correct or the machines do not disclose the biases (e.g., biased accuracy) in their classifications. For the purposes of this work, it is sufficient to note that a different classification of relationships between data points would yield a different sequence S' of relationships, which may contain one or more patterns that differ from the patterns observed in S.

From a pessimistic perspective, it is possible that up to s of the classifications made in the sequence S may be incorrect. If r colors are used, then it is possible to arrive at r^s colorings of a sequence of length s, of which the specific colored sequence S is just one of the sequences. Since $s \geq w_n$, each r^s would have a periodic pattern of at least length n, which would make the pattern significant. While it should be possible to discard the bulk of these r^s colorings as nonsensical, demonstrating that they are all nonsensical would be a mammoth task.

It also possible that a single incorrect classification rule could lead to a pattern that would not have existed. In addition, a pattern depends on the order of the relationships and other pre-processing tasks that are often based on the intuition of the individual who mines a large dataset. If the pattern discovered in S is incriminating evidence, how does the investigator show that a somewhat different – and possibly more accurate – classification of relationships would not have led to the discovery of an equally convincing pattern that may be exculpatory evidence? The converse outcome, where incriminating evidence is overlooked and an exculpatory pattern found – based on a tiny misclassification – is equally serious.

In the context of evidence, the potential existence of meaningful patterns in s^r datasets, where s is already a large number, is sufficient to cast doubt on any pattern found. Unlike the small datasets considered earlier, the sheer number of possible patterns precludes the exploration of each pattern as an alternative and keeping or excluding it. Any finding based on such a pattern should be approached with caution – it is far too easy for the opposing counsel to cast doubt on the conclusions. The obvious exception is when a theoretical basis from forensic science exists that can speak to the significance of specific patterns. However, such patterns should be searched for in cases where they would be of help, rather than be discovered via a process such as data mining.

6.   Conclusions

The increasing volumes of data that pertain to criminal and civil matters is a well-known challenge facing investigators. However, big data techniques thrive on large volumes of data and learning from such data is touted as a viable solution for many problems, even when the problems are not fully understood.

This chapter has used the same logic as Calude and Longo to explore the impact of data size on what may be discovered in the data. Ramsey theory and, more specifically, Van der Waerden's theorem demonstrate that spurious patterns are mathematically guaranteed to exist in large enough datasets. This implies that a discovered pattern may be spurious – in other words, it may be a function of the size of the data instead of the content that the data purportedly represents. The discovery of a pattern does not exclude the discovery of other patterns that may contradict what was inferred from a discovered pattern. And, of course, it is computationally infeasible to find all the patterns in big data.

If forensic conclusions are based on a pattern that has been found, the opposing side has a simple rebuttal for any such conclusion – How does the investigator know that a meaningful pattern has been examined? Without being able to justify the conclusion, there is no way to distinguish between a meaningless result derived from a spurious pattern and a correct, but unreliable, result derived from a meaningful pattern.

Digital forensic practitioners and researchers would be well advised to avoid calls to jump on the big data bandwagon and wantonly use its technologies until the findings can be shown to yield evidence that is compatible with the requirements of presenting the truth, the whole truth, and nothing but the truth, which, by definition, must be free from bias.

References

[1] C. Anderson, The end of theory: The data deluge makes the scientific method obsolete, *Wired*, June 23, 2008.

[2] N. Beebe, Digital forensic research: The good, the bad and the unaddressed, in *Advances in Digital Forensics V*, G. Peterson and S. Shenoi (Eds.), Springer, Heidelberg, Germany, pp. 17–36, 2009.

[3] P. Blair, P. Fleming, D. Bensley, I. Smith, C. Bacon and E. Taylor, Plastic mattresses and sudden infant death syndrome, *Lancet*, vol. 345(8951), p. 720, 1995.

[4] R. Blanch, Report of the Inquiry into the Convictions of Kathleen Megan Folbigg, State of New South Wales, Parramatta, Australia (www.folbigginquiry.justice.nsw.gov.au/Documents/Report%20of%20the%20Inquiry%20into%20the%20convictions%20of%20Kathleen%20Megan%20Folbigg.pdf), 2019.

[5] J. Buolamwini and T. Gebru, Gender shades: Intersectional accuracy disparities in commercial gender classification, *Proceedings of Machine Learning Research*, vol. 81, pp. 77–91, 2018.

[6] C. Calude and G. Longo, The deluge of spurious correlations in big data, *Foundations of Science*, vol. 22(3), pp. 595–612, 2017.

[7] J. Clemens, Automatic classification of object code using machine learning, *Digital Investigation*, vol. 14(S1), pp. S156–S162, 2015.

[8] K. Crawford and T. Paglen, Excavating AI: The Politics of Training Sets for Machine Learning, *Excavating AI* (www.excavating.ai), September 19, 2019.

[9] S. D'Agostino, The architect of modern algorithms, *Quanta Magazine*, November 20, 2019.

[10] England and Wales Court of Appeal (Criminal Division), Regina v. Sally Clark, EWCA Crim 54, Case No: 1999/07495/Y3, Royal Courts of Justice, London, United Kingdom, October 2, 2000.

[11] England and Wales Court of Appeal (Criminal Division), Regina v. Sally Clark, EWCA Crim 1020, Case No. 2002/03824/Y3, Royal Courts of Justice, London, United Kingdom, April 11, 2003.

[12] M. Kestemont, M. Tschuggnall, E. Stamatatos, W. Daelemans, G. Specht and B. Potthast, Overview of the author identification task at PAN-2018: Cross-domain authorship attribution and style change detection, in *Working Notes of CLEF 2018 – Conference and Labs of the Evaluation Forum*, L. Cappellato, N. Ferro, J. Nie and L. Soulier (Eds.), Volume 2125, CEUR-WS.org, RWTH Aachen University, Aachen, Germany, 2018.

[13] W. Knight, Facebook's head of AI says the field will soon "hit the wall," *Wired*, December 4, 2019.

[14] P. Langley, The changing science of machine learning, *Machine Learning*, vol. 82(3), pp. 275–279, 2011.

[15] R. Meadow, Fatal abuse and smothering, in *ABC of Child Abuse*, R. Meadow (Ed.), BMJ Publishing Group, London, United Kingdom, pp. 27–29,1997.

[16] F. Mitchell, The use of artificial intelligence in digital forensics: An introduction, *Digital Evidence and Electronic Signature Law Review*, vol. 7, pp. 35–41, 2010.

[17] F. Mitchell, An overview of artificial intelligence based pattern matching in a security and digital forensic context, in *Cyberpatterns*, C. Blackwell and H. Zhu (Eds.), Springer, Cham, Switzerland, pp. 215–222, 2014.

[18] M. Pollitt and A. Whitledge, Exploring big haystacks, in *Advances in Digital Forensics II*, M. Olivier and S. Shenoi (Eds.), Springer, Boston, Massachusetts, pp. 67–76, 2006.

[19] I. Raji and J. Buolamwini, Actionable auditing: Investigating the impact of publicly naming biased performance results of commercial AI products, *Proceedings of the AAAI/ACM Conference on AI, Ethics and Society*, pp. 429–435, 2019.

[20] F. Ramsey, On a problem of formal logic, *Proceedings of the London Mathematical Society*, vol. s2-30(1), pp. 264–286, 1930.

[21] Royal Statistical Society, Royal Statistical Society concerned by issues raised in Sally Clark case, News Release, London, United Kingdom, October 23, 2001.

[22] J. Smeaton, *Reports of the Late John Smeaton, F.R.S., Made on Various Occasions, in the Course of his Employment as a Civil Engineer, Volume II*, Longman, London, United Kingdom, 1812.

[23] J. Wulff, Artificial intelligence and law enforcement, *Australasian Policing*, vol. 10(1), pp. 16–23, 2018.

Chapter 2

IDENTITY AND SUFFICIENCY OF DIGITAL EVIDENCE

Michael Losavio

Abstract   Digital evidence proffered by prosecutors is subject to the same standards as all other evidence. However, a major concern is that the novelty of digital evidence may lead to less rigor in its application. This chapter discusses issues related to identity and sufficiency of digital evidence, including the need for authenticity and reliability, and concerns about identification via digital evidence.

Keywords: Digital evidence, identification, authentication, hearsay

1.   Introduction

The identification of the responsible party is a core issue in all criminal investigations and prosecutions, including the pursuit of computer and online misconduct. Indeed, the identification of the person who committed the offense is an essential element that the government must establish beyond a reasonable doubt (United States v. Alexander [7]). However, this may be especially challenging for computer and online misconduct because evidence used for identification is often circumstantial or indirect rather than direct (e.g., I saw him do it).

By contrast, in many cases, digital evidence may be used in support of warrants for the search and seizure of direct evidence to establish the identity of the offender. A canonical example is digital contraband such as child pornography. Information about network usage for contraband downloads, such as an IP address, is deemed sufficient for a search warrant of the physical space associated with the IP address. Finding such contraband on a person's device supports an adjudicative finding that identifies the person as the offender with knowing possession of the contraband.

© IFIP International Federation for Information Processing 2020
Published by Springer Nature Switzerland AG 2020
G. Peterson and S. Shenoi (Eds.): Advances in Digital Forensics XVI, IFIP AICT 589, pp. 25–36, 2020.
https://doi.org/10.1007/978-3-030-56223-6_2

But the use of such evidence to establish identification may become attenuated with other forms of computer and network activity, especially misconduct beyond the possession of digital contraband. This may increase the risk of the incorrect identification of an innocent person as the offender.

Often, other evidence may be necessary to establish linkage to the identity of the offender. One example is the use of closed-circuit television camera recordings of device access that link a person physically to the site of activity; this additional evidence can be crucial. However, when only trace identification of a defendant is found or little direct evidence identifies the culprit, the government must prove by additional, sufficient probative facts to infer a culpable rather than accidental connection.

This chapter discusses issues related to identity and sufficiency of digital evidence, including the need for authenticity and reliability, and concerns about identification via digital evidence to prove guilt.

2.   Background

This section discusses the legal foundation for identification using digital evidence. It reviews jurisprudence related to circumstantial or indirect evidence obtained via traditional – non-digital – forensics. The extrapolation is key to developing best practices for the growing body of digital evidence.

In United States v. Jordan [14], the court listed additional and substantial evidence linking the defendant to artifacts of the crime where no direct witness evidence identified him. The indirect evidence included the debit card linked to the account used in the offense, a receipt for the money order used to open the account, a cell phone containing the fraudulent message and a gift card used to pay for the telephone number on the distributed fraudulent documents.

In Mikes v. Bork [10], the court found that, with only fingerprints linking a defendant to a crime, the government must show a further connection that establishes guilt.

These cases imply that in similar scenarios involving computer or online misconduct, where direct witness identification is not possible, the identification of the culprit may be proven by inferential and circumstantial evidence [16, 17]. Network traces of activity are like fingerprints, remnants of activity that may indicate a connection without defining the depth of the connection.

The comment on fingerprint-only cases in Mikes v. Bork [10] is instructive. Often, a profile of electronic data may be assembled to create a functional equivalent of the fingerprint, but this still requires attention to sufficient inferential and circumstantial evidence to make a conclusion of guilt beyond a reasonable doubt. When a defendant has been convicted primarily on the basis of digital evidence, there was additional circumstantial evidence beyond coincident account usage or the use of the defendant's name to connect the defendant to the crime (see, e.g., United States v. Ray [13], United States v. Gonzalez [18] and United States v. Jordan [14]).

For example, in United States v. Ray [13], an email message containing contraband was connected to the defendant by additional evidence in the email, such as pictures of his children, and testimony regarding his access and control of the relevant computer services. In United States v. Gonzalez [18], the defendant engaged in health care fraud and aggravated identity theft via online billing of health insurance companies. Extensive circumstantial text messaging evidence relating to the fraud ultimately established the connection to Gonzalez.

3. Sufficient Evidence of the Act

In United States v. Fraser [11], the U.S. Federal Court of Appeals (Sixth Circuit) discussed proper attribution regarding conduct under Federal Rule of Evidence 404(b) [24]. It did so in the context of other acts such as writings (like metadata) that contain particular facts from which attribution may be inferred.

The parties argued in this case that the other act – a book that the defendant wrote – was not some sort of previous scam, but the act of writing about the scam. Specifically, the defendant did not argue that the trial court should have determined whether he had previously committed the scam described in his book *The Birth of a Criminal*. Moreover, there was no indication that the evidence was admitted for the purpose of showing that he had actually committed the scam in the past.

The trial court made the proper preliminary determination that the defendant wrote *The Birth of a Criminal*. The court noted that the book had the picture of the defendant on the cover, listed him as the author, had a copyright date of 2002, an ISBN of 2972571302 listed on `Amazon.com` and was published by Gutter Publications. The book was further authenticated by the publisher's website, which listed the defendant as the founder of *Gutter Magazine*. The trial court thus, with detailed findings, properly determined as a preliminary matter that the defendant wrote the book.

Proof of *modus operandi* may be used to demonstrate identity, such as permitting signature evidence when identity was "the largest single issue" in the case [12], yet excluding evidence because proof of a *modus operandi* is only relevant when there is an issue regarding the defendant's identity [22]. Together these offer a profile of the types of evidence of computer and network activity that may meet the threshold of sufficient evidence to establish offender identity. A prosecution may mix and match different evidentiary facts to establish who perpetrated a crime, even when direct evidence of the identity of the offender is absent.

4.   Digital Identity Case Study

This section discusses a case study involving the application of evidentiary facts in an electronic fraud prosecution.

4.1   Electronic Fraud Case

A lucrative area of criminal activity is bank and credit card fraud. Electronic banking and e-commerce systems often rely on the reduction of identification to alphanumeric strings that are easily copied or forged. The growth in two-factor authentication helps reduce such misconduct, but the continued reliance on a reduced identifier set assures that these systems will be targets of criminal activity.

One criminal case involved multiple acts of bank and credit card fraud [23]. Online applications for loans, drawdowns of loan funds and credit card and debit card use were conducted using online electronic identification. A related series of acts relating to bank fraud and unauthorized access to automated teller machines (ATMs) included the coincidence of ATM access transactions with photographs maintained by the devices with timestamps of transactions. The configurations of the ATM systems with cameras provided direct time-stamped photographic evidence that identified the culprit. However, beyond the ATM transactions with photographs, there was no other evidence to correlate or identify who was using the debit card for the other transactions and was conducting fraudulent online loan applications and withdrawal actions.

To remedy the gap, the prosecution offered evidence from a senior bank fraud analyst of an online loan application made using a name, date of birth and social security number of a putative relative as the contact and a contact email. The bank fraud analyst recommended denial of the loan application because the date of issuance of the social security number was long before the date of birth of the applicant. However, the analyst acknowledged that he could not tell from the application who was sitting at the computer when it was made.

To continue to frame the identification, another bank officer, who knew one of the victims as she worked to resolve his complaints, testified to handling an online loan application for $15,000 in the victim's name. She also testified to calling the telephone number on the application in order to speak with the fraud victim:

```
"A young gentleman answered the phone."

"He said 'hold on a second' and came back.
It was the same person I asked to talk to Mr. Victim-1 before."

"So I proceeded with the conversation.
I said, 'Victim-1?' and he said 'Yes.'"

"This is a bank officer calling.
I see that you have applied for a $15,000 premier loan with us.
It is approved so I just want to see when you want to come in
and close the loan."

Q. "What did the person on the other end say?"
A. "The person said, 'I'll be in tomorrow.'"

"I said, 'Okay. Come in with your ID.
You'll need to come into the branch and sign.'"

"At that point the person said, 'I have to come to the branch?'"

"I said, 'Yes. You have to bring your ID.
I have to enter it into the computer.'"

"He said, 'Okay. I'll be there tomorrow.'"

Q. "Did the person ever show up?"
A. "No."

Q. "Did the loan ever close?"
A. "No."
```

Additional evidence relating to these indirect actions came from another bank officer, who acknowledged an account note on the compromised joint checking account that said "Victim-1 has verified for [the defendant] to cash checks to $500. Please contact Victim-1 with any questions and ID [the defendant]."

Nevertheless, upon considering all the circumstantial factors relating to misconduct, the identification of the wrongdoer in this case was deemed sufficient by the court (United States v. Vance [21]).

4.2   Fraud Case Analysis

The criminal charging document (indictment) asserted that the defendant used the social security number of another person as the means of identification. The trial court found that the defendant used Victim-1's social security number as a means of identification to open a bank account.

Victim-1 testified that he did not give the defendant permission to use his social security number to open the account. The trial court asserted that the defendant, when using Victim-1's social security number to open the checking account and submit an online loan application in his own name with Victim-1's social security number, was attempting to commit bank fraud.

However, there was little to no evidence to support the finding that defendant had used Victim-1's social security number. The transactions were done in an anonymous manner with insufficient direct connection to the defendant. Indeed, the analysis of the trial court that supported the identification of the defendant as the offender would appear to have gaps.

Despite the fact that no direct evidence connected the defendant to the bank application, the trial court found "sufficient circumstantial evidence that [the defendant] had made the loan application."

Although the business records from the bank and the cable records, which were submitted a few days after the bench trial concluded, and although the records showed that the loan application was submitted from an IP address registered to [another person] and not the defendant, the court concluded there was sufficient circumstantial evidence that it was the defendant, as opposed to someone else, who submitted the loan application using Victim-1's social security number.

Significantly, as it relates to the charge, neither the defendant nor any other defense witness admitted to applying for a loan at the bank in the defendant's name with Victim-1's social security number. In fact, it would have been very odd for someone else to do this.

In effect, the trial court found that, although the IP address used for the fraudulent transactions belonged to someone other than the defendant and there was no direct evidence associating the defendant with the transactions, it is significant and relevant to the defendant's guilt that no one else admitted to the crime. This would appear to violate the basic tenets of a criminal prosecution where the state must prove guilt instead of a defendant having to prove innocence.

The trial court maintained that there was certainly circumstantial evidence from which the court could conclude that the defendant committed the offense of attempted bank fraud when he requested a loan in his own name using someone else's social security number. By using Victim-1's social security number, the defendant was certainly aware that, perhaps, if he had used his own social security number, he would have been unable to obtain the loan because his credit score was not high enough or he could have been denied the loan for some other reason.

Ultimately, the court found that the defendant did attempt to commit bank fraud and that he used some other person's identification during and in relation to the attempted bank fraud. The court concluded that the prosecution had submitted sufficient evidence beyond a reasonable doubt and, therefore, the defendant was found guilty.

In the pursuit of justice, the challenge is to collect and present sufficient evidence to establish guilt or, conversely, show innocence. Beyond this is the reliability of the evidence and the result – avoiding the false positive of convicting an innocent person or the false negative of acquitting a guilty party.

4.3 Sufficiency for Identification

Is there support for the trial court's factual findings about the online identity of the offender? That someone else did not confess to the offense or even that evidence did not point to anyone else do not support that the defendant committed the offense. Given the identity problems with online activities, it is just as likely that the defendant's means of identification – his name – was misappropriated by others. This fundamental failure to sufficiently establish that the defendant committed the act establishes that he should not have been convicted of the crime.

Issues of identity in an online context are significant, leading to the need for greater evidence of real identity in all online contexts using a variety of tools [2]. There was little or no evidence to support the finding that the defendant himself had used Victim-1's social security number. It was all done in an anonymous manner online with insufficient connection to the defendant. There was little or nothing that connected the defendant to the bank application. There was no authentication of the information connecting the name on the application to the real defendant according to Federal Rule of Evidence 901 [27], which requires authentication through proof that an item of evidence is what it is claimed to be.

An identification standard like this does not simply set a low bar on identification, it opens identification to error and manipulation. This case study suggests how false trails of evidence could be created to lead to innocent parties. Unfortunately, many motives are present for such seemingly pointless malice. Harassment, often of a former spouse or significant other, would be a prime beneficiary of this standard of identification proof without connection. That a jury may decide beyond a reasonable doubt is not sufficient protection. U.S. law states that a judge must dismiss if no rational trier of fact could find proof beyond a reasonable doubt [28]. This is critical as online criminality continues to grow. Indeed, it is essential that adequate evidence be established to convict the guilty and protect the innocent.

5.   Authentication and Hearsay Issues

Authentication is a foundational issue for any evidence, digital or otherwise, that establishes identity. To authenticate a fact in evidence is to demonstrate that it is what it is claimed to be. A digital artifact from social media with a defendant's name and photograph must have sufficient facts to authenticate the printout with the name and photograph. In the United States, this is covered by Federal Rule of Evidence 901(a) [8]. For example, evidence of website postings has been held to be insufficiently authenticated when the party offering the evidence failed to show that the sponsoring organization of the website actually posted the statements instead of a third party [9].

The hearsay rule relates to reliability and testability. According to Federal Rule of Evidence 801(c) [25], hearsay is "a statement that: (i) the declarant does not make while testifying at the current trial or hearing; and (ii) a party offers in evidence to prove the truth of the matter asserted in the statement." A U.S. federal court [15] has held that video purporting to demonstrate proper medical procedures was a "statement" offered for the "truth of the matter asserted" under Federal Rule of Evidence 801 [25] and, thus, its admission was impermissible hearsay (error harmless). In a related discussion about the reliability of online artifacts and their authentication as ancient documents per Federal Rule of Evidence 803(16) [26], which assumes age brings reliability, the United States Judicial Committee on Rules of Practice and Procedure noted that "[c]ommittee members unanimously agreed that Rule 803(16) was problematic, as it was based on the false premise that authenticity of a document means that the assertions in the document are reliable – this is patently not the case."

In another case [19], social media postings of pictures of a defendant with a gun, guns and marijuana were out-or-court "statements" that the defendant illegally possessed a firearm as well as drugs, guns and money. This is a multiple hearsay issue because the photographs are statements in themselves that are restated by their posting on Facebook for viewing, restated again by their printouts and restated yet again to the jury. In this case, no foundation was made about the form of the statements or that the statements were made by the defendant. The jury ultimately found that the photographs constituted evidence of the defendant's offense because their admission materially impacted the outcome of the prosecution to prove guilt.

6.   Identification in Online Environments

The challenges to identification using computer and network activity are serious and they may lead to erroneous findings. The errors cut towards the conviction of the innocent as well as the exoneration of the guilty. These are unjust and damaging to the credibility of identification, undermining its utility even as online misconduct grows. It creates an expanded tool for serious and disruptive crimes against all people through the use of forged information and "fake news." The harm from such online misinformation includes harassment, reputation damage and information fraud. Commercial services such as Reputation Defender [4] have been created to alleviate this problem.

In 2008, then vice-presidential candidate Sarah Palin was targeted by online impersonators who sent people to her home for a barbecue [29]. Online impersonation has led to the enactment of criminal prohibitions against online harassment through impersonation [6].

As digital forensics leverages artificial intelligence, machine learning and data mining, more challenges will arise that must be addressed before the innocent are hurt. The Los Angeles Police Department has suspended the use of predictive policing tools due to inconsistent implementation [5]. A law enforcement technology vendor recently empaneled experts to review the use of artificial intelligence for policing, only to have the panel advise against any implementation using available technologies [1]. An algorithm-driven, robo-adjudication, anti-fraud system was found to produce erroneous decisions in more than 80% of fraud determinations before it was suspended, albeit after causing financial damage to many people [20]. Each of these presents questions of accuracy, reliability and justice. Each of these offers significant, if not essential, support for public safety in this online era.

Failure to address the potential problems posed by advanced technologies will undermine law enforcement activities as well as public safety. Strong steps must be taken or the future may well be dystopian [3].

7.   Conclusions

The identification of online criminals has been a troublesome issue over the entire lifetime of digital forensics. Increased online criminal activity, whether domestic or transnational, exacerbates the challenges to identifying the true entities responsible for crimes. The allure of simple, alphanumeric authentication and identification for online transactions has contributed to the explosion of cyber crime. Nevertheless, the need to prosecute criminals should not weaken the resolve to ensure that the right persons are held responsible for their crimes. It is imperative that protocols are created for the accurate identification and authentication of online misconduct and online miscreants.

References

[1] Axon AI and Policing Technology Ethics Board, First Report of the Axon AI and Policing Technology Ethics Board, Axon, Scottsdale, Arizona, 2019.

[2] J. Blue, J. Condell, T. Lunney and E. Furey, Bayesian-chain: Intelligent identity authentication, *Proceedings of the Twenty-Ninth Irish Signals and Systems Conference*, 2018.

[3] T. Maughan, *Infinite Detail*, Farrar, Straus and Giroux, New York, 2019.

[4] Reputation Defender, About Reputation Defender, Redwood City, California (www.reputationdefender.com/about), 2020.

[5] M. Smith, Review of Selected Los Angeles Police Department Data-Driven Policing Strategies, BPC #19-0072, Office of the Inspector General, Los Angeles Police Commission, Los Angeles, California (www.lapdpolicecom.lacity.org/031219/BPC_19-0072.pdf), 2019.

[6] State of Texas, Texas Penal Code §33.07. Online impersonation, Austin, Texas (codes.findlaw.com/tx/penal-code/penal-sect-33-07.html), 2020.

[7] United States Court of Appeals (Ninth Circuit), United States v. Alexander, *Federal Reporter, Third Series*, vol. 48, pp. 1477–1484, 1995.

[8] United States Court of Appeals (Second Circuit), United States v. Vayner, *Federal Reporter, Third Series*, vol. 769, pp. 125–131, 2014.

[9] United States Court of Appeals (Seventh Circuit), United States v. Jackson, *Federal Reporter, Third Series*, vol. 208, pp. 633–637, 2000.

[10] United States Court of Appeals (Sixth Circuit), Mikes v. Bork, *Federal Reporter, Second Series*, vol. 947, pp. 353–361, 1991.

[11] United States Court of Appeals (Sixth Circuit), United States v. Fraser, *Federal Reporter, Third Series*, vol. 448, pp. 833–842, 2006.

[12] United States Court of Appeals (Sixth Circuit), United States v. Perry, *Federal Reporter, Third Series*, vol. 438, pp. 642–652, 2006.

[13] United States Court of Appeals (Sixth Circuit), United States v. Ray, *Federal Appendix*, vol. 189, pp. 436, 449–450, 2006.

[14] United States Court of Appeals (Sixth Circuit), United States v. Jordan, *Federal Reporter, Third Series*, vol. 544, pp. 656–671, 2008.

[15] United States Court of Appeals (Sixth Circuit), United States v. Martinez, *Federal Reporter, Third Series*, vol. 588, pp. 301–317, 2009.

[16] United States Court of Appeals (Sixth Circuit), United States v. Boyd, *Federal Appendix*, vol. 447, pp. 684–690, 2011.

[17] United States Court of Appeals (Sixth Circuit), United States v. Davis, *Federal Appendix*, vol. 531, pp. 601–607, 2013.

[18] United States Court of Appeals (Sixth Circuit), United States v. Gonzalez, *Federal Appendix*, vol. 560, pp. 554–559, 2014.

[19] United States Court of Appeals (Sixth Circuit), United States v. Farrad, *Federal Reporter, Third Series*, vol. 895, pp. 859, 875–880, 2018.

[20] United States Court of Appeals (Sixth Circuit), Cahoo et al. v. SAS Analytics Inc. et al., *Federal Reporter, Third Series*, vol. 912, pp. 887–897, 2019.

[21] United States Court of Appeals (Sixth Circuit), United States v. Vance, No. 19-5160, Decided and Filed, April 17, 2020.

[22] United States Court of Appeals (Tenth Circuit), Chavez v. City of Albuquerque, *Federal Reporter, Third Series*, vol. 402, pp. 1039–1046, 2005.

[23] United States District Court (Eastern District of Kentucky), United States v. Vance, Transcript of Trial, Case No. 18-CR-10, R. 72, Ewald, Transcript of Trial, 9/5/2018, pp 48–49, 2018.

[24] United States Government, Rule 404. Character evidence; crimes or other acts, Federal Rules of Evidence, Washington, DC (www.law.cornell.edu/rules/fre/rule_404), 2020.

[25] United States Government, Rule 801. Definitions that apply to this article; exclusions from hearsay, Federal Rules of Evidence, Washington, DC (www.law.cornell.edu/rules/fre/rule_801), 2020.

[26] United States Government, Rule 803. Exceptions to the rule against hearsay, Federal Rules of Evidence, Washington, DC (`www.law.cornell.edu/rules/fre/rule_803`), 2020.

[27] United States Government, Rule 901. Authenticating or identifying evidence, Federal Rules of Evidence, Washington, DC (`www.law.cornell.edu/rules/fre/rule_901`), 2020.

[28] United States Supreme Court, Jackson v. Virginia, *U.S. Supreme Court*, vol. 443, pp. 307–339, 1979.

[29] J. Velasco, Four Case Studies in Fraud: Social Media and Identity Theft, *Socialnomics Blog* (`socialnomics.net/2016/01/13/4-case-studies-in-fraud-social-media-and-identity-theft`), January 13, 2016.

II

FORENSIC TECHNIQUES

Chapter 3

INTERACTIVE TEMPORAL DIGITAL FORENSIC EVENT ANALYSIS

Nikolai Adderley and Gilbert Peterson

Abstract   Current digital forensic tools and applications lack the capability to visually present high-level system events and their associated low-level traces in a user interpretable form. This chapter describes the Temporal Analysis Integration Management Application (TAIMA), an interactive graphical user interface that renders graph-based information visualizations for digital forensic event reconstruction. By leveraging correlation and abstraction as core functions, TAIMA reduces the manual, labor-intensive efforts needed to conduct timeline analyses during digital forensic examinations. A pilot usability study conducted to evaluate TAIMA supports the claim that correlation and abstraction of low-level events into high-level system events can enhance digital forensic examinations.

Keywords: Automated event reconstruction, information visualization

1.   Introduction

The discipline of digital forensics has been under constant pressure as advancements in digital device technology outpace the technical capabilities of digital forensic tools and applications [20]. Exacerbating the issue is the increased use of computers in the commission of crimes [10]. Continuous increases in the amount of heterogeneous data involved in investigations have made digital forensic analyses complex and time-consuming.

Current digital forensic analysis applications are primarily trace-based and force practitioners to rely on manual, labor-intensive practices for performing correlations and reconstructing events [18, 20]. As a result, it is difficult to establish a holistic understanding of an entire system

© IFIP International Federation for Information Processing 2020
Published by Springer Nature Switzerland AG 2020
G. Peterson and S. Shenoi (Eds.): Advances in Digital Forensics XVI, IFIP AICT 589, pp. 39–55, 2020.
https://doi.org/10.1007/978-3-030-56223-6_3

image and to identify patterns and anomalies in a reasonable amount of time.

Information visualization (InfoVis) and abstraction leverage human perceptual and intellectual capabilities to reduce forensic practitioner workload and analysis time [23]. Specifically, information visualization takes advantage of human visual and analytical capabilities to explore data; data exploration is conducted using visual displays that offer flexible data encodings in perceptually effective environments [8]. Abstraction reduces the amount of data displayed to users and minimizes the adverse effects of text-based information overload [19, 22]. Studies that combine information visualization and abstraction reveal that digital forensic practitioners appreciate displays that minimize the number of items for review, but still present relevant information [9].

This chapter describes the Temporal Analysis Integration Management Application (TAIMA), a proof-of-concept information visualization application that enhances digital forensic investigations with an emphasis on the analysis phase of the digital forensic process. TAIMA leverages temporal system event reconstruction and information visualization to enrich a graphical timeline with discrete high-level system events. The information visualization component enables a practitioner to adjust the focus from a case-wide overview to a detailed view of low-level traces. The detailed view enables the practitioner to confirm the accuracy of reconstruction.

A usability study of TAIMA was conducted in which digital forensic practitioners completed a simulated digital forensic analysis task. During the study, all the participants were able to locate all the evidence items. The post-task survey results reveal that all the participants found TAIMA to be intuitive and easy to learn. Additionally, the participants felt that the visualization was effective at helping them complete their tasks. The results demonstrate the power of correlation and abstraction in supporting timeline analyses.

2.   Related Work

Timeline analysis of digital system events helps identify when events occurred and the order in which they occurred. Timestamp data from multiple data sources (e.g., registry files, event logs, link files and prefetch files) help clarify the temporal proximity of system traces, test investigative hypotheses and identify additional system traces of interest that would have been overlooked without timeline examination [11].

Despite the critical role that timelines play in forensic investigations, most industry-standard digital forensic applications merely focus on data

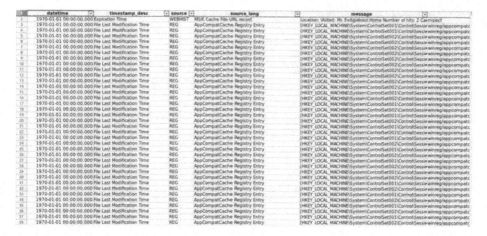

Figure 1. `log2timeline` CSV output.

collection. After importing artifacts into their applications, practitioners are left with vast amounts of low-level traces. The majority of industry applications either have limited capabilities for generating timelines or entirely lack the capabilities [3]. The applications that do generate timelines often provide static timelines or histograms, or simply export digital artifacts as comma-separated value (CSV) reports (Figure 1).

For example, Encase (version 8.07) [7] generates a calendar timeline with individual artifacts represented as dots on the calendar (Figure 2). Forensic Toolkit (FTK) [1] generates a histogram timeline (Figure 3).

Previous work in digital forensic visualization has highlighted the difficulty in handling the vast amounts of extracted data involved in timeline analyses [19]. Carbone and Bean [3] describe the lack of intuitive GUIs and integrated timelines when dealing with large heterogeneous datasets. Without careful planning, visualizations quickly become overwhelming; the overcrowded displays cause information overloads. Gudjonsson [6] notes that practitioners often struggle to complete forensic analyses using timelines that are overcrowded and stresses the importance of reducing the amount of reviewed data to facilitate timeline analyses.

Olsson and Boldt [18] demonstrate the advantages of using the Cyber-Forensics TimeLab (CFTL) graphical timeline tool over Forensic Toolkit (FTK); the post questionnaire from their study reveals that participants solved a hypothetical case "significantly faster using CFTL than when using FTK." Teelink and Erbacher [23] demonstrate that visualization techniques assist practitioners in the forensic data analysis process. The two studies combined interactive capabilities with visualization tools. The combination resulted in practitioners experiencing improvements

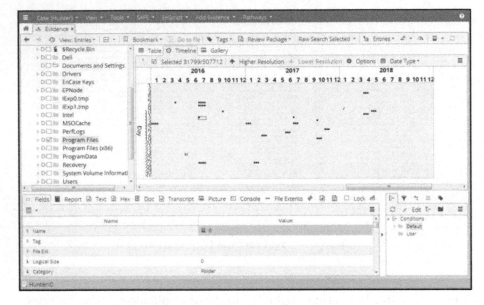

Figure 2.   Encase timeline view.

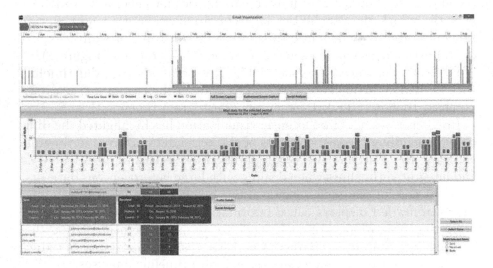

Figure 3.   Forensic Toolkit timeline view.

in the digital forensic process and reductions in the time required to identify suspicious files.

As a visualization tool, TAIMA enhances digital forensic examinations by providing practitioners with an interactive environment integrated with visual representations of digital evidence. The interactive capabilities and visualizations enabled practitioners to answer all the investigative questions posed in a user evaluation study.

3. TAIMA

TAIMA displays digital evidence on a graph-based timeline to enhance forensic analyses and facilitate event reconstruction. The primary purpose of TAIMA is to provide an overview of the types of system events that exist on a media image. TAIMA's intuitive GUI precludes users from having to learn a programming language or use a command line interface.

At the core of TAIMA is the rendering of a graph-based timeline that overcomes the effects of information overload. Using only a date/time range as a search parameter, a practitioner is able to identify suspicious files and events without labor-intensive manual exploration, or any plugins or code. TAIMA displays high-level system events on a single screen along with the locations of the traces that are related to the high-level events.

User accessibility was a core function goal during the TAIMA design phase. The application was intended to be used by technical as well as non-technical practitioners. Industry tools that provide extensive features and capabilities can be overwhelming. For example, Encase is not user friendly enough for non-technical practitioners. TAIMA, which is backed by the Neo4j graph-based database, provides non-technical users with the ability to issue database queries using only date/time ranges; no programming skills or additional plugins are required.

3.1 Design Principles

The development strategy for TAIMA followed Shneiderman's interactive GUI design principles [22]. Shneiderman proposed a user-centered GUI design guide model that supports the use of information visualization in digital forensic applications. He stresses the importance of providing a modern information visualization GUI that supports the processing of large volumes of heterogeneous data.

The TAIMA development process also followed the Visual Information Seeking Mantra (overview first, zoom and filter, details on demand) [19]. The mantra specifies information visualization design techniques and interactive controls for presenting data in an organized and intuitive manner that enables easy traversal. To fulfill the mantra requirements, TAIMA first presents an overview of all the high-level system events in a time-span as discrete color-coded tiles on a timeline. The graph-based timeline display enables a practitioner to view the temporal proximity

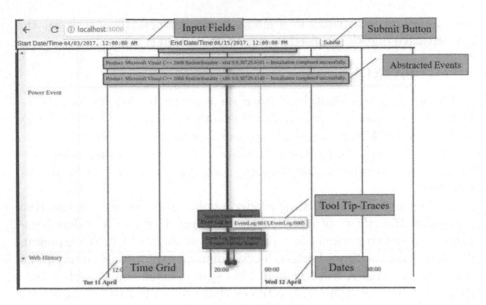

Figure 4.   TAIMA GUI.

of system events quickly and also provides an easy way to identify (at a glance on a single screen) clusters of system events. Moreover, the practitioner can adjust the point-of-view by zooming in on a timeline to adjust the scale for detailed views of specific time intervals.

TAIMA was designed to minimize the effects of large, complex (heterogeneous) data volumes on the digital forensic investigation process, especially during the analysis phase. Accordingly, TAIMA was built using the GRANDstack (GraphQL, React, Apollo, Neo4j Database) architecture. GRANDstack is an ecosystem of software applications that are used to create full-stack web and mobile GUIs [5]. The integration of the applications allows for a scalable JavaScript web application backed by a Neo4j database [16]. An important advantage of the GRANDstack ecosystem is its provision of a modern web browser, which reduces the TAIMA learning time.

3.2   GUI Timeline

Graph-based digital forensic timelines mitigate many of the challenges encountered when attempting to analyze vast volumes of data [4, 8, 18].

Figure 4 shows the principal TAIMA GUI interactions. The user is presented with the React GUI front-end to enter a time interval of interest (start time and end time). Clicking the submit button sends a GraphQL query via the GraphQL service with the timestamps as search parameters to the Neo4j database. GraphQL is a query language that enables developers to specify schema definitions to express the data to be requested from a datastore. The Apollo client integrates with GraphQL to process and route data requests to the Neo4j database [2]. The GraphQL server implements the logic for querying the modeled Neo4j database (via the addition of abstraction nodes) to search for high-level events based on their temporal attributes. After fetching the data, the Apollo client sends the results to the GraphQL server. The React GUI integration with the Apollo client is configured to store the results of the query within a React component to render the visualization. The database query results are automatically converted to graphical form and presented to the user on a graph-based timeline.

The TAIMA information visualization timeline component shown in Figure 4 displays discrete high-level system events chronologically. The graph-based timeline enables a practitioner to identify patterns and anomalies during data analysis while providing an overview that facilitates the overall understanding of system events.

Figure 4 also shows the various parts of a timeline: input fields, submit button, high-level events, traces via a tooltip, time grid and dates. The tooltip dialog box satisfies the "details on demand" interactive GUI requirement specified by Shneiderman [22]. This requirement enables a practitioner to view additional information about events by placing the mouse pointer over the event tile. A text-box displays the trace artifacts responsible for the event.

The visualization in Figure 4 shows four abstracted events. These include two program installation events (blue titles), denoted by "Installation Completed Successfully." Additionally, there are two power events (purple titles), denoted by "System Uptime Report/Event Log Service Started." The temporal proximity of the four high-level system events suggests that the system of interest was restarted due to the installation of Microsoft Visual C++ 2008 on 11 April 2017 at approximately 8PM local system time.

Figure 5 shows an overview of the activities on the timeline for the time interval 03 April 2017 12:00 AM to 15 June 2017 12:00 PM. Note that various programs (EXEs) were executed on the system of interest on 3 April 2017 and 11 April 2017.

3.3   Abstraction Technique

The abstraction technique implemented by TAIMA leverages the graph database generated via property graph event reconstruction (PGER) [21]. This technique extracts temporal traces from a media image and imports

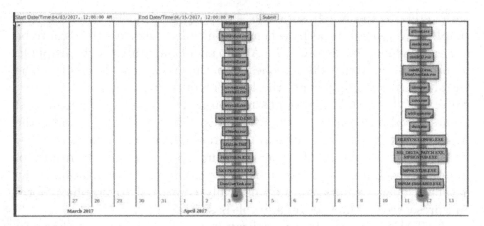

Figure 5. TAIMA global view.

them into a native labeled property graph that stores system events as nodes linked via cause-effect relationships. The links enable the temporal traces to be rapidly correlated and abstracted into a single narrative.

As a proof-of-concept tool, TAIMA supports five high-level abstraction system events: (i) program installation; (ii) power (startup/shutdown); (iii) program execution; (iv) file download; and (v) web history. The overall logic for creating abstraction events and relationships involves searching a time window for the declared low-level events. The time window is subsequently searched for related events. If the declared low-level events are found in the time window, then a high-level system event abstraction node is created; this creates a link. Multiple trace matching enforces the credibility of the high-level system event abstraction event. In addition to creating relationships, the low-level traces are used to enrich the abstracted event.

Program Installation. The Cypher query shown in Figure 6 creates a program installation abstraction node that is a relational correlation of four low-level traces associated with the particular program installation event.

Lines 1 through 5 of the Cypher query find all the action and object nodes associated with the event log entries that occurred within a ten-second window. Line 6 filters the object nodes down to three event log entries: (i) MsiInstaller/11707; (ii) MsiInstaller/1042; and (iii) MsiInstaller/1033. In Lines 7 through 8, the COLLECT command aggregates the action and object nodes based on time, and the DISTINCT commands filter the list to include only unique timestamps. This eliminates having multiple entries for a given timestamp; only unique timestamps

```
1    MATCH (:parser {parserName: "eventLog"}) <-[:PARSER] -
     (act:action)-[:EFFECTS]->(event:object)
2    MATCH (act)-[:AT_TIME]->(sec:Second)
3    MATCH p = (sec)-[:NEXT *10]->()
4    WITH p, event
5    UNWIND nodes(p) AS secNodes
6    MATCH (secNodes)<-[:AT_TIME]-(act:action)--(obj2:object)
7    WHERE obj2.filename IN ["MsiInstaller/1107",
     "MsiInstaller/1042", "MsiInstaller/1033"]
8    WITH act.timestamp as timestamp, COLLECT(DISTINCT
     act.message) as messages, COLLECT(DISTINCT obj2.filename)
     as filenames, COLLECT(DISTINCT act) as acts
9    CREATE (a:Abstraction{Event: 'Program Installation',
     Trigger:filenames, Description:messages, timestamp:timestamp})
10   FOREACH (act in acts | MERGE (act)-
     [:LVL1_ABSTRACTION_LINK]->(a))
     FOREACH (set in obj2s | MERGE (set)-
     [:LVL1_ABSTRACTION_LINK]->(a))
```

Figure 6. Program installation query.

are tracked. Line 9 creates the abstraction nodes. Finally, Line 10, creates a relationship (LVL1_ABSTRACTION_LINK) to the action (red) and object (blue) nodes associated with the program installation.

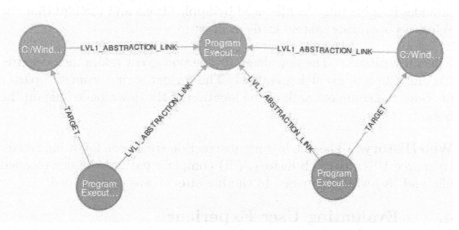

Figure 7. Program installation abstraction node linked to four traces.

Figure 7 shows a graph representation of the query result. The center node is the abstraction node, which is connected to four low-level nodes. High-level system events (i.e., center nodes) are only created

and added to the graph model if the criteria imposed by expert rules
are satisfied. The event logs, MsiInstaller/11707, MsiInstaller/1042 and
MsiInstaller/1033, constitute evidence that a program installation event
occurred. New relationships (e.g., LVL1_ABSTRACTION_LINK) are
added to the abstraction node to correlate the low-level traces connected
to the program installation event. Aggregating low-level events and linking them to higher-level events reduce the amount of data presented to
the practitioner and also increases the efficiency of the application (i.e.,
lower computational cost).

Power. Power events (shutdown, startup and sleep) are established
by tracking the start and stop of the Windows Customer Experience
Improvement (CEI) and Windows Event logs. The combination of these
two traces is a strong indicator of power events. EventLog/6013 logs
the total system running time after system boot-up. EventLog/6005
generates a log entry message that the Windows Event Log service was
started.

Program Execution. The program execution abstraction is based
on identifying prefetch file artifacts. The prefetch file, which is created
every time an application is executed on a Windows system, contains
information about the files associated with the application. Windows
uses the prefetch information to reduce and optimize the loading time of
the application during subsequent executions. Analyzing prefetch files
provides insights into the files used by applications and the files that the
Windows operating system loads at startup.

File Download. The download abstraction event nodes include Firefox and Chrome event log entries. The format string from the parser
provides the complete path of the location of the downloaded file on the
host.

Web History. The web history abstraction tracks the following traces:
(i) source URL; (ii) web history; (iii) complete path of the downloaded
file; and (iv) what happened to the file after it was downloaded.

4.   Evaluating User Experience

TAIMA applies novel information visualization concepts and methods
to digital forensic investigations. A usability evaluation study was conducted in order to examine their effectiveness. The study followed the
user experience evaluation guidelines specified by Lam et al. [13]. Such
an evaluation includes assessments that analyze individual responses and

attitudes towards a visualization [12]. The user evaluation performed in this research combined usability testing (UX) and the broadly-used post-study system usability questionnaire (PSSUQ), thereby drawing on their collective strengths [14].

The original PSSUQ comprises 19 items. However, this study employed a modified version that included 15 items. Since error handling was not implemented in TAIMA, the four related questions were removed from the PSSUQ.

Data from the user study included participant performance and open-ended feedback provided by a post-task questionnaire. The participant performance metrics included the task performance expressed in terms of the task completion time and completion rate (i.e., percentage of the six hacking software traces that were correctly found by a participant). Additionally, a subjective user satisfaction rating, captured via the post-task questionnaire, provided insights into the participants' overall satisfaction with TAIMA. The questionnaire also included an open-ended section for the participants to provide feedback about TAIMA.

4.1   Study Participants

According to Nielsen [17], approximately 90% of usability problems are discovered in usability evaluation studies with no more than five participants. This study had five participants, all of whom were either computer crime investigators or digital forensic analysts with one to two years of experience using industry-standard tools to analyze digital evidence.

Statistical analysis of the outcome was not appropriate due to the small sample size. The simulated hacking scenario reflected tasks that are typically performed in a digital forensic investigation. The participants also provided feedback on enhancing TAIMA.

4.2   Procedure

The usability testing portion of the evaluation employed a scenario involving an abandoned notebook computer suspected of being used for hacking purposes [15]. The participants were tasked with conducting a digital forensic analysis using TAIMA to identify hacking software applications on the abandoned computer. The task was deemed successful if all six hacking software applications were discovered.

Before starting their tasks, the participants were provided access to TAIMA to explore the visualization features and capabilities. The testing officially started after the participants verbally expressed that they

Table 1.   Post-study system usability questionnaire (PSSUQ) usability metrics.

Item		Rating
1	Overall, I was satisfied with how easy it was to use this system	6.2
2	It was simple to use this system	6.4
3	I was able to complete the tasks and scenarios quickly using this system	5.8
4	I felt comfortable using this system	6.4
5	It was easy to learn to use this system	7.0
6	I believe I could become productive quickly using this system	6.4
7	Whenever I made a mistake using the system, I could recover easily and quickly	6.0
8	It was easy to find the information I needed	6.4
9	The visualization provided by the system was easy to understand	6.6
10	The visualization was effective at helping me complete the tasks and scenarios	6.6
11	The organization of information on the interface was clear	6.2
12	The interface of this system was pleasant	6.0
13	I liked using the interface of this system	6.0
14	This system has all the functions and capabilities I expect it to have	5.0
15	Overall, I was satisfied with this system	6.2

felt comfortable using TAIMA. After completing the task, the participants completed the PSSUQ.

The user study assessed two goals:

- Effectiveness of TAIMA at assisting forensic analyses by presenting digital evidence using best practice information visualization techniques.

- Effectiveness of the TAIMA infrastructure and processes at reducing the challenges associated with the examination and presentation of vast volumes of digital evidence.

The results of the assessment provided insights into the participants' attitudes towards the information visualization. Additionally, the assessment determined if TAIMA improved the analysis and presentation of large volumes of digital evidence.

4.3   Results

Table 1 and Figure 8 present the PSSUQ results. Note that higher scores denote better usability.

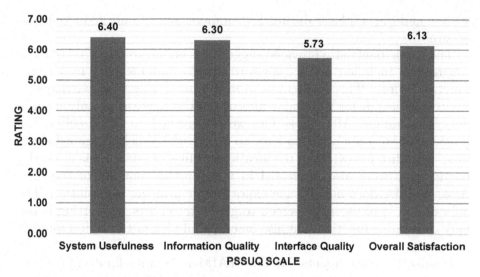

Figure 8. Post-study system usability questionnaire (PSSUQ) subscores.

The survey results reveal that the participants were highly satisfied with the usability of TAIMA – as indicated by a 100% (7 out of 7) rating for Item 5 (It was easy to learn to use this system). Item 9 (The visualization provided by the system was easy to understand) and Item 10 (The visualization was effective at helping me complete the tasks and scenarios) received the next highest rating of 94% (6.6 out of 7).

All the participants noted that they enjoyed not having to conduct an extensive search to find relevant artifacts. They also appreciated that important and relevant information was presented to them on one screen. Additionally, the participants found TAIMA to be easy to use due to its straightforward controls and intuitive display. This highlights the visualization effectiveness achieved by the intuitive display that reduces the data presented while still providing the critical information needed to complete the task.

One participant commented that the visualization was "extremely beneficial" and that it made observations of system activity "easy and fast." Another participant noted that it was easy to understand the visualization. This suggests that the integration of exploratory information visualization and abstraction techniques provides an accurate means to reconstruct timelines despite the challenges imposed by data complexity and data volume in digital forensic investigations.

Some items received low scores. The lowest score was received by Item 14 (This system has all the functions and capabilities I expect it to have). But this is a reasonable score because TAIMA is a prototype system and the emphasis during development was on data reduction and accuracy.

The participants also provided suggestions on improving TAIMA. The suggestions included adding keyword search and file content viewing functionalities. This is because, during the testing, the participants wanted to search for particular files of interest instead of only using a data/time range. After these files were identified on the timeline, the participants did not want to have to search the timeline again for the files. In addition to viewing the locations of files of interest via a tooltip, participants were also interested in viewing the contents of the files. Also, TAIMA does not provide exporting or printing capabilities. The only option is to use print-screen to generate reports. Reporting is not only a desirable function, but also an essential part of the digital forensic process.

Finally, the participants felt that TAIMA provides limited functionality. They wanted more ways to customize TAIMA and wanted more control over the interface. For example, they wanted more filtering options. Also, after the results are returned and populated on the timeline, the participants wanted the ability to eliminate system events that were not of interest.

5.   Conclusions

Establishing timelines is vital in digital forensic investigations. However, most digital forensic tools and applications merely present timelines as histograms or as raw trace entries in files. Additionally, traditional timeline analysis uses static text-based timelines that force practitioners to employ labor-intensive manual practices that often miss significant pieces of evidence.

The TAIMA prototype described in this chapter was specifically developed to mitigate these challenges. It leverages information visualization concepts and techniques to automate the creation of graph-based timelines of high-level system events. TAIMA enriches timelines with discrete high-level system events by presenting temporal data attributes in a practitioner-focused GUI.

The high usability ratings obtained by TAIMA in the user evaluation study reveal that it is intuitive, easy to learn, effective and accurate. These results satisfy the primary goal of the research – to address the significant challenges introduced by data complexity and data volume in digital forensic investigations.

Much of the future research and development activities related to TAIMA will be driven by the feedback received from the usability study participants. Priorities include providing printing and data export capabilities. Even more important is supporting report generation, which is an essential component of the digital forensic process.

One of strengths of TAIMA is its ability to filter and reduce the numbers of events on timelines. Enabling users to customize filtering according to their needs should make the application even more effective. Future activities will also focus on the robust testing of TAIMA using a large image with real-world activities and complex system events.

References

[1] AccessData, Forensic Toolkit (FTK), Orem, Utah (`accessdata.com/products-services/forensic-toolkit-ftk`), 2020.

[2] Apollo Docs, Configuring the Cache, Apollo, San Francisco, California (`www.apollographql.com/docs/react/advanced/cach ing`), 2020.

[3] R. Carbone and C. Bean, Generating Computer Forensic Super-Timelines under Linux: A Comprehensive Guide for Windows-Based Disk Images, Technical Memorandum TM2011-216, Defence R&D Canada, Valcartier, Canada, 2011.

[4] Y. Chabot, A. Bertaux, C. Nicolle and T. Kechadi, Automatic timeline construction and analysis for computer forensic purposes, *Proceedings of the IEEE Joint Intelligence and Security Informatics Conference*, pp. 276–270, 2014.

[5] GRANDstack, Build Full Stack Graph Applications with Ease (`grandstack.io`), 2020.

[6] K. Gudjonsson, Mastering the Super Timeline with `log2timeline`, Information Security Reading Room, SANS Institute, Bethesda, Maryland, 2010.

[7] Guidance Software, EnCase Forensic User Guide, Version 8.07, Pasadena, California, 2018.

[8] G. Hales, Visualization of device datasets to assist digital forensic investigations, *Proceedings of the International Conference on Cyber Situational Awareness, Data Analytics and Assessment*, 2017.

[9] H. Hibshi, T. Vidas and L. Cranor, Usability of forensic tools: A user study, *Proceedings of the Sixth International Conference on IT Security Incident Management and IT Forensics*, pp. 81–91, 2011.

[10] P. Hitlin, Internet, social media use and device ownership in U.S. have plateaued after years of growth, *Fact Tank – News in Numbers*, Pew Research Center, Washington, DC, September 28, 2018.

[11] B. Inglot, L. Liu and N. Antonopoulos, A framework for enhanced timeline analysis in digital forensics, *Proceedings of the IEEE International Conference on Green Computing and Communications*, pp. 253–256, 2012.

[12] T. Isenberg, P. Isenberg, J. Chen, M. Sedlmair and T. Moller, A systematic review of the practice of evaluating visualization, *IEEE Transactions on Visualization Computer Graphics*, vol. 19(12), pp. 2818–2827, 2013.

[13] H. Lam, E. Bertini, P. Isenberg, C. Plaisant and S. Carpendale, Empirical studies in information visualization: Seven scenarios, *IEEE Transactions on Visualization and Computer Graphics*, vol. 18(9), pp. 1520–1536, 2012.

[14] J. Lewis, Psychometric evaluation of the post-study system usability questionnaire: The PSSUQ, *Proceedings of the Human Factors and Ergonomics Society Annual Meeting*, vol. 36(16), pp. 1259–1260, 1992.

[15] National Institute of Standards and Technology, Hacking Case, Gaithersburg, Maryland (`www.cfreds.nist.gov/Hacking_Case.html`), April 16, 2018.

[16] Neo4j, Introducing Neo4j, San Mateo, California (`neo4j.com`), 2020.

[17] J. Nielsen, Why you only need to test with 5 users, Nielsen Norman Group, Fremont, California (`www.nngroup.com/articles/why-you-only-need-to-test-with-5-users`), March 18, 2000.

[18] J. Olsson and M. Boldt, Computer forensic timeline visualization tool, *Digital Investigation*, vol. 6(S), pp. S78–S87, 2009.

[19] G. Osborne and J. Slay, Digital forensic infovis: An implementation of a process for visualization of digital evidence, *Proceedings of the Sixth International Conference on Availability, Reliability and Security*, pp. 196–201, 2011.

[20] G. Osborne, B. Turnbull and J. Slay, The "Explore, Investigate and Correlate" (EIC) conceptual framework for digital forensic information visualization, *Proceedings of the International Conference on Availability, Reliability and Security*, pp. 629–634, 2010.

[21] D. Schelkoph, G. Peterson and J. Okolica, Digital forensic event graph reconstruction, *Proceedings of the International Conference on Digital Forensics and Cyber Crime*, pp. 185–203, 2018.

[22] B. Shneiderman, The eyes have it: A task by data type taxonomy for information visualizations, *Proceedings of the IEEE Symposium on Visual Languages*, pp. 336–343, 1996.

[23] S. Teerlink and R. Erbacher, Improving the computer forensic analysis process through visualization, *Communications of the ACM*, vol. 49(2), pp. 71–75, 2006.

Chapter 4

ENHANCING THE FEATURE PROFILES OF WEB SHELLS BY ANALYZING THE PERFORMANCE OF MULTIPLE DETECTORS

Weiqing Huang, Chenggang Jia, Min Yu, Kam-Pui Chow, Jiuming Chen, Chao Liu and Jianguo Jiang

Abstract   Web shells are commonly used to transfer malicious scripts in order to control web servers remotely. Malicious web shells are detected by extracting the feature profiles of known web shells and creating a learning model that classifies malicious samples. This chapter proposes a novel feature profile scheme for characterizing malicious web shells based on the opcode sequences and static properties of PHP scripts. A real-world dataset is employed to compare the performance of the feature profile scheme against state-of-art schemes using various machine learning algorithms. The experimental results demonstrate that the new feature profile scheme significantly reduces the false positive rate.

Keywords: Web shells, feature profiles, text vectorization, machine learning

1.   Introduction

High profile web attacks have highlighted the importance of preventing web application penetrations that serve as springboards for compromising networks [12]. A web shell is often the first step in setting up a backdoor for web application penetration – it is a web script that is placed in a publicly-accessible web server to enable an attacker to obtain web server root permissions and remote control [7].

Accurately detecting web shells in web servers could significantly reduce web application penetration attacks. However, attackers insert hidden functionality in web shells to hinder detection. As a result, evidence pertaining to web shell attacks is difficult to find among the massive

© IFIP International Federation for Information Processing 2020
Published by Springer Nature Switzerland AG 2020
G. Peterson and S. Shenoi (Eds.): Advances in Digital Forensics XVI, IFIP AICT 589, pp. 57–72, 2020.
https://doi.org/10.1007/978-3-030-56223-6_4

amounts of normal data. Forensic practitioners have to search for web shells manually, a task that is laborious and time-consuming.

Researchers have proposed several methods for detecting malicious web shells. A common approach is to extract features and construct feature profiles that characterize web shells, following which a classification model is developed using a machine learning algorithm.

Liu et al. [5] have proposed a detection model based on convolutional and recurrent neural networks that does not consider the attacker's intentions or require payload sample labeling. Although these learning models may exhibit good performance for specific types of web shells, the models often yield large false positive rates when applied to real-world datasets. Moreover, researchers often ignore the feature profiles and potential behaviors of web shells, and merely view detection as a black-box operation. This makes it difficult to apply and evaluate the detection models in real-world environments. As a result, forensic practitioners have to manually sift through large volumes of data to detect malicious web shells hidden among numerous false positives.

This chapter compares the detection performance of multiple feature profile schemes and machine learning models to identify the reasons for the differences. A general test platform based on real-world web shells collected from public datasets is used to evaluate the performance of the feature profiles and learning models. The experiments reveal that web shell detection performance is affected by feature profiles, text vectorization methods and machine learning models. A novel feature profile scheme is proposed for characterizing malicious web shells based on the opcode sequences and static properties of PHP scripts. The evaluation results demonstrate that the detection method significantly improves malicious web shell classification as well as the ability to detect custom web shell functionality.

2.   Related Work

A web shell is a malicious script that attempts to maintain persistent access in an exploited web application [1]. It is assigned to the post-exploitation stage of the attack chain. A web shell does not have any exploitability on its own, but it can be leveraged by attacks such as SQL injection, remote file inclusion and cross-site scripting. Its functions include facilitating persistent remote access, privilege escalation, antivirus software evasion and zombie botnet control.

A web shell can be written in any language that is supported by a web server. Typical examples include PHP, JSP and ASP. Some web shells are tiny, needing only a single line of code whereas others are full-featured with thousands of lines of code. Well-known web shell families are c99, r57, b374k and barc0de [8].

Wang et al. [14] have used a multi-layer perceptron neural network to detect web shells. They converted sample source code to byte code using a compiler, following which they used bigrams and the term-frequency-inverse-frequency (TF-IDF) statistic to obtain a frequency matrix that was passed to the multi-layer perceptron. Their multi-layer perceptron approach yielded 90% detection accuracy.

Wrench and Irwin [15] have determined the similarity levels between PHP malware samples using four measures to create representative similarity matrices. The malware samples were decoded, the contents of user-defined function bodies and names of user-defined functions were extracted, and file fuzzy hash values were created for similarity analysis.

Yong et al. [16] have employed a deep neural network that detects server-side web shells with good results. Fang et al. [4] have used random forest machine learning with the fastText library to obtain excellent web shell detection results.

Several tools have been developed for web shell detection. One example is CloudWalker for Linux and macOS systems [2]. Web Shell Detector is a PHP script that identifies PHP, CGI(Perl), ASP and ASPX web shells [3]. The `php-malware-finder` tool is designed to crawl filesystems and analyze files against a set of YARA malware identification rules [13]. WebShell.Pub employs traditional features and cloud-based large data dual-engine killing technology [10]. D Shield is an active defense software tool designed for Microsoft IIS systems [11]; it prevents invasions of websites and web servers by applying internal and external protections.

3. Proposed Web Shell Detection Method

This section describes the proposed web shell detection method. It has two components: (i) web shell feature extraction; and (ii) learning model creation.

3.1 Web Shell Feature Extraction

Figure 1 shows the web shell feature extraction process. The model uses PHP opcode sequences of execution path features, opcode sequences of code features and static features to distinguish web shells.

Two types of features are extracted from PHP samples: (i) opcode sequence features; and (ii) static features. The opcode sequences of PHP scripts are obtained using the PHP VLD extension [9] to hook into the Zend engine and dump the opcodes (execution units) of the scripts. Next, the opcode sequences based on execution paths in the PHP scripts

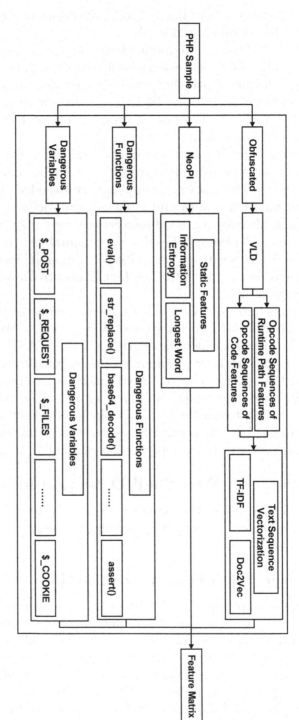

Figure 1.   Web shell feature extraction.

```
0.      <?php
1.          echo ''hello world'';
2.      ?>
```

Figure 2. Simple PHP script.

Table 1. VLD execution results.

Line	Opcode#	Opcode	Branch	Lines	Sop-Eop	Path
1	0	EXT_STMT	0	1-2	0-2	1
	1	ECHO				
2	2	RETURN				

and the opcode sequences corresponding to the code are obtained. TF-IDF and the Doc2Vec tool are used to vectorize opcode sequences of the PHP scripts. Static features such as the longest string, entropy and dangerous functions and variables are also extracted. Finally, the two feature matrices are combined to create a single feature matrix.

Opcode Sequence Features. Opcode arrays generated by a PHP compiler from source code are similar to assembler code generated by a C compiler. However, instead of being directly executed by the CPU, opcode arrays are executed by a PHP interpreter.

The PHP VLD extension is often used for web shell detection [9]. The extension yields two parts. One is the opcode sequences corresponding to the PHP code. The other is the opcode sequences of the execution paths in the code. If only opcode sequences from the first part are considered, interference by certain opcodes causes some PHP code not to be executed, which renders it benign. Therefore, the second part is employed to abstract the opcode sequences.

Figure 2 shows a simple PHP script. Table 1 shows the VLD execution results. The left portion of Table 1 shows the opcodes corresponding to each line of the PHP script. In this portion of the table, Line refers to the line number in the PHP script, Opcode# refers to the opcode number and Opcode refers to the opcode name.

The right portion of the table shows the branches and paths of code execution. Branch refers to the number of the branch, Lines refers to the line numbers in the PHP script corresponding to the branch, Sop-Eop refers to the starting and ending opcode numbers of the branch, and Path refers to the path number of the branch. In this case, there is only one path, which starts at Line 0 and continues in Lines 1 and 2. The opcode sequence of the code is determined from the Line 0 opcode to Line 2 opcode. The opcode sequence of the path is: EXT_STMT, ECHO and RETURN.

The opcode sequences of the PHP scripts are generated in the form of text. TF-IDF and the Doc2Vec tool are used to vectorize the text to a matrix of fixed dimensions for input to a machine learning algorithm.

Static Features. The static features include: (i) longest string; (ii) information entropy; and (iii) dangerous functions and variables:

- **Longest String:** Web shells maintain stealth using techniques such as encryption, encoding and stitching to obfuscate strings. Normal PHP scripts mostly comprise short strings whereas obfuscated code often contains long strings. The longest string feature is computed as the length of the longest string divided by ten.

- **Information Entropy:** Information entropy is the average rate at which a stochastic source of data produces information. Encryption and compression increase the randomness and information entropy. An obfuscated web shell typically has high information entropy.

- **Dangerous Functions and Variables:** Certain PHP functions are deemed to be high risk. Examples are `eval`, `system`, `assert` and `cmd_shell` that make system calls. Also, `fopen`, `fwrite` and SQL, which can modify files.

3.2　　Learning Model Construction

The features extracted from PHP scripts, namely, opcode sequences of code, opcode sequences of runtime paths and static features, are input to TF-IDF and the Doc2Vec tool that vectorize the text for input to a machine learning algorithm. Figure 2 shows the machine learning models employed in the web shell detection framework developed in this research. The models include the support vector machine (SVM), random forest (RF) and k-nearest neighbor (KNN) models.

The dataset was randomly divided to create a training dataset with 70% of the overall data and a testing dataset with the remaining 30% of the data. The training dataset was input to the three learning models to obtain the trained models. The testing dataset was then input to the trained models as well as commercial web shell detection products to evaluate the detection performance.

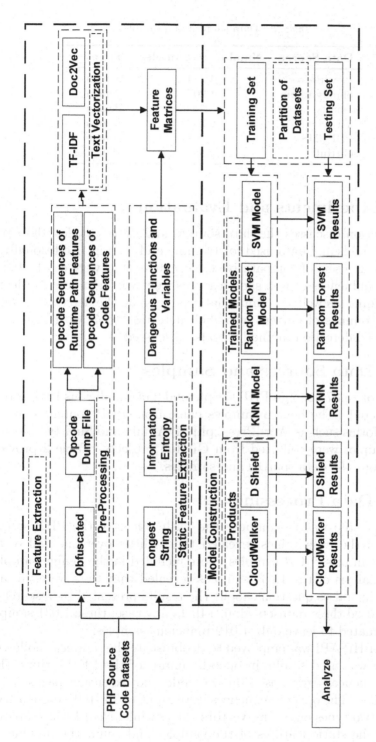

Figure 3. Web shell detection framework.

Table 2.   Data sources and samples.

Data Source	Number of Samples	Type
WordPress	4,244	Benign
phpMyAdmin	1,207	Benign
Smarty	213	Benign
Yii	6,202	Benign
PHPCMS	1,207	Benign
GitHub	2,050	Malicious

4.   Experiments and Evaluation

This section discusses the data sources and data samples, data processing methods and data used for training and testing. Additionally, it describes three sets of comparative experiments that were conducted to assess the influences of web shell features, text vectorization and learning algorithms (as well as commercial products) on the detection results. The shortcomings of current web shell detection tools with respect to the proposed detection method are also discussed.

4.1   Data Sources and Samples

A total of 13,073 benign PHP scripts and 2,050 malicious PHP scripts were collected. The benign samples came from PHP content management platforms such as WordPress, phpMyAdmin and Smarty. The malicious samples were collected from GitHub projects. Table 2 provides details about the data sources and samples.

4.2   Data Processing

The first step was to compute the hash values of the PHP scripts. Analysis of the hash values revealed that a little over one-half of the malicious samples (1,031 samples) were included in the benign samples. Manual analysis of the 1,031 samples revealed that they were, in fact, benign – this raises questions about the results presented by researchers who have used these datasets [4, 6, 14]. In any case, these 1,031 samples were eliminated to leave only 1,019 malicious samples.

The UnPHP API was employed to deobfuscate the samples. Following this, VLD was used to obtain opcode dumps of the PHP scripts. The opcode sequences were based on the code and execution paths in the dumped files. The opcode sequences were input to TF-IDF and Doc2Vec to obtain two types of feature vectors. Meanwhile, NeoPI was employed to obtain the static features of the samples and count the numbers of

Table 3. Dataset summary.

Category	Property	Value
Dataset	Number of samples	12,309
	Number of benign samples	11,397
	Number of malicious samples	912
Number of Input Features	TF-IDF	$181 + 23 = 214$
	Doc2Vec	$10 + 23 = 33$
Training Set (70%)	Number of benign samples	7,979
	Number of malicious samples	646
Testing Set (30%)	Number of benign samples	3,418
	Number of malicious samples	266

malicious functions and variables in each sample. Since some scripts could not be analyzed by NeoPI, the number of malicious samples was reduced to 912. Finally, the vectorized and static features were combined to obtain the final sample features.

Table 3 provides details about the final dataset, numbers of input features, and the training and testing datasets.

4.3   Evaluation of Feature Sets

This section discusses the effects of input features on the classification results. In order to compare the classification results for different feature sets, TF-IDF was used for text vectorization and random forest (RF) was selected as the learning model.

Figure 4 shows the detection results obtained using two types of opcode sequences (path_seq and code_seq) and static features. The path_seq feature yielded the best accuracy, recall and F1 score metrics whereas the static features yielded poor results for these metrics.

Table 4 shows the true positive (TP), false negative (FN), false positive (FP) and true negative (TN) values for combinations of opcode sequence and static features with TF-IDF vectorization compared with static features alone. Note that using an opcode sequence feature with static features produced better results than using only static features.

Analysis of the false negative samples revealed that the opcode sequence features can distinguish some malicious samples with static features that are not obvious. This was especially noticeable in the case of custom malicious functions used to create backdoors; examples include database write operations and file entry operations. A normal database operation directly stores the data from a form to the database. How-

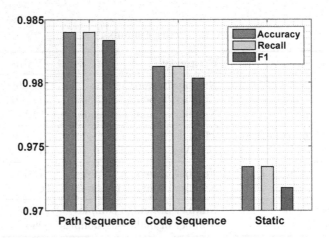

Figure 4. Evaluation of feature sets.

Table 4. Detection performance for various feature sets.

Feature Sets	TP	FN	FP	TN
path_seq + static + TF-IDF + RF	3,410	8	51	215
code_seq + static + TF-IDF + RF	3,409	9	68	198
static + RF	3,400	18	80	186

ever, a malicious database operation decrypts the data from the form and then operates on the database based the decrypted string. When only static features were used, the malicious operations were classified as normal because there were no malicious features aside from the decryption function. For these reasons, 35 malicious samples could be detected using the static features alone.

The 26 samples that were only detected using opcode sequence features were also analyzed. Most of the samples could not be detected using only static features because they employed custom malicious functions instead of common malicious functions. This shows the relative advantage of using opcode sequence features based on runtime paths.

Table 5 shows the numbers of malicious functions that were detected when opcode sequence and static features were used in combination, but were not detected when static features were used alone. The samples are divided into six categories based on the malicious functions: (i) command line; (ii) file read and write; (iii) file search; (iv) database backdoor; (v) encrypted communication; and (vi) password acquisition.

Table 5. Sample misclassification (opcode + static features vs. static features).

Category	Malicious Functions in Misclassified Samples
Command Line	14
File Read and Write	12
File Search	4
Database Backdoor	2
Encrypted Communication	9
Password Acquisition	2

4.4 Evaluation of Text Vectorization Methods

Three comparative experiments were conducted to verify the suitability of the TF-IDF and Doc2Vec text vectorization methods. In order to compare the two text vectorization methods, the opcode sequences of execution path features and static features were combined to create the input features, and random forest was used as the learning model. TF-IDF and two Doc2Vec versions, Doc2Vec10 and Doc2Vec181, that generated ten and 181 vector parameters, respectively, were evaluated.

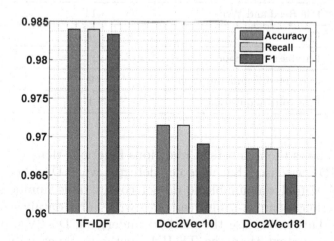

Figure 5. Evaluation of text vectorization methods.

Figure 5 demonstrates that TF-IDF performed better than both versions of Doc2Vec in terms of accuracy, recall and the F1 score.

Table 6. Detection performance for various text vectorization methods.

Vectorization Method	TP	FN	FP	TN
TF-IDF	3,410	8	51	215
Doc2Vec10	3,409	9	93	173
Doc2Vec181	3,410	8	108	158

Table 6 shows that the true positive rates are similar for TF-IDF and the two Doc2Vec versions, but the false positive and true negative rates are significantly lower for both Doc2Vec versions.

The comparative experiment using Doc2Vec10 and Doc2Vec181 to generate ten vectors and 181 vectors, respectively, was conducted to prove that static features have higher weights among all the features. The results in Figure 5 and Table 6 indicate that the presence of too many Doc2Vec vectors weakened the proportion of static features, leading to a decrease in detection performance.

Table 7. Sample misclassification (TF-IDF vs. Doc2Vec).

Category	Malicious Functions in Misclassified Samples
Command Line	17
File Read and Write	14
File Search	4
Database Backdoor	11
Encrypted Communication	9
Password Acquisition	1

Table 7 shows the numbers of malicious functions that were detected when TF-IDF was used, but were not detected when Doc2Vec was used. The Doc2Vec tool was unable to detect considerable numbers of command line (long samples), file read and write, and database backdoor functions. This is because the method underlying Doc2Vec pays more attention to context than the TF-IDF method. Since only one path in the code sequences of a malicious sample may be malicious, there is considerable interference by non-malicious paths on the features. This also explains why researchers have suggested that the Doc2Vec detection performance is below par [6].

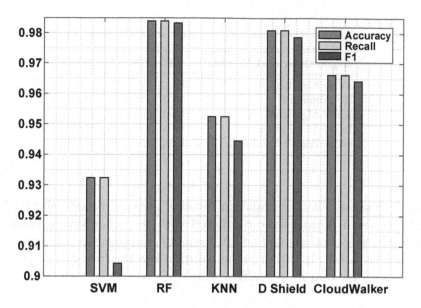

Figure 6. Evaluation of detection algorithms and commercial products.

4.5 Evaluation of Algorithms and Products

The experiments described above demonstrated that opcode sequence features combined with static features and TF-IDF are the best combination for detecting malicious web shells. This section discusses the detection results obtained for various machine learning algorithms with the best feature set combination and TF-IDF along with the detection results obtained using two commercial web shell detection products. The machine learning algorithms included the support vector machine (SVM), random forest (RF) and k-nearest neighbor (KNN) algorithms. The commercial products included D Shield [11] and CloudWalker [2].

The results in Figure 6 demonstrate that the random forest algorithm based web shell detection solution yielded much better detection performance compared with the support vector machine and k-nearest neighbor algorithm based solutions in terms of accuracy, recall and the F1 score. This is because the random forest algorithm, which is an ensemble learning model based on decision trees, has better generalization ability than single models like the support vector machine and k-nearest neighbor algorithms. Figure 6 also shows that the random forest algorithm based solution was slightly better than the D Shield product and moderately better than CloudWalker in terms of accuracy, recall and the F1 score.

Table 8. Detection performance of various algorithms and commercial products.

Algorithms and Products	TP	FN	FP	TN
SVM Algorithm	3,417	1	248	18
RF Algorithm	3,410	8	51	215
KNN Algorithm	3,410	18	157	109
D Shield Product	3,410	8	108	158
CloudWalker Product	3,392	26	98	168

Table 8 shows that the random forest algorithm based solution has the best overall performance compared with the other two learning algorithm based solutions and the two commercial products. Specifically, the random forest algorithm based solution has the lowest combination of false negative and false positive values.

Table 9. Sample misclassification (random forest solution vs. D Shield).

Category	Malicious Functions in Misclassified Samples
Command Line	7
File Read and Write	9
File Search	3
Database Backdoor	1
Encrypted Communication	7
Password Acquisition	1

Table 9 shows the numbers of malicious functions that were detected when the random forest algorithm based solution was used, but were not detected by D Shield. Analysis of these samples revealed that D Shield is poor at detecting web shells with custom malicious functions. The results also reveal that using opcode sequences of execution path features enhance malicious web shell detection.

However, 15 malicious samples that were detected by D Shield were missed by the random forest algorithm based solution. Analysis of these samples revealed that the random forest based solution was hindered by the inclusion of functions such as `eval()` and `phpinfo()`. These functions also appeared in a small number of positive samples, which may be the reason for their misclassification.

5. Conclusions

This chapter has proposed a malicious web shell detection method that leverages opcode sequence and static features of PHP scripts along with text vectorization and machine learning. Experiments using a general web shell detection framework relying on real-world data collected from public datasets reveal that the detection performance is affected by feature profiles, text vectorization methods and machine learning models. The experimental evaluations demonstrate that using the combination of opcode sequence and static features along with TF-IDF vectorization and the random forest machine learning algorithm outperforms other machine learning algorithm based solutions as well as the D Shell and CloudWalker commercial web shell detection products. In particular, the low false positive rate renders the proposed method useful and efficient in forensic investigations.

Acknowledgement

This research was supported by the Natural Science Foundation of China under Grant no. 61402476 and by the National Key R&D Program of China under Grant no. 2017YFB0801900.

References

[1] Acunetix, An Introduction to Web-Shells, London, United Kingdom (www.acunetix.com/websitesecurity/introduction-web shells), 2016.

[2] Chaitin Tech, CloudWalker Platform, GitHub (github.com/chai tin/cloudwalker), March 7, 2020.

[3] M. Emposha, PHP-Shell-Detector, GitHub (github.com/emposha/ PHP-Shell-Detector), October 5, 2015.

[4] Y. Fang, Y. Qiu, L. Liu and C. Huang, Detecting web shells based on random forest with fastText, *Proceedings of the International Conference on Computing and Artificial Intelligence*, pp. 52–56, 2018.

[5] H. Liu, B. Lang, M. Liu and H. Yan, CNN and RNN based payload classification methods for attack detection, *Knowledge-Based Systems*, vol. 163, pp. 332–341, 2019.

[6] Z. Lv, H. Yan and R. Mei, Automatic and accurate detection of web shells based on convolutional neural networks, *Proceedings of the China Cyber Security Annual Conference*, pp. 73–85, 2018.

[7] MITRE Corporation, Web Shell, Bethesda, Maryland (`attack.mitre.org/techniques/T1100`), 2019.

[8] T. Moore and R. Clayton, Evil searching: Compromise and recompromise of Internet hosts for phishing, *Proceedings of the International Conference on Financial Cryptography and Data Security*, pp. 256–272, 2009.

[9] D. Rethans, More Source Analysis with VLD (`derickrethans.nl/more-source-analysis-with-vld.html`), February 19, 2010.

[10] ShellPub.com, Webshell.Pub, Beijing, China (`www.shellpub.com`), 2020.

[11] Shenzhen Di Element Technology, D Shield, Shenzen, China (`www.d99net.net`), 2020.

[12] O. Starov, J. Dahse, S. Ahmad, T. Holz and N. Nikiforakis, No honor among thieves: A large-scale analysis of malicious web shells, *Proceedings of the Twenty-Fifth International Conference on World Wide Web*, pp. 1021–1032, 2016.

[13] J. Voisin, `php-malware-finder`, GitHub (`github.com/nbs-system/php-malware-finder`), May 26, 2020.

[14] Z. Wang, J. Yang, M. Dai, R. Xu and X. Liang, A method for detecting web shells based on multi-layer perception, *Academic Journal of Computing and Information Science*, vol. 2(1), pp. 81–91, 2019.

[15] P. Wrench and B. Irwin, Towards a PHP web shell taxonomy using de-obfuscation-assisted similarity analysis, *Proceedings of the Information Security for South Africa Conference*, 2015.

[16] B. Yong, X. Liu, Y. Liu, H. Yin, L. Huang and Q. Zhou, Web behavior detection based on deep neural networks, *Proceedings of the IEEE SmartWorld, Ubiquitous Intelligence and Computing, Advanced and Trusted Computing, Scalable Computing and Communications, Cloud and Big Data Computing, Internet of People and Smart City Innovation Conferences*, pp. 1911–1916, 2018.

Chapter 5

A NOVEL APPROACH FOR GENERATING SYNTHETIC DATASETS FOR DIGITAL FORENSICS

Thomas Göbel, Thomas Schäfer, Julien Hachenberger, Jan Türr and Harald Baier

Abstract   Increases in the quantity and complexity of digital evidence necessitate the development and application of advanced, accurate and efficient digital forensic tools. Digital forensic tool testing helps assure the veracity of digital evidence, but it requires appropriate validation datasets. The datasets are crucial to evaluating reproducibility and improving the state of the art. Datasets can be real-world or synthetic. While real-world datasets have the advantage of relevance, the interpretation of results can be difficult because reliable ground truth may not exist. In contrast, ground truth is easily established for synthetic datasets.

This chapter presents the `hystck` framework for generating synthetic datasets with ground truth. The framework supports the automated generation of synthetic network traffic and operating system and application artifacts by simulating human-computer interactions. The generated data can be indistinguishable from data generated by normal human-computer interactions. The modular structure of the framework enhances the ability to incorporate extensions that simulate new applications and generate new types of network traffic.

Keywords: Synthetic dataset generation, network traffic, operating system data

1.   Introduction

Advanced, accurate and efficient digital forensic tools are vital to processing the large volumes of complex digital evidence encountered in digital forensic investigations. In order to be admissible in court, open source digital forensic tools must meet four criteria: (i) tools, techniques and procedures are thoroughly tested to assess the occurrences of false negatives and false positives; (ii) results are verifiable and falsifiable in

© IFIP International Federation for Information Processing 2020
Published by Springer Nature Switzerland AG 2020
G. Peterson and S. Shenoi (Eds.): Advances in Digital Forensics XVI, IFIP AICT 589, pp. 73–93, 2020.
https://doi.org/10.1007/978-3-030-56223-6_5

order to specify possible error rates; (iii) new procedures are discussed in the scientific community and subjected to objective peer reviews; and (iv) new procedures are accepted by the digital forensic community [4].

In order to evaluate a suitable digital forensic tool (e.g., for network traffic forensics), appropriate forensic testing and evaluation datasets comprising correctly-labeled data that are similar to real-world data are required. Tool testing, as suggested by Carrier [4], can only be performed if suitable datasets are available to assess the accuracy and generalizability of the results. NIST's Computer Forensic Tool Testing (CFTT) Program [13] is responsible for developing test methods for digital forensic tools and producing appropriate test data. The main criteria for digital evidence admissibility in court are that appropriate tests should be repeatable and reproducible. These criteria cannot be achieved without high-fidelity testing and evaluation datasets for forensic tools, techniques and procedures.

A number of datasets have been proposed for testing and evaluating digital forensic tools. Ring et al. [15] identify a broad spectrum of network-based datasets that have been released from 1998 through 2019. However, datasets quickly become outdated. They are often too academic, too specific, too synthetic (and thus too unrealistic) and/or too anonymized. Additionally, there is a lack of good real-world datasets.

Grajeda et al. [7] stress the relevance of up-to-date datasets and the importance of sharing them in the digital forensics community. Their research reveals that 198 of the 351 analyzed datasets (56.4%) were experimentally generated, where researchers considered *ad hoc* scenarios to create data for their experiments. Only 129 (36.7%) were real-world datasets and 16 (4.6%) were computer-generated datasets (e.g., using algorithms, bots or simulators). Grajeda and colleagues also noted that 45.6% (160 out of 351) of the datasets were newly created, but only 3.8% of them (6 of 160) were released to the public due to concerns about releasing digital forensic data, especially real-world data. According to some researchers [1, 7], barriers to publishing datasets include data protection laws, privacy and intellectual property concerns, lack of resources and/or capabilities, and lack of understanding of the importance of sharing.

Aside from the availability and standardization of datasets, the process of generating data is of crucial importance. The generated datasets must be reliable and realistic. Additionally, the more extensive the datasets, the better they are for education and training, and for the application of machine learning algorithms.

Meanwhile, the heterogeneity and complexity of modern infrastructures require the use of a variety of forensic acquisition and analysis methods. Sophisticated analyses involve attack attribution based on recurring attack patterns and the correlation of diverse information from multiple data sources. Therefore, from a data synthesis point of view, it is not enough to merely generate network traffic in PCAP files, but also digital evidence from other sources (e.g., server-side information in Apache log files, client-side information in syslog/event logs and even memory dumps).

This chapter describes the `hystck` framework for generating synthetic evaluation corpora for digital forensics using a novel approach that allows the modeling of a complete infrastructure with a realistic network environment. Although the main goal is to generate benign and malicious network traffic, the proposed framework offers a more holistic data synthesis approach compared with existing traffic generators. Specifically, it simulates entire operating system sequences and applications via synthetic human-computer interactions, generating a ground truth that is realistic and comprehensive to the extent possible. The framework also enables researchers to generate network traffic as well as relevant digital evidence and artifacts in operating systems, such as data that is typically stored in application-dependent log files and in main memory.

The open source nature of the framework with complete source code and documentation can be leveraged by researchers to generate synthetic digital forensic corpora that are comparable to real-world corpora. The framework supports the generation of a reliable ground truth using a holistic approach with a real-world context that simulates a complete infrastructure with multiple running operating systems, application types and network protocols. An open API enables the synthetic generation of traffic to be programmed. Finally, the framework is modular and extensible, enabling researchers to simulate new operating systems, applications and network protocols.

2. Related Work

Demand for datasets has always been great in the intrusion detection community for evaluating new techniques and comparing their performance against existing ones. As a result, several approaches have been proposed for generating intrusion detection datasets. Molnar et al. [12] reveal that a large number of network traffic generators are available, but most of them are focused on specific application areas, which makes comparative evaluations extremely difficult. Other approaches generate synthetic traffic by mimicking human user activity, but the generated traffic typically is restricted to a single protocol or application type, or only contains data without context.

ID2T [6] is a Python-based network dataset synthesizer that was developed to overcome the shortcomings of the infamous KDD Cup 1999. ID2T essentially creates a new dataset by merging two PCAP-based network traffic dumps, one containing benign traffic and the other containing malicious traffic. During the merging process, ID2T accounts for network characteristics to avoid the artifacts seen in the KDD Cup 1999 dataset [9]. FLAME [2] is similar to ID2T, but it requires NetFlow-based traffic dumps. However, both ID2T and FLAME do not address the problem of generating initial network dumps.

Moirai [3] is a testbed creation framework that supports the emulation of Windows and Linux hosts. The framework uses an INI configuration file to define an "experiment" that has rudimentary support for installation routines, host process control and file exchange, but does not provide keyboard/window manager based controls. In addition, most commits were made during a short period of time, after which the testbed no longer appears to be maintained.

Emulab [8] is a network testbed that enables researchers to define and perform tests of virtual network environments. Emulab simultaneously refers to the open source platform for defining and controlling experimental environments, as well as the actual entity that runs the virtualized systems. A user interface and Python-based scripting language are provided for creating experimental hardware, software and network setups. Emulab supports GENI RSpec to enhance interoperability. DETER is an extension of Emulab that focuses on security-sensitive experiments. It incorporates several architectural changes to prevent malware from compromising other experiments and the underlying infrastructure. However, both Emulab and DETER do not provide opportunities for modeling and simulating user activities.

The LARIAT testbed [16] developed by MIT Lincoln Laboratory supports the modeling of benign and malicious activities in networked environments. Wright et al. [19] have further extended LARIAT to record and replay user activity at the user interface level using Markov chains. This provides a more realistic network footprint compared with the original LARIAT implementation, which was based on statistically-derived network events combined with an application protocol generator. While LARIAT receives good scores for its ability to simulate user activity, a major drawback is its limited accessibility – it is neither open source nor publicly available.

Related work on the automated generation of persistent disk images also deserves mention. NIST [14] has released reference datasets that provide forensic practitioners with simulated digital evidence for examination. Moch et al. [10, 11] have developed the Forensic Image Generator Generator (Forensig2) that generates filesystem images for digital forensics training courses. Another similar tool is ForGe – Forensic Test Image Generator [18]. Yet another similar system is EviPlant [17], which facilitates the efficient creation, manipulation, storage and distribution of digital forensic challenge problems for education and training purposes. However, all these tools are prototypes. Only the source code of ForGe is available, but the last commit was five years ago.

Traffic generators and image generators are disparate – traffic generators exclusively generate traffic and image generators do not produce traffic. Since the primary goal is to develop a holistic data synthesis framework that generates more than just network traffic and forensic disk images, existing generators are unsatisfactory. The aforementioned approaches do not provide mechanisms for dynamically modeling an entire infrastructure in a modular manner, nor are they open source and maintained or enable the automation of user activity. Indeed, the review of the literature reveals that no generator comparable to `hystck` combines all these features, and synthesizes network traffic and operating system and application artifacts based on human-computer interactions.

3. Framework Architecture and Functionality

This section describes the architecture and functionality of the `hystck` framework.

3.1 Overview

The `hystck` framework is designed to generate network traffic and other relevant digital evidence – that do not differ from real network traffic and disk images – by simulating human-computer interactions. Therefore, a special user interaction model was developed to capture and articulate human-computer interactions. The framework generates datasets by executing user interaction models. In order for user interaction models to generate network traffic, a solution with an operating system and graphical user interface is required. Additionally, it should be possible to install new software that can be executed by a user interaction model at a later time.

Virtualization was chosen when designing the framework because any operating system and applications can be installed on a virtual machine. The Kernel-based Virtual Machine (KVM) is employed for virtualization and `libvirt` is used for KVM administration. Other hypervisors supported by `libvirt` (e.g., VirtualBox) may be integrated into the framework. Since the framework must simulate the behavior of multi-

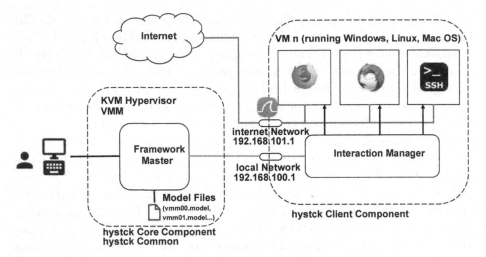

Figure 1. Framework architecture.

ple operating systems, a platform-independent programming language is required. This is why the framework was developed entirely in Python.

3.2   Framework Architecture

The framework engages a client-server architecture. The server-side has a framework master that manages the virtual machines. The client-side has an interaction manager, an agent that runs in the background and controls the graphical user interfaces of the virtual machines.

Figure 1 shows the interactions between the two main components. The framework master communicates with the interaction manager running on a virtual machine via a TCP socket on port 11000. The connection is used to send commands that control applications running on the virtual machine (e.g., start, close and window change) as well as keystrokes and mouse events.

The framework is divided into two parts to ensure that simulations work correctly. One is the server-side (physical machine) on which a specific scenario is implemented. The other part comprises the client-side virtual machines that execute commands in the scenario. Traffic produced by the virtual machines and sent to the Internet (internet network) is captured in the PCAP format using the tcpdump tool. To ensure that captures do not contain non-relevant control traffic, in addition to the internet network, a second network named local is created. The local network is used for communications between the framework master and interaction manager.

A separate virtual machine (guest) is created for each computer or user to be simulated. Therefore, virtual machine template files for Linux and Windows systems must be created in advance. All the images of the guest virtual machines are derived from the template files so that each simulated user works in an isolated execution environment and can use different software. The interaction manager currently supports the Linux, Windows 7 and Windows 10 operating systems.

The `constants.py` configuration file is used to adapt the framework settings. The configuration file contains information such as the number of virtual machines to be created, the names of the template files, the IP addresses of the `local` network (`192.168.100.1` in Figure 1) and `internet` network (`192.168.101.1` in Figure 1), and the MAC addresses of the virtual machine network interfaces for IP address assignment using DHCP.

The framework initiates the cloning of a virtual machine and establishes the connection to the guest (through which the guest sends and receives commands) based on its MAC address. This is accomplished using the `GuestListener` helper class. After the communications path has been established, the `Guest` class is invoked with the appropriate parameters to actually clone and start the virtual machine. After the virtual machine has started, the network interfaces are extracted and sniffers for the correct interfaces are started. The last key component is the `Agent` class, which handles the connection between the host and a virtual machine by having an agent running as an instance in the guest. At this point, commands may be invoked to start applications and perform tasks.

3.3 Data Synthesis Procedure

Figure 2 provides details about the operation of the framework.

1. The `VMM` class functions as a setup environment to create and control guests. It ensures that the default guest parameters (IP address, MAC address, template, `tcpdump`, etc.) are set to successfully clone templates. Also, it creates sockets on all the interfaces for the agents to listen on the guests.

2. The `Guest` class loads the parameters from the `constants.py` configuration file. The class creates and controls the guests using the template files.

3. The MAC addresses are linked to IP addresses and stored in the network configuration files for use by `libvirt`.

4. The `local` and `internet` networks are created by `libvirt`.

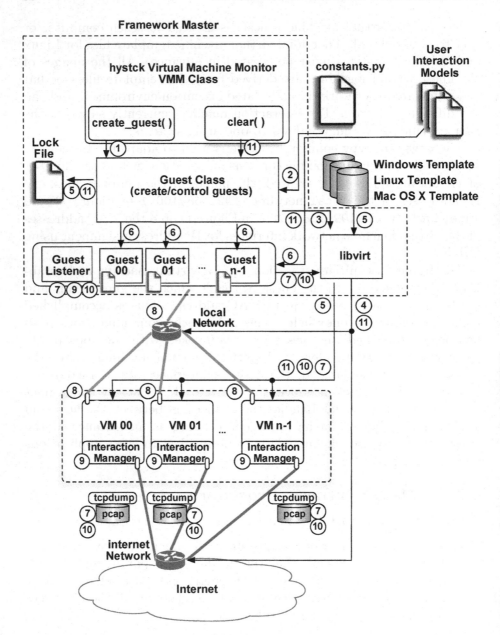

Figure 2. Data synthesis procedure.

5. The Guest class creates the virtual machines based on the templates using libvirt. In addition, a lock file is created.

6. The Guest class causes each guest to load its user interaction model.

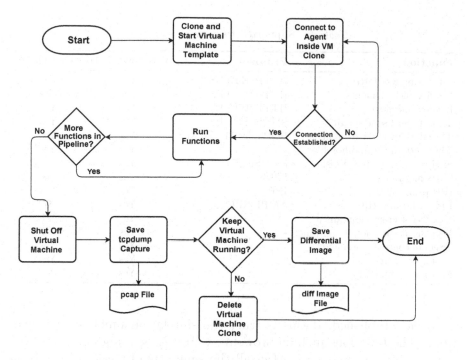

Figure 3. Framework flow diagram.

7. The user interaction models are executed in the guests. This causes the virtual machines to be started by `libvirt`. The `tcpdump` tool is started on the host for each virtual machine in order to record network traffic.

8. The guest instances connect to the virtual machine.

9. The process flow of each user interaction model proceeds, whereby the interaction manager controls the graphical user interface and simulates the desired behavior using the operating system and its applications (e.g., Firefox and Thunderbird).

10. The simulation is complete. The virtual machines are shut down by `libvirt` and `tcpdump` stops capturing traffic.

11. Finally, the virtual machines and the `local` and `internet` network interfaces are deleted by `libvirt`. The lock file is also deleted.

The flow diagram in Figure 3 shows the most important steps in the workflow. The workflow begins with cloning, starting and connecting to the virtual machine. Next, a test is made to check if the connection

Table 1. Supported framework features.

Function	Protocol	Windows 7/10	Ubuntu 19
Firefox browse URL	HTTP/HTTPS	Yes	Yes
Firefox click elements	HTTP/HTTPS	Yes	Yes
Firefox download	HTTP/HTTPS	Yes	Yes
Thunderbird send email	SMTP/SMTPS	Yes	Yes
Thunderbird receive email	POP3/IMAP/IMAPS	Yes	Yes
Thunderbird fill mailbox file	–	Yes	Yes
SSH connection/file transfer	SSH/SFTP	Yes	Yes
SMB file transfer	SMB	Yes	Yes
IPP print job	IPP	Yes	Yes
Pidgin IM and IRC	XMPP/IRC	Yes	No
VeraCrypt create container	–	Yes	NT
VeraCrypt (un)mount container	–	Yes	NT
Execute console commands	–	Yes	Yes
Change system clock	–	Yes	Yes
Multiuser capability	–	Yes	No

has been established; if this is true, the simulation functions are executed. The functions include browsing websites, sending email and exchanging instant messages. After all the simulation functions have been executed, the virtual machine is shut down. Following this, a parameter value is checked to determine if the virtual machine should remain in **virtmanager** or if it should be deleted. For example, the virtual machine image should be maintained if it is desired to correlate network traffic with operating-system-dependent traces. Finally, **tcpdump** is closed and the capture files are saved.

3.4　Supported Features

The framework currently simulates common applications and traffic types. Table 1 shows the list of supported features, including the simulation activities in the operating systems. Note that "NT" means that the feature was not tested. The following details are provided about the supported features:

- **Firefox:** Certain behavior by the Firefox web browser can be simulated. The most important feature is the ability to browse websites. With the support of the web browser environment, it is possible to simulate common traffic types, including typical traffic patterns such as those involving streaming platforms. It is also possible to interact with websites using an **xpath** component to trigger click events on website objects.

- **Thunderbird:** A Thunderbird module is available for creating email traffic. The module supports basic Thunderbird activities such as logging into an email account, and sending and receiving email.

- **SSH/SFTP:** The SSH protocol is widely used to securely log into and transfer files across enterprise server infrastructures. This is easily simulated because the framework provides full Linux Bash shell and Windows command line functionality.

- **Pidgin:** The Pidgin chat client supports a variety of chat services. It is possible to simulate instant messaging traffic (e.g., IRC) such as sending and receiving chat messages.

- **Botnets:** A module is available for simulating botnet attacks by Zeus, Asprox, Mariposa and Waledac. It is possible to generate network dumps of entire attacks from the victims' perspectives.

- **VeraCrypt:** A module is available for simulating the creation of encrypted containers. The module is only used in the image generation part.

3.5   Network Traffic Synthesizer

As mentioned above, the guest systems and virtual machines have two network interfaces. The `local` interface is for transmitting `hystck` commands while the `internet` interface is a bridge to the Internet. From the traffic generation point of view, the `internet` interface is interesting because all relevant traffic flows through it. The separation was implemented to prevent framework communications from showing up in network captures. Specifically, it ensures that all framework communications, such as telling a guest to browse a website, are handled by the `local` interface and everything else, such as actually browsing the website and sending and receiving email, are handled by the `internet` interface.

To obtain a traffic dump, `hystck` searches for a specific IP address and starts `tcpdump` with the corresponding network interface as a parameter. The `tcpdump` tool then captures every packet traveling through the network, outgoing as well as incoming. The tool continues to capture all the packets as long as the guest operating system is running and dumps them into a specified file.

In an experiment with Firefox, only two websites were visited, but the captured traffic exceeded 17,000 network packets. Many of the packets were related to the Firefox landing page (about 20 pages are loaded when

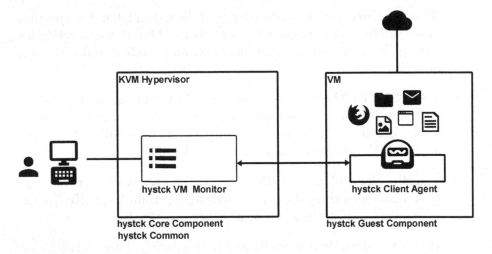

Figure 4.   Generating persistent disk images.

the browser is opened). However, another large – and more important – group comprised packets associated with Windows services and updates that executed in the background from the time the operating system was started. Clearly, much more traffic would be captured when simulating complete operating system behavior. Thus, the framework can generate more realistic datasets than other traffic generators.

3.6   Disk Image Generator

In addition to network traffic, the framework can be used to generate persistent disk images as in [10, 11, 17, 18]. Depending on the user interaction model, the framework can partially automate forensic image generation, including background data and planted evidence.

Figure 4 shows how the framework can emulate a number of applications on the guest systems; this is highly versatile. Additionally, the modular architecture enables new applications to be added. It is possible to specify and emulate a variety of user behaviors on guests using simple user interaction models. Many plugins for web browsing, program execution and file injection are provided. System time can be altered automatically to simulate system usage over a large interval of time. The framework also creates a report of all the activities performed on the image with hash values. At first glance, an image would be indistinguishable from the image of an actual system operated by a user. This is advantageous for education and training purposes where a variety of datasets can be created in an automated manner. Only one large base image is necessary in the framework. The distribution of the actual im-

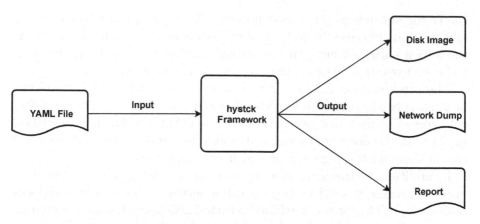

Figure 5. Generator workflow.

age is performed via snapshots in the QEMU-based file format, which are less than 1 GiB and only include the differences from the base image.

Locard's exchange principle states that every contact leaves a trace. This poses a problem during image generation. Every interaction with the operating system leaves a trace – usually multiple traces. These were seen in the framework components inside a virtual machine (e.g., Python installation, hystck agent source code, third party libraries, Bash scripts for the startup process and network connections to the virtual machine monitor). Future research will attempt to reduce the presence of these artifacts in images.

4. Generator and Reporter

This section describes the automated generation of images and network dumps. Also, it describes the reporting function, which summarizes everything that occurred in a virtual machine.

4.1 Generator

The hystck generator can almost automatically produce large amounts of traces and traffic. For example, the generator could instruct the framework to send hundreds of email messages and to browse numerous websites in order to generate benign and malicious data. Benign data corresponds to the generated haystack of good files. Malicious data corresponds to needles inserted in the haystack for subsequent detection.

The generator produces a variety of data types – normal, suspicious and malicious data (e.g., PDFs, images and text). As Figure 5 demonstrates, the generator takes in a YAML file and calls the functions associated with the YAML tags. The YAML configuration file helps setup the traffic and image generation process. Next, several action suites are created that describe the order and protocols under which files are sent; the action suites execute on the virtual machines. If desired, the data to be sent over the network may be selected randomly.

The configuration file grants wide access to framework functionality because special programming expertise is not needed to generate different types of traffic. Moreover, every portion of the YAML file is described in detail in the documentation, which enables users to understand what can be done with the generator and how it can be done.

In addition to the generator, a separate virtual machine is used to provide necessary services (e.g., Samba server, print server and local mail server). The virtual machine is started headless without a graphical user interface. If the virtual machine is installed as specified in the documentation, then the framework knows exactly where to find all the relevant services.

Users who have good understanding of Python and the `hystck` codebase have the option of manually scripting scenarios without using the generator. An example of manually-generated user interaction model source code is shown later (Figure 7). Note that it is not necessary to develop models independently because tweaking the YAML file of the `hystck` generator could produce the same outcome or even richer outcomes as the operations are configurable.

4.2   Reporter

The framework and its generator make it easy to produce datasets with hundreds or thousands of executed operations. This would make it very difficult to manually keep track of every detail of every operation. The `hystck` reporter keeps track of what happened and when, maintaining information about every benign and malicious operation. The reporting function is very useful for education and training, enabling instructors to tailor images and/or network dumps to their teaching goals. Additionally, the reporter could produce an XML document that assists an instructor in grading student work (e.g., providing all the details about a scenario). This document could then be viewed via the web viewer integrated in the framework or using a tool that can parse XML files.

5.   Framework Validation

As mentioned above, the `hystck` framework was specifically designed to simulate human-computer interactions in order to generate forensic images and network traffic that would at best be indistinguishable

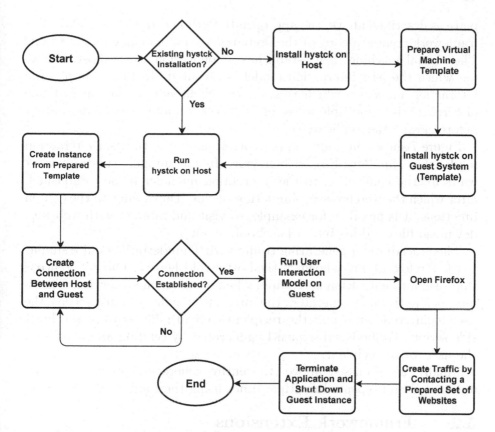

Figure 6. Traffic generation using Firefox.

from real-world human-computer interactions. This section describes two practical scenarios involving the generation of web and mail traffic using the framework. The section also shows how simulations of other applications can be integrated into the framework. Not every function can be discussed here, which is why interested readers are referred to the GitHub repository (`github.com/dasec/hystck`) for technical details.

5.1 Web Traffic and Mail Traffic Generation

While the modular structure of the framework supports the development and implementation of custom user interaction models to generate traffic and images for a variety of scenarios, several implemented models can inspire the creation of new scenarios with the same or different applications. This section describes two implemented models involving Firefox and Thunderbird.

Figure 6 shows traffic generation using the Firefox application. After installing the **hystck** framework and preparing the virtual machine tem-

plate as described above, the appropriate Python script is executed. The
framework creates a copy of the prepared virtual machine and starts it.
The virtual machine then establishes a connection to the host, following which the user interaction model is executed. In this example, the
interaction manager, which runs on the client-side, opens an instance
of Firefox, visits multiple websites in succession and downloads content
before closing the application.

Figure 7 shows the code snippet corresponding to the user interaction
model that simulates Firefox behavior. In the snippet, the framework
waits for the connection to the interaction manager to be established,
after which the web browser simulation begins. Depending on the chosen
functions, it is possible, for example, to visit and interact with websites,
download files and log into a Facebook account.

The procedure for generating traffic with Thunderbird is quite similar
to the Firefox example shown at the bottom of Figure 7. One difference is
that user authentication is required when using an email service. Therefore, before traffic is generated, the interaction manager must receive the
user login credentials and the recipient's email address from the host-
side script. Traffic is subsequently generated by sending an email from
the user to the recipient.

Finally, as discussed above, the entire generation process is easily
automated and repeated multiple times using the framework generator.

5.2   Framework Extensions

The framework is designed with extensibility in mind. A variety of
user activities and operating system behaviors based on new applications can be generated at any time. The applications may be added using the `skeleton.py` file located in the application folder in the GitHub
repository. The file provides developers with a basic structure of four
classes. However, only two classes, `SkeletonVmmSideCommands` and
`SkeletonGuestSideCommands`, are relevant. The other two classes are
only for command parsing and do not need to be altered.

The `SkeletonVmmSideCommands` class is responsible for the host-side
assembly of commands; it implements the functions that send the appropriate commands. The `SkeletonGuestSideCommands` class is the actual
implementation. Everything written in this class is executed by the
virtual machine and causes actions by an application or the operating
system.

Two functions are provided in the skeleton to facilitate the addition of
applications. The `open` and `close` functions trigger the corresponding
actions in the application. Additional assistance for integrating custom

```
1   from hystck.core.vmHelper import vmHelper
2   from hystck.core.vm import vm
3
4   vmhelper = vmHelper()
5   vmobj = vmhelper.createVM(vmname="windows-vm01", template=
        "windows")
6
7   #wait for vm
8   for vm in vmhelper.vms:
9       while vm.state != "connected"
10          time.sleep(0.1)
11
12      # vm.state == "connected":
13      # Email login data for Thunderbird
14      mail.add_imap_account("imap.web.de", "smtp.web.de",
15          "anonymous_sender@web.de", "password", "Sender Name",
16          "Example Subject", 2, 3, 1, 3)
17      ...
18      # begin of firefox session by opening the application
            and visiting a website
19      browserobj = vm.openBrowser("firefox", "www.h-da.de")
20      # downloading via firefox
21      browser_obj.download_from(
22          'https://www.nist.gov/itl/ssd/software-quality-group/' +
23          'computer-forensics-tool-testing-program-cftt/' +
24          'computer-forensic-0-0-2',
25          'Video dd files (zip format)')
26      # login for facebook via firefox
27      browserobj.facebook_login(username="user@domain.de",
            password="password")
28      browserobj.close()
29      ...
30      # enter recipient address and message and send email
31      mail.send_mail(message="testmail", subject="testmail",
32          receiver="anonymous_receiver@web.de")
```

Figure 7.   User interaction model code simulating Firefox and Thunderbird behavior.

applications is available in the template class files and framework documentation.

6.   Future Work

While the framework is versatile and supports diverse tasks, it will never cover all the use cases because new operating systems, applications and protocols will always have to be integrated. However, the modular architecture facilitates extensibility by enabling new user interaction models and scenarios to be incorporated. The framework can be made more functional by increasing the number of supported applications, including applications that use protocols such as FTPS, SIP and VoIP, and messenger applications such as WhatsApp Desktop and Skype. Many applications are cloud-based or require network connections to function and, therefore, generate traffic in the background almost "automatically." In addition to generating benign traffic, it is also necessary to simulate network attacks for attack traffic generation. The first steps in this direction have already been implemented by inserting malicious data (needles) into the network stream using the generator and by incorporating the botnet component.

As far as the core components of the framework are concerned, an important future task is to add data synthesis support for macOS. Framework agents will also be developed for Android and iOS.

Since the framework is based on the client-server model, it is cumbersome to test code changes quickly. This will be addressed by developing an efficient test base and debugging mechanisms. Another important task is to reduce artifacts in the generated images (e.g., agent source code and virtual machine monitor connections). In addition, it is necessary to integrate automated memory dump processes for Linux and Windows virtual machines to correlate relevant information with data captured by `tcpdump` and data stored in virtual machine persistent storage.

Other research problems are modeling normal user behavior and simulating daily routines and environment interactions in network infrastructures. Chinchilla et al. [5] describe some characterizations of Internet traffic and perform a user classification. Studies will be performed on user behavior to produce high-fidelity user simulations. It will also be necessary to develop metrics for dataset quality, including comparing synthetically-generated and real-world datasets.

7.   Conclusions

The `hystck` framework offers a novel approach for generating digital forensic datasets. The data synthesis approach is more holistic than existing traffic generators. The framework models and simulates real human-computer interactions to generate network traffic and forensic images.

A key advantage of the framework is its extensibility. The modular, plugin-based design involving user interaction models enables users to write and integrate plugins for custom system interactions and realistic traffic generation. Another advantage is scalability – it is possible to simulate a network of computers with diverse operating systems, users, applications and protocols, each running in their own virtual machines. More systems can be added to the network environment at any time by simply introducing more virtual machines. The framework also offers an efficient image distribution feature because only small differential images need to be shared. Furthermore, the framework operates in a time-independent manner as the system time can be changed at will; this makes it possible to simulate multiple user interactions during a desired time interval. Additionally, the framework is case independent in that it is not necessary to model user behavior manually; an API is provided to automatically interact with the framework.

As the future research tasks are implemented, the framework will evolve to become a powerful dataset generator. These datasets can be used for new network traffic analysis tools and network forensic approaches, simulating realistic user interactions for classical drive forensics, analyzing memory dumps and investigating network usage and data storage by mobile device applications.

The latest version of the framework source code is downloadable from the GitHub repository (`github.com/dasec/hystck`). The framework documentation, an installation guide and details about framework features and adding custom code for simulating other application types are available at `hystck/docs`. The pre-compiled documentation is available at `hystck/docs/src/_build/html/index.html`.

Acknowledgements

This research was supported by the German Federal Ministry of Education and Research (BMBF) under Forschung an Fachhochschulen (Contract No. 13FH019IB6) and by the Hessen State Ministry for Higher Education, Research and the Arts (HMWK) under CRISP. The authors also wish to thank Reinhard Stampp and Sascha Kopp, who played important roles in implementing the framework.

References

[1] S. Abt and H. Baier, Are we missing labels? A study of the availability of ground truth in network security research, *Proceedings of the Third International Workshop on Building Analysis Datasets and Gathering Experience Returns for Security*, pp. 40–55, 2014.

[2] D. Brauckhoff, A. Wagner and M. May, FLAME: A flow-level anomaly modeling engine, *Proceedings of the Conference on Cyber Security Experimentation and Test*, article no. 1, 2008.

[3] G. Brogi and V. Tong, Sharing and replaying attack scenarios with Moirai, presented at the *Rendezvous de la Recherche et de l'Enseignement de la Sécurité des Systèmes d'Information (Information Systems Security Research and Education Meeting)*, 2017.

[4] B. Carrier, Open Source Digital Forensic Tools: The Legal Argument, @stake, Cambridge, Massachusetts, 2002.

[5] R. Chinchilla, J. Hoag, D. Koonce, H. Kruse, S. Osterman and Y. Wang, Characterization of Internet traffic and user classification: Foundations for the next generation of network emulation, *Proceedings of the Tenth International Conference on Telecommunications Systems, Modeling and Analysis*, 2002.

[6] C. Cordero, E. Vasilomanolakis, N. Milanov, C. Koch, D. Hausheer and M. Muhlhauser, ID2T: A DIY dataset creation toolkit for intrusion detection systems, *Proceedings of the IEEE Conference on Communications and Network Security*, pp. 739–740, 2015.

[7] C. Grajeda, F. Breitinger and I. Baggili, Availability of datasets for digital forensics – And what is missing, *Digital Investigation*, vol. 22(S), pp. S94–S105, 2017.

[8] M. Hibler, R. Ricci, L. Stoller, J. Duerig, S. Guruprasad, T. Stack, K. Webb and J. Lepreau, Large-scale virtualization in the Emulab network testbed, *Proceedings of the USENIX Annual Technical Conference*, pp. 113–128, 2008.

[9] M. Mahoney and P. Chan, An analysis of the 1999 DARPA/Lincoln Laboratory evaluation data for network anomaly detection, *Proceedings of the International Workshop on Recent Advances in Intrusion Detection*, pp. 220–237, 2003.

[10] C. Moch and F. Freiling, The Forensic Image Generator Generator (Forensig^2), *Proceedings of the Fifth International Conference on IT Security Incident Management and IT Forensics*, pp. 78–93, 2009.

[11] C. Moch and F. Freiling, Evaluating the Forensic Image Generator Generator, *Proceedings of the International Conference on Digital Forensics and Cyber Crime*, pp. 238–252, 2011.

[12] S. Molnar, P. Megyesi and G. Szabo, How to validate traffic generators? *Proceedings of the IEEE International Conference on Communications Workshops*, pp. 1340–1344, 2013.

[13] National Institute of Standards and Technology, Computer Forensic Tool Testing (CFTT) Program, Gaithersburg, Maryland (www.nist.gov/itl/ssd/software-quality-group/computer-forensics-tool-testing-program-cftt), 2019.

[14] National Institute of Standards and Technology, The CFReDS Project, Gaithersburg, Maryland (`www.cfreds.nist.gov`), 2019.

[15] M. Ring, S. Wunderlich, D. Scheuring, D. Landes and A. Hotho, A survey of network-based intrusion detection datasets, *Computers and Security*, vol. 86, pp. 147–167, 2019.

[16] L. Rossey, R. Cunningham, D. Fried, J. Rabek, R. Lippmann, J. Haines and M. Zissman, LARIAT: Lincoln adaptable real-time information assurance testbed, *Proceedings of the IEEE Aerospace Conference*, 2002.

[17] M. Scanlon, X. Du and D. Lillis, EviPlant: An efficient digital forensics challenge creation, manipulation and distribution solution, *Digital Investigation*, vol. 20(S), pp. S29–S36, 2017.

[18] H. Visti, S. Tohill and P. Douglas, Automatic creation of computer forensic test images, in *Computational Forensics*, U. Garain and F. Shafait (Eds.), Springer, Cham, Switzerland, pp. 163–175, 2015.

[19] C. Wright, C. Connelly, T. Braje, J. Rabek, L. Rossey and R. Cunningham, Generating client workloads and high-fidelity network traffic for controllable repeatable experiments in computer security, *Proceedings of the International Workshop on Recent Advances in Intrusion Detection*, pp. 218–237, 2010.

Chapter 6

DETECTING ATTACKS ON A WATER TREATMENT SYSTEM USING ONE-CLASS SUPPORT VECTOR MACHINES

Ken Yau, Kam-Pui Chow and Siu-Ming Yiu

Abstract   Critical infrastructure assets such as power grids and water treatment plants are monitored and managed by industrial control systems. Attacks that leverage industrial control systems to disrupt or damage infrastructure assets can impact human lives, the economy and the environment. Several attack detection methods have been proposed, but they are often difficult to implement and their accuracy is often low. Additionally, these methods do not consider the digital forensic aspects.

This chapter focuses on the use of machine learning, specifically one-class support vector machines, for attack detection and forensic investigations. The methodology is evaluated using a water treatment testbed, a scaled-down version of a real-world industrial water treatment plant. Data collected under normal operations and attacks are used in the study. In order to enhance detection accuracy, the water treatment process is divided into sub-processes for individual one-class support vector machine model training. The experimental results demonstrate that the trained sub-process models yield better detection performance than the trained complete process model. Additionally, the approach enhances the efficiency and effectiveness of forensic investigations.

Keywords: Machine learning, one-class SVM, forensics, water treatment system

1.   Introduction

Industrial control systems, which combine distributed computing and physical process monitoring and control [9], are commonly used to operate critical infrastructure assets such as power grids and water treatment plants. Industrial control systems make it convenient to operate infrastructure assets remotely, but the added convenience comes at the cost of increased vulnerabilities [13]. Specifically, an attacker can compro-

© IFIP International Federation for Information Processing 2020
Published by Springer Nature Switzerland AG 2020
G. Peterson and S. Shenoi (Eds.): Advances in Digital Forensics XVI, IFIP AICT 589, pp. 95–108, 2020.
https://doi.org/10.1007/978-3-030-56223-6_6

mise a corporate network using conventional network security attacks
and leverage the access to pivot and target industrial control systems.
A widely-reported attack on a Ukrainian power grid in December 2015
caused a power outage to more than 200,000 customers [10]. The attackers leveraged spear phishing email, variants of the BlackEnergy 3
malware and Microsoft Office documents containing malware to pene-
trate information technology networks and launch attacks on electrical
substations.

Digital forensics is increasingly engaging artificial intelligence to analyze large amounts of complex data [11]. Meanwhile, machine learning
techniques have been shown to be very effective at detecting anomalies and attacks in industrial control systems. Supervised learning has
yielded results with high precision, but the approach requires labeled
(normal and attack) data for training. Class labeling is a challenging
task because it is time consuming for large datasets and often requires
manual efforts of the part of control system experts. Moreover, it is
difficult or impossible to collect attack data. While some attacks may
be simulated, it is not possible to simulate all possible attacks [19].

To address these challenges, this research employs a semi-supervised
machine learning methodology in which a one-class support vector machine (OC-SVM) model is trained using normal data, following which
data that deviate from the trained model are identified as attacks. This
methodology does not need class labeling. Moreover, normal data for
training is readily obtained.

An important aspect of the proposed methodology is that the physical process is divided into sub-processes and a one-class support vector
machine model is created for each sub-process, which improves attack
detection performance. Additionally, the division renders forensic investigations more effective. Instead of investigating the entire system at
one time, a forensic practitioner can focus on individual sub-processes as
needed. Since each trained sub-process model is responsible for detecting
specific attacks, the practitioner is able to narrow the scope to perform
data collection and investigate each sub-process individually. Experiments with a water treatment testbed demonstrate the improvements in
attack detection and effectiveness of incident investigations.

2.   Related Work

Attack detection in industrial control systems has been the subject
of considerable research. Machine learning is one of the successful approaches for implementing attack detection.

Yau et al. [21, 22] have proposed forensic solutions for a simulated traffic light system that leverage machine learning techniques. They captured the values of relevant memory addresses used by the programmable logic controller that monitored and managed the traffic light system. The memory values were stored in a log file for model training and the trained model was used to identify anomalous programmable logic controller behavior. Although the solutions achieved high attack detection accuracy, the simulated system used in the research did not approach the scale and complexity of a real-world traffic light system.

Inoue et al. [8] have evaluated the application of unsupervised machine learning methods to anomaly detection in cyber-physical systems. Specifically, they compared two methods, deep neural networks and one-class support vector machines, for detecting anomalies in the same water treatment testbed used in this research. The results reveal that the two methods have various advantages and disadvantages with regard to detection performance and accuracy.

Mounce et al. [12] have employed supervised machine learning with support vector regression to detect novel events in time series data pertaining to water flow and pressure. The novel events include pipe bursts, hydrant flushing and sensor failure. Their research demonstrates that the methodology provides faster alert generation than approaches using artificial neural networks and fuzzy inference.

Schuster et al. [15] have applied one-class support vector machines to a number of real-world industrial control system traffic traces. Their experimental results show that one-class support vector machines are effective at analyzing network packets and packet sequences to detect anomalies.

Kravchik and Shabtai [9] have developed a methodology for detecting anomalies and attacks in industrial control systems using a 1D convolutional neural network and autoencoders. Convolutional neural networks are a popular machine learning technique used in image processing applications. An autoencoder is a neural network that is trained to reproduce its input, thereby learning useful properties of the data. Applications of the methodology to several popular public datasets reveal that the detection results match or exceed previously-published results while featuring a small footprint and short training and detection times, and providing more generality.

The methodology presented in this chapter is distinct from other approaches in that it divides a complex process into sub-processes for one-class support vector machine model training in order to increase attack detection performance and accuracy. The data used in this research was collected from a testbed that closely mimics a real-world water treat-

Figure 1. Secure Water Treatment (SWaT) testbed [3].

ment plant. A sliding window method is employed to process time series datasets for one-class support vector machine model training. Additionally, the methodology enhances forensic investigations of industrial control system incidents.

3.   Secure Water Treatment Testbed

The Secure Water Treatment (SWaT) testbed shown in Figure 1 is set up at the iTrust Centre for Research in Cyber Security at Singapore University of Technology and Design. The testbed closely mimics a real-world water treatment plant [3]. The testbed takes raw water as input, executes a series of treatments and outputs recycled water.

The water treatment process comprises six sub-processes or stages P1 through P6 (Figure 2) [20]. Raw water enters the raw water tank (P1) from where it is pumped to chemical tanks. After chemical dosing and static mixing (P2), the water is passed to an ultrafiltration (UF) system (P3) and ultraviolet (UV) lamps (P4). Following this, the water is fed to a reverse osmosis (RO) system (P5). Finally, a backwash process cleans

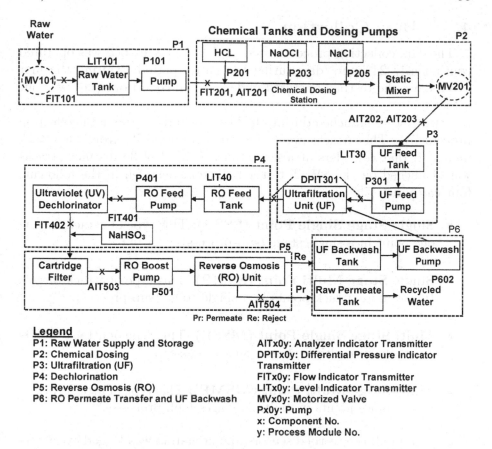

Figure 2. Six-stage water treatment process [3].

the membranes of the ultrafiltration system using the water produced by the reverse osmosis system (P6).

Sensors are employed at each sub-process; the sensor values are passed to a programmable logic controller, which monitors the states of the sub-processes. Based on the sensor values, the programmable logic controller directs actuators to manipulate the states of the sub-processes. For example, in the case of sub-process P1, the sensor LIT101 monitors the water level in the raw water tank. The programmable logic controller reads the sensor value and decides whether or not to change the state of the actuator, valve MV-101. If the LIT-101 sensor value is above a threshold, the programmable logic controller may deactivate valve MV-101, which stops raw water flow into the tank.

4.   Data Collection

The data collection process lasted 11 days. The testbed was operated continuously 24 hours/day during the entire period. During the first seven days, the testbed operated under normal conditions (i.e., without attacks).

Attacks were launched during the last four days of the data collection process [7]. The attacks were created systematically from an attack model [1] that considers attacker intent. A total of 36 distinct attacks were launched on the SWaT testbed. The attacks fell in the following four categories [7]:

- **Single Stage Single Point (SSSP):** This type of attack targets one point in a single stage (sub-process).

- **Single Stage Multi Point (SSMP):** This type of attack targets two or more attack points in a single stage (sub-process).

- **Multi Stage Single Point (MSSP):** This type of attack targets one point in multiple stages (sub-processes).

- **Multi Stage Multi Point (MSMP):** This type of attack targets two or more points in multiple stages (sub-processes).

Data from all the testbed sensors and actuators was logged every second and stored in a historian. A total of 946,722 data samples involving 51 attributes (e.g., FIT101, LIT101 and P101) were collected over the 11-day period. Figure 3 shows sample data that was collected during the experiments.

5.   One-Class Support Vector Machine

Machine learning builds an automated analytical model using algorithms that learn from data iteratively. Based on the model, machine learning enables the automated discovery of hidden insights without explicit programming [14]. A one-class support vector machine is a semi-supervised learning model that is widely used to detect anomalous events. The one-class support vector machine essentially finds the maximal margin hyperplane using an appropriate kernel function to map most of the training data to one side of the hyperplane [2]. Thus, it is trained using only data from only one (normal) class. After being trained with normal data, the one-class support vector machine classifies test data as normal data or abnormal (i.e., attack) data.

Timestamp	FIT101	LIT101	MV101	P101	P102	AIT201	AIT202	AIT203	FIT201	...
22/ 12/ 2015 4:30:00 PM	0	124.3135	1	1	1	251.9226	8.313446	312.7916	0	...
22/ 12/ 2015 4:30:01 PM	0	124.392	1	1	1	251.9226	8.313446	312.7916	0	...
22/ 12/ 2015 4:30:02 PM	0	124.4705	1	1	1	251.9226	8.313446	312.7916	0	...
22/ 12/ 2015 4:30:03 PM	0	124.6668	1	1	1	251.9226	8.313446	312.7916	0	...
22/ 12/ 2015 4:30:04 PM	0	124.5098	1	1	1	251.9226	8.313446	312.7916	0	...
22/ 12/ 2015 4:30:05 PM	0	123.921	1	1	1	251.9226	8.313446	312.7916	0	...
22/ 12/ 2015 4:30:06 PM	0	123.5284	1	1	1	251.9226	8.313446	312.7916	0	...
22/ 12/ 2015 4:30:07 PM	0	123.4107	1	1	1	251.9226	8.313446	312.7916	0	...
22/ 12/ 2015 4:30:08 PM	0	123.2144	1	1	1	251.9226	8.312805	312.7916	0	...
22/ 12/ 2015 4:30:09 PM	0	123.3322	1	1	1	251.9226	8.310242	312.7916	0	...
22/ 12/ 2015 4:30:10 PM	0	123.7247	1	1	1	251.9226	8.30896	312.8685	0	...
22/ 12/ 2015 4:30:11 PM	0	124.2742	1	1	1	251.9226	8.30896	312.9198	0	...
22/ 12/ 2015 4:30:12 PM	0	124.4705	1	1	1	251.9226	8.30896	312.9198	0	...
22/ 12/ 2015 4:30:13 PM	0	124.863	1	1	1	251.9226	8.30896	312.9198	0	...
22/ 12/ 2015 4:30:14 PM	0	125.0593	1	1	1	251.9226	8.30896	312.9198	0	...
22/ 12/ 2015 4:30:15 PM	0	124.5883	1	1	1	251.9226	8.30896	312.9198	0	...
22/ 12/ 2015 4:30:16 PM	0	124.392	1	1	1	251.9226	8.30896	312.9198	0	...

Figure 3. Sample data.

6.   Methodology

In the experiments, data from the first seven days (without attacks) was used to train the one-class support vector machine. Data from the last four days (with attacks) was used to evaluate the one-class support vector machine performance.

Since the scales of the various testbed features (attributes) were different (Figure 3), the min-max scaling method was used to normalize the values of the features to a scale of 0 to 1 in order to achieve better model training performance. Min-max scaling is performed as follows:

$$x' = \frac{x - min(x)}{max(x) - min(x)}$$

where x is the original value and x' is the normalized value.

Since the data was logged as a time series, the sliding window method was used to convert the data into individual feature vectors [6, 8]. Assume that l_i is the ith log entry and w is the window size, then the window W_i is given by:

$$W_i = l_i, l_{i+1}, \ldots, l_{i+w-1}$$

If there are k entries $l_1, l_2, \ldots, l_k$, then $k - w + 1$ windows $W_i, W_2, \ldots, W_{k-w+1}$ are generated. A window is labeled as an attack window if at

Timestamp	FIT101	UT101	M V101	P101	P102		RT601	P601	P602	P603	Normal/Attack
28/12/2015 10:29:10 AM	2.428979	815.9471	2	1	1	...	0.000128	1	1	1	Normal
28/12/2015 10:29:11 AM	2.424174	816.1041	2	1	1	...	0.000128	1	1	1	Normal
28/12/2015 10:29:12 AM	2.424174	816.3788	2	1	1	...	0.000128	1	1	1	Normal
28/12/2015 10:29:13 AM	2.447234	816.8499	2	1	1	...	0.000128	1	1	1	Normal
28/12/2015 10:29:14 AM	2.493675	817.6742	2	1	1	...	0.000128	1	1	1	Attack
28/12/2015 10:29:15 AM	2.535951	817.9490	2	1	1	...	0.000128	1	1	1	Attack
28/12/2015 10:29:16 AM	2.535951	817.9490	2	1	1	...	0.000128	1	1	1	Attack
28/12/2015 10:29:17 AM	2.569900	818.4592	2	1	1	...	0.000128	1	1	1	Attack
28/12/2015 10:29:18 AM	2.610575	818.8911	2	1	1	...	0.000128	1	1	1	Attack
28/12/2015 10:29:19 AM	2.635557	818.6948	2	1	1	...	0.000128	1	1	1	Attack
28/12/2015 10:29:20 AM	2.657336	819.3228	2	1	1	...	0.000128	1	1	1	Attack
28/12/2015 10:29:21 AM	2.663741	819.7938	2	1	1	...	0.000128	1	1	1	Attack

$W_1 = <l_1, l_2, l_3>$, Normal
$W_2 = <l_2, l_3, l_4>$, Normal
$W_3 = <l_3, l_4, l_5>$, Attack

Figure 4.   Sliding log entries into windows of size three.

least one of the log entries $l_i, l_{i+1}, \ldots, l_{i+w-1}$ in the window is labeled as an attack; otherwise, the window is labeled as a normal window.

Figure 4 shows how the log entries slide into windows of size three. Each window is fed to the trained model to classify it as normal or attack. The experiments compared the trained model performance achieved for different window sizes.

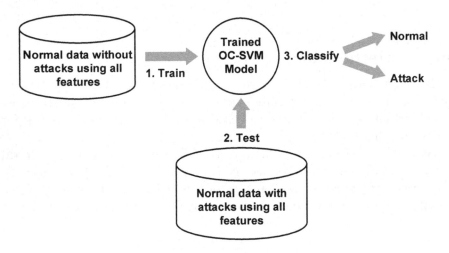

Figure 5.   Approach 1: Model training for the entire SWaT process.

In general, there are two approaches for model training. Approach 1 creates a trained a model using the entire process with all the data features (Figure 5). The trained model is then used to determine if any attacks were launched against the water treatment system. However, this approach cannot identify the sub-processes that were attacked.

The second approach, Approach 2, trains the models for the sub-processes separately using their own features. Figure 6 shows the details of the approach. For example, the model M_{P1} is trained using only

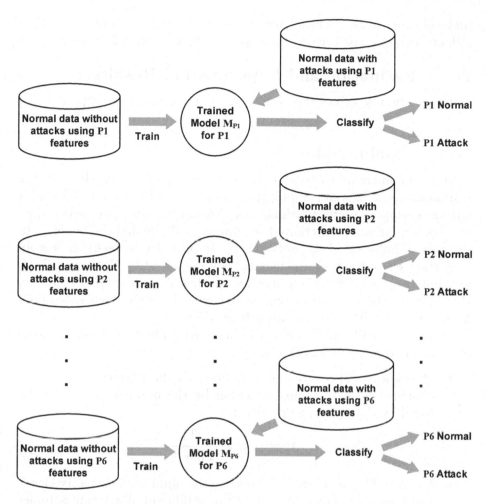

Figure 6. Approach 2: Model training for each of the six SWaT sub-processes.

P1 features (FIT101, LIT101, MV101, P101 and P102). The trained model M_{P1} is then used to detect attacks on sub-process P1. The one-class support vector machine used in the experiments was implemented using the scikit-learn machine learning library [16] on TensorFlow [18], an end-to-end open source machine learning platform.

Optimum one-class support vector machine classifiers for attack detection were realized using the parameters: (i) nu = 10^{-5}; (ii) gamma = auto; and (iii) kernel = sigmoid. Note that nu is an upper bound on the fraction of training errors and a lower bound on the fraction of support vectors; gamma defines the influence of a single training sample (default value is auto, which corresponds to the reciprocal of the number of features); and the kernel type may be linear, poly, rbf or sigmoid.

7.   Evaluation and Experimental Results

This section describes the evaluation procedure and the experimental results.

7.1   Evaluation

Since an imbalance exists between normal and attack data in the testing dataset, it is not appropriate to measure the performance of a one-class support vector machine model using the accuracy metric (i.e., number of correct predictions from among all predictions made). In the case of imbalanced datasets, when the minority (attack) class is an important class, the performance metrics suggested by Bekkar et al. [4] are more appropriate. These metrics are based on a confusion matrix that reports the number of true positives (TP), true negatives (TN), false positives (FP) and false negatives (FN).

Precision, recall and F-score were used to evaluate the performance of a classifier on the minority class [5, 17]:

- **Precision:** This measure is defined as the number of correctly classified positive samples divided by the number of samples labeled by the system as positive:

$$\text{Precision} = \frac{\text{TP}}{\text{TP} + \text{FP}}$$

- **Recall:** This measure is defined as the number of correctly classified positive samples divided by the number of all relevant samples (i.e., all the samples that should have been identified as positive):

$$\text{Recall} = \frac{\text{TP}}{\text{TP} + \text{FN}}$$

- **F-score:** This measure is defined as the harmonic mean of the precision and recall:

$$\text{F-score} = 2 \times \frac{\text{Precision} \times \text{Recall}}{\text{Precision} + \text{Recall}}$$

7.2   Experimental Results

According to Dietterich [6], the sliding window method converts a sequential supervised learning problem into a classical supervised learning problem, which yields adequate performance in many applications.

Table 1. Approach 1 classification performance.

Window Size	Precision (%)	Recall (%)	F-score (%)
N/A	88.07	99.96	93.63
3	88.08	99.96	93.64
5	88.08	99.96	93.64

Table 2. Approach 2 classification performance.

Sub-Process	Window Size	Precision (%)	Recall (%)	F-score (%)
P1 (5 Features)	N/A	98.28	99.86	99.07
	3	98.28	99.86	99.06
	5	98.28	99.86	99.06
P2 (11 Features)	N/A	99.25	100.00	99.63
	3	99.25	100.00	99.63
	5	99.25	100.00	99.63
P3 (9 Features)	N/A	90.29	100.00	94.89
	3	90.44	99.98	94.97
	5	90.47	99.95	94.98
P4 (9 Features)	N/A	99.07	99.89	99.48
	3	99.07	99.89	99.48
	5	99.08	99.89	99.48
P5 (13 Features)	N/A	99.49	99.91	99.70
	3	99.49	99.91	99.70
	5	99.49	99.91	99.70
P6 (4 Features)	N/A	99.82	99.99	99.91
	3	99.82	99.99	99.91
	5	99.82	99.99	99.91

However, the experimental results demonstrate that the sliding window method applied to the entire process (Approach 1 in Table 1) and to individual sub-processes (Approach 2 in Table 2) does not improve the performance of the one-class support vector machine classifiers for attack detection when the window sizes are set to three and five. On the other hand, the precision and F-score values are significantly increased for Approach 2 (Table 2), which divides the entire process into six sub-processes for model training. Note that identical parameter settings (nu = 10^{-5}, gamma = auto and kernel = sigmoid) were employed for one-class support vector machine training in Approach 1 and Approach 2.

An advantage of the proposed methodology is that the parameter settings can be adjusted individually for training each sub-process classifier in order to achieve the best performance. Moreover, this methodology results in better attack detection performance, and increases the efficiency and effectiveness of forensic investigations. Since the timestamps, durations and activity sequences of sub-process attacks are recorded in a log file during the classification process (Figure 6), a forensic investigator is able to obtain more evidence about the case from the classification log file when the attack log activities and time sequences are correlated with other system/network logs and the activity logs on a suspect's computer.

8.   Conclusions

Detecting and investigating attacks on industrial control systems are vital to securing critical infrastructure assets. This chapter has described a semi-supervised machine learning methodology in which a one-class support vector machine model is trained using normal data, following which attacks are identified as data that deviates from the trained model. The methodology eliminates the need to employ labeled (normal and attack) data for training – class labeling is time consuming for large datasets and it is difficult, if not impossible, to collect attack data. Another important aspect is that the methodology divides a physical process into sub-processes, and a one-class support vector machine model is created for each sub-process.

Experimental results using a water treatment testbed demonstrate that the trained sub-process models yield better attack detection performance than the trained complete process model. Additionally, the division into sub-processes renders forensic investigations more effective. Instead of investigating the entire system at one time, a forensic practitioner can focus on individual sub-processes as needed. Since each trained sub-process model is responsible for detecting specific attacks, the practitioner is able to narrow the scope to perform data collection and investigate each sub-process individually.

Future research will attempt to improve attack detection performance using machine learning on large, real-world datasets. Additionally, it is will attempt to use artificial intelligence techniques to support forensic investigations of industrial control systems.

Acknowledgement

The authors wish to thank the iTrust Centre for Research in Cyber Security at Singapore University of Technology and Design for providing the datasets used in this research.

References

[1] S. Adepu and A. Mathur, An investigation into the response of a water treatment system to cyber attacks, *Proceedings of the Seventeenth IEEE International Symposium on High Assurance Systems Engineering*, pp. 141–148, 2016.

[2] S. Amraee, A. Vafaei, K. Jamshidi and P. Adibi, Abnormal event detection in crowded scenes using a one-class SVM, *Signal, Image and Video Processing*, vol. 12(6), pp. 1115–1123, 2018.

[3] K. Aung, Secure Water Treatment Testbed (SWaT): An Overview, iTrust Centre for Research in Cyber Security, Singapore University of Technology and Design, Singapore, 2015.

[4] M. Bekkar, K. Djemaa and T. Alitouche, Evaluation measures for model assessment over imbalanced datasets, *Journal of Information Engineering and Applications*, vol. 3(10), pp. 27–38, 2013.

[5] A. Bottenberg and J. Ward, Applied Multiple Linear Regression, Technical Documentary Report PRL-TDR-63-6, Air Force Systems Command, Lackland Air Force Base, Texas, 1963.

[6] G. Dietterich, Machine learning for sequential data: A review, *Proceedings of the Joint IAPR International Workshops on Statistical Techniques in Pattern Recognition, and Structural and Syntactic Pattern Recognition*, pp. 15–30, 2002.

[7] J. Goh, S. Adepu, K. Junejo and A. Mathur, A dataset to support research in the design of secure water treatment systems, *Proceedings of the International Conference on Critical Information Infrastructures Security*, pp. 88–99, 2016.

[8] J. Inoue, Y. Yamagata, Y. Chen, M. Poskitt and J. Sun, Anomaly detection in a water treatment system using unsupervised machine learning, *Proceedings of the IEEE International Conference on Data Mining Workshops*, pp. 1058–1065, 2017.

[9] M. Kravchik and A. Shabtai, Efficient Cyber Attack Detection in Industrial Control Systems using Lightweight Neural Networks, Department of Software and Information Systems Engineering, Ben-Gurion University of the Negev, Beer-Sheva, Israel, 2019.

[10] M. Lee, M. Assante and T. Conway, Analysis of the Cyber Attack on the Ukrainian Power Grid, TLP: White, SANS Industrial Control Systems, Bethesda, Maryland, and Electricity Information Sharing and Analysis Center, Washington, DC, 2016.

[11] F. Mitchell, The use of artificial intelligence in digital forensics: An introduction, *Digital Evidence and Electronic Signature Law Review*, vol. 7, pp. 35–41, 2010.

[12] S. Mounce, R. Mounce and J. Boxall, Novelty detection for time series data analysis in water distribution systems using support vector machines, *Journal of Hydroinformatics*, vol. 13(4), pp. 672–686, 2011.

[13] D. Ramotsoela, A. Abu-Mahfouz and G. Hancke, A survey of anomaly detection in industrial wireless sensor networks with critical water system infrastructure as a case study, *Sensors*, vol. 18(8), article E2491, 2018.

[14] SAS Institute, Machine learning: What it is and why it matters, Cary, North Carolina (`www.sas.com/en_us/insights/analytics/machine-learning.html`), 2019.

[15] F. Schuster, A. Paul, R. Rietz and H. Koenig, Potential of using a one-class SVM for detecting protocol-specific anomalies in industrial networks, *Proceedings of the IEEE Symposium Series on Computational Intelligence*, pp. 83–90, 2015.

[16] scikit-learn, Machine learning in Python (`scikit-learn.org`), 2019.

[17] M. Sokolova and G. Lapalme, A systematic analysis of performance measures for classification tasks, *Information Processing and Management*, vol. 45(4), pp. 427–437, 2009.

[18] TensorFlow, TensorFlow: An end-to-end open source machine learning platform (`www.tensorflow.org`), 2019.

[19] R. Vlasveld, Introduction to One-Class Support Vector Machines (`rvlasveld.github.io/blog/2013/07/12/introduction-to-one-class-support-vector-machines`), July 12, 2013.

[20] J. Wang, J. Sun, Y. Jia, S. Qin and Z. Xu, Towards "verifying" a water treatment system, in *Formal Methods*, K. Havelund, J. Peleska, B. Roscoe and E. de Vink (Eds.), Springer, Cham, Switzerland, pp. 73–92, 2018.

[21] K. Yau and K. Chow, PLC forensics based on control program logic change detection, *Journal of Digital Forensics, Security and Law*, vol. 10(4), pp. 59–68, 2015.

[22] K. Yau and K. Chow, Detecting anomalous programmable logic controller events using machine learning, in *Advances in Digital Forensics XIII*, G. Peterson and S. Shenoi (Eds.), Springer, Cham, Switzerland, pp. 81–94, 2017.

III

FILESYSTEM FORENSICS

Chapter 7

A DIGITAL MEDIA SIMILARITY MEASURE FOR TRIAGE OF DIGITAL FORENSIC EVIDENCE

Myeong Lim and James Jones

Abstract   As the volume of potential digital evidence increases, digital forensic practitioners are challenged to determine the best allocation of their limited resources. While automation will continue to partially mitigate this problem, the preliminary question about which media should be examined by human or machine remains largely unsolved. This chapter describes and validates a methodology for assessing digital media similarity to assist with digital media triage decisions. The application of the methodology is predicated on the idea that unexamined media is likely to be relevant or interesting to a practitioner if the media is similar to other media that were previously determined to be relevant or interesting. The methodology builds on prior work using sector hashing and the Jaccard index of similarity. These two methods are combined in a novel manner and the accuracy of the resulting methodology is demonstrated using a collection of hard drive images with known ground truth. The work goes beyond interesting file and file fragment matching. Specifically, it assesses the overall similarity of digital media to identify systems that might share applications and thus be related, even if common files of interest are encrypted, deleted or otherwise unavailable. In addition to triage decisions, digital media similarity may be used to infer links and associations between disparate entities.

Keywords: Drive similarity, link discovery, sector hashing, Jaccard index

1.   Introduction

Digital forensic practitioners extract and process evidence from digital sources and media, often during the course of criminal investigations. Digital evidence is fragile and volatile, and requires the attention of a

Published by Springer Nature Switzerland AG 2020
G. Peterson and S. Shenoi (Eds.): Advances in Digital Forensics XVI, IFIP AICT 589, pp. 111–135, 2020.
https://doi.org/10.1007/978-3-030-56223-6_7

trained specialist to ensure that content of evidentiary value can be effectively isolated and extracted in a forensically-sound manner. One of the roles of a digital forensic practitioner is to find supporting evidence by recovering data such as files, email and photographs from computer hard drives as well as from cell phones, flash drives, RAM chips and network devices. Cloud computing has expanded data storage to multiple geographically-dispersed systems such as game consoles, Internet of Things devices and embedded systems, which are also the targets of digital forensic investigations.

As more digital data is created and digital storage systems grow in size, forensic practitioners are overwhelmed by the volume of data to be analyzed and backlogs in digital forensic laboratories are common. According to an FBI Regional Computer Forensics Laboratory Program report [23], more than 15,000 digital devices and storage media were previewed and six petabytes of data were processed by the FBI in 2017 alone, and several Regional Computer Forensics Laboratories set the reduction of backlogs as an explicit goal. In 2018, the Digital Forensics Unit of the Department of Homeland Security Cyber Crime Center processed seven petabytes of data.

Digital forensic practitioners seek to prioritize the data sources to be analyzed given limited time, and human and computing resources. Manual and forensic-tool-based analyses may take many hours to complete for each data source. Even with automated tools such as EnCase [6], FTK and Autopsy, additional human review time is required before forensic analyses of drives can be conducted. Practitioners often do not have adequate information to make decisions about which media to work on first, something that can only be determined by spending valuable time and resources on each candidate source. The lack of efficient tools and knowledge about potential evidence on a device cause inefficiencies that can lead to critical deadlines being missed and delays in disseminating actionable information.

With limited time, digital forensic practitioners must pick and choose which digital media to review from among the many available, making media triage a necessity. While triage tools exist for explicit tasks such as finding substrings of interest and specific files, a general purpose triage method based on a similarity measure between arbitrary-sized content and a labeled collection of digital media images is required. For example, a hard drive image that shows high similarity to a cluster of previously-labeled drive images of interest can be prioritized for further analysis. The similarity may be used to infer relationships between entities and as the basis for examining additional media.

This chapter proposes a digital media similarity measure based on sector hashing and a variant of the Jaccard index to help address these challenges. The similarity measure enables forensic practitioners to quickly and accurately measure the similarity of unexamined digital media to other images that are known to be relevant or interesting. A similar image is more likely to contain evidence of interest and may be used to discover previously-unknown links between entities.

2. Background

The proposed method relies on a modified Jaccard index similarity measure computed over digital media sector hashes. The similarity is computed based on the sectors present in digital media after adjusting for known common sectors (e.g., operating system and low entropy sectors) and weighting based on sector frequency. A sector size of 512 bytes is used regardless of the actual sector size so that fragments can match across devices with different sector sizes; these are assumed to be 512 bytes or 4,096 bytes in most cases. It is also assumed that files are stored on sector (cluster) boundaries, which is generally accepted to be true. Of course, sector hashing and other content-specific techniques, including the proposed methodology, cannot be used to match identical data that is encrypted with different keys.

Cryptographic hashing computes a fixed size output for an arbitrary length input. Changes in input have unpredictable and equally significant effects on the output regardless of the scope and nature of the input changes.

Sector hashing computes the hashes of data stored in digital media sectors. File hashing computes the hashes of data stored in digital media files. Advantages of sector hashing over file hashing are that sector hashing does not require filesystem interpretation and the entire file to be present for the presence of common data to be inferred. In general, finding more content in a file increases the likelihood that the entire file is present. This facilitates analysis, but recovering entire files is not necessary to conduct triage and useful analyses. In this work, matching sectors may be the result of deleted and partially-overwritten data as well as other activity (e.g., temporary files and swap space files).

The Jaccard index (JI) is a simple and widely used similarity measure that is applied to arbitrary sets of data [24]. The index, which measures the similarity between finite sample sets, is computed as follows:

$$JI(A, B) = \frac{|A \cap B|}{|A \cup B|} = \frac{|A \cap B|}{|A| + |B| - |A \cap B|} \quad 0 \leq JI(A, B) \leq 1$$

where JI(A, B) is the cardinality of the intersection of sets A and B divided by the cardinality of the union of sets A and B. In this work, the sets A and B comprise sector hashes from digital media of potential interest.

3.   Use Cases

The following two use cases are considered in this research:

- I have a collection of digital media. Are any of these items similar to media I have seen before and about which I care (or not care)?

- I have a collection of digital media and I know where they came from. Are any of these items similar to each other? Can their similarity tell me anything about connections between people and/or devices?

Breitinger et al. [5] state that resemblance (R) and containment (C) are two common types of similarity queries, and that a similarity identification algorithm should handle one of four use cases: (i) object similarity detection (R); (ii) cross correlation (R); (iii) embedded object detection (C); and (iv) fragment detection (C). The two use cases considered in this work are similarity detection and cross correlation between hard drive images, which are routinely encountered in law enforcement and national security investigations. In both the use cases, digital forensic practitioners may or may not know the sources of the evidentiary items and their relationships to the active investigations.

4.   Previous Work

Many forensic tools and algorithms use string searches as their basis. The strings may be user-specified regular expressions that match features such as email addresses, telephone numbers, social security numbers, credit card numbers, network IP addresses and other kinds of information that might correspond to pseudo-unique identifiers [12, 15, 21, 31]. Garfinkel [11] defines a pseudo-unique identifier as "an identifier that has sufficient entropy such that within a given corpus it is highly unlikely that the identifier will be repeated by chance."

Garfinkel [11] also identified an issue with typical forensic analysis – that a hard drive image does not correlate with other images. In particular, he listed three problems: (i) improper prioritization; (ii) lost opportunities for data correlation; and (iii) improper emphasis on document recovery. He attempted to address these problems via cross-drive analysis that used pseudo-unique information such as social security numbers, credit card numbers and email addresses. In his approach, feature extractors analyzed the string files and wrote their results to feature files. The extracted features were then applied to a multi-drive corpus to identify associations between different drives.

In the case of second-order cross-drive analysis, a different question is raised: Which drives in the corpus have the largest number of features in common? To answer this question, Garfinkel [11] implemented the Multi Drive Correlator (MDC). The input to MDC is a set of drive images with a feature to be correlated and the output is a list of (feature, drive-list) tuples. The MDC program reads multiple feature files and generates a report, which shows the number of drives on which each feature was seen, the total number of times each feature was seen on the drives and the list of drives on which each feature occurred.

Beverly et al. [1] extended this work using Ethernet media access control (MAC) addresses extracted from validated IP packets. They treated the MAC addresses and drive images as nodes, and addresses on a hard drive image as links in a graph. From the partitioned graph, they were able to obtain distinct clusters in the collection of drive images.

Young et al. [32] introduced a file-agnostic approach that leverages the speed of hashing. They employed sector hashes instead of file hashes. They compared blocks (fixed-sized file fragments) against a large data set of sector hashes, and considered individual sectors and collections of contiguous sectors (blocks or clusters). Their method is based on two hypotheses:

- If a block of data from a file is distinct, then a copy of the block found on a data storage device is evidence that the file is or was present.

- If the blocks of a file are shown to be distinct with respect to a large and representative corpus, then the blocks can be treated as if they are universally distinct.

Young et al. [32] suggest that analyses of digital media would be more accurate and faster if a database of hash values computed from fixed-sized blocks of data is used. They employed large corpora such as Govdocs [13] and the NSRL RDS [18] to populate the hash value database. Three types of sectors – singleton, paired and common sectors – were analyzed to understand the root causes of non-distinct blocks. They discovered that the major reason for encountering common sectors was that the same block existed in many files due to malware code reuse and common file container formats. In order to implement a field deployment on a laptop, Young and colleagues considered sampling sectors instead of processing all the media sectors. Several database implementations were considered and a Bloom filter front-end was ultimately implemented to speed up generic query times [3]. Young et al. analyzed several filesystems to demonstrate the generality of their approach. However, encrypted files and filesystems were found to be problematic because the same data of interest is stored differently when encrypted.

Garfinkel and McCarrin [14] have proposed hashing blocks instead of entire files; this block hashing method inspired the similarity measure methodology proposed in this chapter. Garfinkel and McCarrin also specified the HASH-SETS algorithm that identifies the existence of files and the HASH-RUN algorithm that reassembles files using a database of file block hashes. A fixed block size (e.g., 4 KiB) may present a problem due to filesystem alignment. However, this is addressed by hashing overlapping blocks with a 4 KiB sliding window over the entire drive and moving the window one sector at a time.

Taguchi [29] experimented with different sample sizes using random sampling and sector hashing for drive triage. Given a drive, the goal was to provide a practitioner with information about the utility of continuing an investigation. If a block hash value of target data is in the database, then it is very probable that the target file is on the drive. However, if no hashes are found during sampling, then a confidence level is computed that indicates the likelihood that the target data is not on the drive.

The **spamsum** program developed by Tridgell [30] performs context-triggered piecewise hashing to find updates of files. It identifies email messages that are similar to known spam. The **ssdeep** program developed by Kornblum [16], which is based on **spamsum**, computes and matches context-triggered piecewise hash values. It is more effective than **spamsum** for relatively small objects that are similar in size. However, it is vulnerable to attacks that insert trigger sequences at the beginning of files, exploiting the fact that an **ssdeep** signature value can have at most 64 characters [4].

Roussev and colleagues [25–27] have developed a similarity digest hashing method that is implemented in a program called **sdhash**. The program finds the features from a neighborhood with the lowest probability of being encountered by chance. Each selected feature, which is a 64-byte sequence, is hashed and placed in a Bloom filter. When a filter reaches full capacity, a new filter is generated. Thus, a similarity digest is a collection of a sequence of Bloom filters.

Oliver et al. [19] have proposed a locality-sensitive hashing methodology called TLSH. TLSH populates an array of bucket counts by processing an input byte sequence using a sliding window. Quartile points are computed from the array, following which the digest header and body are constructed. The digest header values are based on the quartile points, file length and checksum. The digest body comprises a sequence of bit pairs determined by each bucket value in relation to the quartile points. A distance score is assigned between two digests; this score is a summed-up distance between the digest headers and digest bodies. The distance between two digest headers is based on file lengths and quartile ratios. The distance between two digest bodies is computed as the Hamming distance. Experiments indicate that TLSH is more robust to random adversarial manipulations than ssdeep and sdhash.

Penrose et al. [22] have used a Bloom filter for rapid contraband file detection. The Bloom filter reduces the size of the database (hashes in this case) by an order of magnitude, but incurs a small false positive rate. Penrose and colleagues subsequently implemented a larger Bloom filter for faster access, achieving 99% accuracy while scanning for contraband files in minutes using a test dataset.

Bjelland et al. [2] present three common scenarios where approximate matching can be applied: (i) search; (ii) streaming; and (iii) clustering. In a search scenario, the data space is large compared with a streaming scenario. In a clustering scenario, the input and data spaces are the same. Approximate matching is impractical for large datasets due to its high latency.

Moia and Henriques [17] have presented steps for developing new approximate matching functions. Approximate matching functions overcome the limitations of cryptographic hash functions that cannot detect non-identical, but similar, data.

The main goal of the research described in this chapter is to compute digital media image similarity measures for efficient triage. The proposed methodology does not replace approximate hashing and other methods; instead, it employs and potentially augments them. Most similarity methods operate at the file or object levels. In contrast, the proposed methodology works at the sector level, rendering it robust to deleted and partially-overwritten data. However, the proposed methodology is vulnerable to attacks that: (i) selectively delete and overwrite content that is common with another digital device; (ii) plant false fragments to mislead the algorithm and practitioners; and (iii) wipe digital media at a low level.

5. Methodology

The proposed digital media similarity measure uses sector hashes to compute a Jaccard index, but with three modifications: (i) whitelist for removing operating system and low-entropy (non-discriminatory) sectors; (ii) frequency weight that reflects content uniqueness; and (iii)

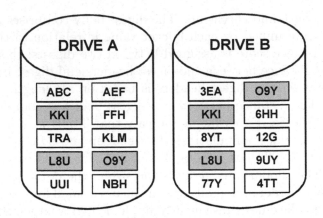

Figure 1. Two hard drives with three common sectors.

normalization that accounts for differences in media size. This section presents the Jaccard index computation over sector hashes, and the whitelist that is used to remove non-discriminatory sectors. It discusses the similarity computations for a single comparison drive and a set of comparison drives. It proceeds to show how the similarity computations are modified to account for hash frequency (i.e., sector content uniqueness). Finally, the section demonstrates the normalization of similarity computations to account for differences in digital media size.

5.1   Jaccard Index of Similarity

The basic Jaccard index is computed as the number of common sectors in two sources (e.g., hard drives A and B) divided by the number of sectors in the two sources minus the number of common sectors in the two sources. Figure 1 shows hard drives A and B, each with ten sectors. Each value denotes the hash value of the sector. The two hard drives have three of the same sectors (shaded). Thus, the Jaccard index is computed as $3/(10 + 10 - 3) = 0.1765$.

Each hard drive is divided into sectors. For example, if a hard drive has 1 terabyte (2^{40} bytes) capacity and the sector size is 512 bytes, then the drive has 2^{31} sectors. If both hard drives are exactly the same (e.g., one hard drive contains the image copied from the other hard drive), then the Jaccard index is one, indicating perfect similarity. If the two hard drives have no common sectors, then the Jaccard index is zero, indicating no similarity.

In order to compute the similarity measure, the sets of sectors in the basic Jaccard index computation are replaced by the sets of hash values

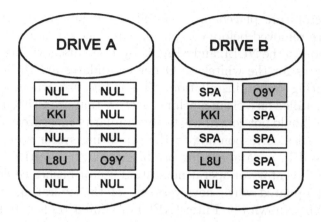

Figure 2. Whitelisted sectors (NUL and SPA).

of the sectors. The Jaccard index is thus computed as:

$$JI(A, B) = \frac{|A \cap B|}{|A \cup B|} = \frac{|A \cap B|}{|A| + |B| - |A \cap B|}$$

where A and B are the sets of hash values of the sectors in the first drive and second drive, respectively.

5.2   Whitelist

Figure 2 shows that the seven non-matching sectors in drive A contain only NULL bytes and the seven non-matching sectors in drive B contain only SPACE characters. For convenience, assume that the hash value of a NULL byte sector is NUL and the hash value of a SPACE sector is SPA. If the general method for computing the Jaccard index is employed, then the index value would be the same as in Figure 1 (i.e., 0.1765).

However, the similarity measure in Figure 2 should be higher than that in Figure 1 because all the meaningful sectors match in Figure 2 (NULL and SPACE sectors are not meaningful). In fact, the similarity measure in Figure 2 should have the maximum value of one. If this situation is considered when computing the Jaccard index, a more realistic similarity measure would be obtained.

In practice, it is better to report that the two drives match exactly instead of providing a low similarity level based on the unadjusted Jaccard index of 0.1765. This is achieved by eliminating the NULL and SPACE byte sectors from the sets being compared. When these sectors are eliminated from consideration, each drive has three sectors that match exactly, yielding a Jaccard index of one. Thus, the NULL and

SPACE sectors are placed in a whitelist and all the members of the whitelist are removed before computing the Jaccard index.

In addition to the NULL and SPACE byte sectors, low entropy sectors are candidates for the whitelist. Other candidates are the sectors in a clean operating system installation. This is because, when an operating system is installed on a clean machine, sectors that are written during the installation should not contribute to the similarity measure computation.

Sector hashes corresponding to the operating systems on test drives may be saved in a database for pre-filtering (exclusion) purposes. In practice, an inventory of operating system sector hashes could be maintained and updated when new versions of the operating systems are installed. The Known File Filter (KFF) or similar tools may be used for filtering.

5.3   Similarity between Two Drives

Computing a similarity measure between two drives is straightforward, but it relies on the construction of a good whitelist. This is because the Jaccard index is computed after the sectors in the whitelist are filtered. The term "target drive" refers to the drive that is triaged using a similarity measure against a known and established "source drive."

5.4   Similarity against a Cluster of Drives

During triage, the focus is on the similarity of one target drive against multiple groups of sources that might represent different priorities, levels of interest, or specific staff members and organizations. The drives in a cluster may have been confiscated from terrorist groups or could be collections of hard drives containing malicious programs of interest. In other words, multiple different groups of source media would typically exist. After the whitelist is created and saved in a database, the sectors of the target drive and clusters of interest can be scanned and ignored based on the database. This procedure enhances the speed and accuracy of the similarity measure computations.

Given an image of interest and cluster of labeled drives, one approach to assess the image of interest is to first compute the Jaccard index values between pairs of drives in the cluster. Table 1 shows the comparison chart for a cluster of k drives. Note that JI(i, j) = JI(j, i) in the table.

The image of interest may be compared against each drive in the cluster and the Jaccard index values may be computed. Table 2 shows the corresponding comparison chart. The last row d_t may be compared against the rows d_i. Examining the values in these two sets yields a statistically meaningful assessment.

Table 1. Comparison of a cluster of drives.

	d_1	d_2	...	d_k
d_1	1	JI(1, 2)	...	JI(1, k)
d_2	JI(2, 1)	1	...	JI(2, k)
...	...	...	1	...
d_k	JI(k, 1)	JI(k, 2)	...	1

Table 2. Comparison of a target drive against a cluster of drives.

	d_1	d_2	...	d_k
d_1	1	JI(1, 2)	...	JI(1, k)
d_2	JI(2, 1)	1		JI(2, k)
...	...	...	1	...
d_k	JI(k, 1)	JI(k, 2)	...	1
d_t	JI(t, 1)	JI(t, 2)	...	JI(t, k)

Table 3. Comparison of a target drive against an imaginary drive.

	Imaginary Drive
d_1	JI(1, I)
d_2	JI(2, I)
...	...
d_k	JI(k, I)
d_t	JI(t, I)

Another approach is to create an imaginary drive that contains all the sectors in the cluster of drives. This imaginary drive is merely the union of all the sectors in all the drives in the cluster. However, sectors that are shared by multiple drives are only counted once. The Jaccard index values are computed between the target sectors and the imaginary drive. Table 3 shows the corresponding comparison chart.

5.5   Similarity with Frequency

To simplify the analysis, an imaginary drive I is used as the source drive. The imaginary drive I is created by combining three drives C1, C2 and C3 in a cluster. Table 4 shows the sectors in the three cluster drives. Table 5 shows the imaginary drive sectors along with their frequencies.

Table 4. Sectors in cluster drives C1, C2 and C3.

C1	C2	C3
A	A	A
B	B	C
C	E	E
D	F	G

Table 5. Sectors and frequencies in imaginary drive I.

Imaginary Drive I	
A	3
B	2
C	1
D	1
E	2
F	1
G	1
Total	11

Now consider two target drives T_A and T_F, each with a single sector, A and F, respectively. Sector A in the imaginary drive I is present in every cluster drive whereas sector F is present in only one cluster drive (C2). Clearly, target drive T_A should have more similarity than T_F in a cluster comparison because sector A is present in every cluster drive. Therefore, the frequency of each sector must be used as an adjusting factor when computing the Jaccard index.

In order to illustrate the modified Jaccard index computations, two target drives T1 and T2 are compared against the imaginary drive I (and, by extension cluster drives C1, C2 and C3). Table 6 shows the sectors in the two target drives along with their frequencies in the imaginary drive.

The standard Jaccard index values for JI(T1, I) and JI(T2, I) are computed as $4/8 = 0.5$. However, T1 is more similar to I than T2 because T1 has sector A, which is shared by all three cluster drives (C1, C2 and C3), and it has sector E, which is shared by two cluster drives (C2 and C3).

Thus, the modified Jaccard index with frequency JIWF between two drives, D1 and D2, is computed as:

Table 6. Sectors and frequencies in target drives T1 and T2.

T1		T2	
A	3	C	1
E	2	D	1
F	1	F	1
G	1	G	1
H	1	H	1
Total	8	**Total**	5

$$\text{JIWF(D1, D2)} = \frac{\text{Number of Common Sectors with Frequency in D1 and D2}}{\text{Number of All Sectors with Frequency in D1 and D2}}$$

When computing JIWF, if a sector is shared by n drives, then the sector is counted n times. The numerator of JIWF(T1, I) is 7 because there are four common sectors (A, E, F and G) and sector A is counted three times and sector E is counted twice. The denominator of JIWF(T1, I) is 12 because there are a total of eight sectors (A, B, C, D, E, F, G and H) and A is counted three times and sectors B and E are each counted twice. Thus, JIWF(T1, I) is computed as $7/12 = 0.583$. JIWF(T2, I) is computed in a similar manner as $4/12 = 0.333$. The incorporation of sector frequencies in the JIWF computations yields a better result because T1 (0.583) is more similar to the cluster (source) drives than T2 (0.333).

5.6   Similarity with Normalized Frequency

The JIWF similarity measure is computed under the assumption that the sizes of the target and cluster drives are similar. However, if the target and cluster drives are significantly different in size – for example, the target is a thumb drive and the cluster drive is several terabytes – then, considering sector frequencies alone is inadequate when computing a good measure of similarity.

The standard Jaccard index computation employs intersection and union. The new Jaccard index computation employs modified definitions, Intersection* (I^*) and Union* (U^*), which are given by:

$$\text{Intersection}^*(\text{N1, N2}) = \text{Min}(|\text{N1}|, |\text{N2}|)$$

$$\text{Union}^*(\text{N1, N2}) = \text{Max}(|\text{N1}|, |\text{N2}|)$$

where N1 and N2 are normalized frequencies.

Table 7.   Hash values and frequencies of source drive S and target drive T.

Source Drive S			Target Drive T		
Hash Value	Frequency	Normalized Frequency	Hash Value	Frequency	Normalized Frequency
A	5	0.3333	A	1	0.0667
B	4	0.2667	B	2	0.1333
C	3	0.2	C	3	0.2
D	2	0.1333	D	4	0.2667
E	1	0.0667	E	5	0.3333
Total	15	1	**Total**	15	1

The new Jaccard index computation employs the normalized frequency to account for the difference in the sizes of the target and cluster drives. The normalized frequency N_f is given by:

$$N_f = \frac{F_i}{S_T}$$

where F_i is the frequency of a sector hash value i and S_T is the total number of sectors in a drive.

The resulting Jaccard index with normalized frequency JINF requires two normalized values to be computed for each distinct hash value, one for the source and the other for the target. In general, the JINF similarity value is computed as:

$$\text{JINF}(S, T) = \frac{\text{Sum of all Intersection}^*(S, T)}{\text{Sum of all Union}^*(S, T)}$$

where S and T are the source and target drives, respectively.

Table 7 shows the hash values, sector frequencies and normalized sector frequencies for hypothetical source and target drives.

Table 8 shows the Intersection* and Union* values computed for the hypothetical source and target drives using the normalized frequency values in Table 7. The sum of Intersection* values over all the hashes is 0.6. Likewise, the sum of all Union* values is 1.4. The resulting JINF value is 0.6/1.4 = 0.4286. Note that the JINF value is one for identical drives because the Intersection* and Union* values computed using the normalized frequency of each sector hash are identical.

Table 9 shows how the JINF values change when the frequency of sector hash A is successively increased by one in target drives T2, T3 and T4 (the normalized frequencies of the drives are not shown). As the frequency of the first block A in the target drive moves toward the

Table 8. Intersection* and Union* of two normalized frequency values.

Hash Value	Normalized Frequency of Source	Normalized Frequency of Target	Intersection*	Union*
A	0.3333	0.0667	0.0667	0.3333
B	0.2667	0.1333	0.1333	0.2667
C	0.2	0.2	0.2	0.2
D	0.1333	0.2667	0.1333	0.2667
E	0.0667	0.3333	0.0667	0.3333
Total			0.6	1.4
JINF			0.4286	

Table 9. JINF values of target drives T2, T3 and T4.

| Hash | Freq | T2 | | Freq | T3 | | Freq | T4 | |
		I*	U*		I*	U*		I*	U*
A	2	0.125	0.3333	3	0.1764	0.3333	4	0.2222	0.3333
B	2	0.125	0.2667	2	0.1176	0.2667	2	0.1111	0.2667
C	3	0.1875	0.2	3	0.1764	0.2	3	0.1667	0.2
D	4	0.1333	0.25	4	0.1333	0.2352	4	0.1333	0.2222
E	5	0.0667	0.3125	5	0.0666	0.2941	5	0.0667	0.2778
Sum	16	0.6375	1.3625	17	0.6705	1.3294	18	0.7	1.3
JINF		0.4678			0.5044			0.5384	

frequency of the same sector hash A in the source drive, the similarity should increase. Each block is essentially a new target drive that is being checked against the source drive. For each block, the JINF similarity increases when the frequency of sector hash A increases. Note also that the total number of blocks increases by one as the frequency of sector hash A is increased by one. This increase in the total number of blocks reduces the similarity because the portion of each block against the total number of blocks decreases. In contrast, the positive effect of increasing the frequency of sector hash A is greater than the negative effect of increasing the total number of blocks.

Table 10 shows how the similarity levels increase when the frequencies of sector hash A are considered. T6 is a new target drive created from target drive T5, where the frequency of sector hash E in drive T6 is reduced by one (= 4) from 5 in drive T5. Target drive T6 has a JINF

Table 10. JINF values of target drives T5, T6 and T7.

Hash	Freq	T5 I^*	U^*	Freq	T6 I^*	U^*	Freq	T7 I^*	U^*
A	5	0.2631	0.3333	5	0.2778	0.3333	10	0.0667	0.3333
B	2	0.1052	0.2667	2	0.1111	0.2667	20	0.1333	0.2667
C	3	0.1578	0.2	3	0.1667	0.2	30	0.2	0.2
D	4	0.1333	0.2106	4	0.1333	0.2222	40	0.1333	0.2667
E	5	0.0667	0.2631	4	0.0667	0.2222	50	0.0667	0.3333
Sum	19	0.7263	1.2736	18	0.7556	1.2444	150	0.6	1.4
JINF		0.5702			0.6071			0.4286	

value of 0.6071, which is higher than the JINF value of 0.5702 of target T5. This is because the total number of blocks in target drive T6 is closer to the number in the source drive and has less negative impact on the JINF value computation compared with target drive T5.

Target drive T7 in Table 10 demonstrates how well the methodology copes when the target and source drives have different sizes. The frequency of each block is copied from target drive T shown in the right-hand side of Table 7 and multiplied by 10. The JINF values of target drives T and T7 are the same because the normalized frequency of each hash block is the same for both drives. Therefore, the proposed methodology does not require the sizes of the drives to be measured.

6.   Validation

The proposed similarity measure was validated using the 2009 M57-Patents Scenario dataset [13], which comprises 68 hard drive images with known similarity. The images were taken from four distinct systems (named after four users, Pat, Terry, Jo and Charlie) over a 25-day period. Each system was imaged 17 times during the 25-day experiment.

For the purposes of this validation, each of the four systems represents a similar set of images. This is because they are, in fact, the same source systems with the only differences arising from normal use during the experiment. For the validation, sets of similar images were created using a subset of one user's images, following which one of the user's other images was compared with the set. High similarity was anticipated, which, in fact, occurred.

The validation was intended to serve as a preliminary confirmation that the proposed similarity measure is computationally correct, and not as a scalability test. Additional testing is planned against the Real

Data Corpus, which contains thousands of disparate media sources with no ground truth [10].

6.1   Initial Validation

The initial validation employed sequential snapshots of a single drive. On a clean drive, the following sequence of actions was performed after the Windows operating system was installed:

(a) An application was installed.

(b) An application was opened.

(c) An application was closed.

(d) An application was uninstalled.

(e) The system was rebooted.

The procedure was repeated for three clean drives with three applications, Wireshark, Firefox and Safari, whose generic drives were labeled, WS, FF and SA, respectively. A snapshot of the hard drive image were saved for each drive after each step in the sequence. In the case of drive WS, the snapshots were named WS_a, WS_b, WS_c, WS_d and WS_e. For example, WS_c denotes the snapshot of drive WS after Wireshark was closed, corresponding to action (c) in the sequence. The snapshots of the other two drives were named in a similar manner. Note that all the snapshots corresponding to a generic drive (e.g., WS) were designated as belonging to the same category, and different from the categories corresponding to the other generic drives (FF and SA).

6.2   Whitelist Sector Removal

As described above, sectors collected after the installation action (a) correspond to whitelist candidates. Therefore, sectors from snapshots WS_a, FF_a, SA_a were added to the whitelist database. The elimination of these sectors from consideration reduces the computational effort and enhances the accuracy of the Jaccard index.

6.3   JIWF Computation

The `hashdb` tool [14] was employed in this research. In order to compute the Jaccard index between two drives, A and B, the Windows operating system sectors from each drive were removed. Following this, the hash values h-A and h-B, were computed for the slimmed drives. The intersection of the hash values Int(h-A, h-B) was created using the hashdb command: intersect hash(h-A, h-B). Similarly, the union of the hash values Un(h-A, h-B) was created using the hashdb command: add_multiple(h-A, h-B).

The size command provides the number of entries in the LMDB database [7]. In particular, it returns two values – hash data store value and hash store value. The LMDB hash store is a highly compressed optimized store of all the block hashes in the database. When scanning for a hash, if it is not in this store, then it is not in the database. Because of the degree of optimization, there can be false positives. To compensate for this, when a hash is found in the LMDB hash store, hashdb reads the LMDB hash data store to check that the hash actually exists. The LMDB hash data store is a multi-map store of all the hashes and their associated data and source information [8].

The hash store value was used in the Jaccard index computations. The Jaccard index JI was computed as follows:

$$\text{JI(A, B)} = \frac{\text{hash store value of Int(h-A, h-B)}}{\text{hash store value of Un(h-A, h-B)}}$$

This Jaccard index JI was used to approximate the Jaccard index with frequency JIWF.

The add_multiple command in hashdb was used to create an imaginary drive I(h-A, h-B, h-C) from hard drive images A, B and C:

$$\text{I(h-A, h-B, h-C)} = \text{add\_multiple(h-A, h-B, h-C)}$$

Next, the Jaccard index values for all pairs of snapshots – $\text{JI}(WS_b, WS_c)$, $\text{JI}(WS_b, WS_d)$, $\text{JI}(WS_b, WS_e)$, $\text{JI}(WS_c, WS_d)$, $\text{JI}(WS_c, WS_e)$ and $\text{JI}(WS_d, WS_e)$ – were computed. The Jaccard index values between WS_b and other instances became smaller after each sequence of actions. This was expected because a drive with an installed application and a drive with the same application uninstalled are less similar. After uninstallation and system rebooting, the previously matching sectors were overwritten and no longer matched. A similar trend was observed between WS_c and other instances.

The Jaccard index values of any two drives in different categories were very low compared with the Jaccard index values for any two drives in the same category.

The next set of tests employed realistic datasets, including the 2009 M57-Patents Scenario dataset [9]. The 2009 M57-Patents Scenario was created by modeling actions at a fictitious small company named M57 that was engaged in prior art searches involving patents. The dataset records actions by four employees – (i) Pat (CEO); (ii) Charlie (patent researcher); (iii) Jo (patent researcher); and (iv) Terry (IT administrator) – over a 17-day period in November-December 2009. The hard drive in each employee's workstation was imaged daily, except for weekends and holidays. Terry's workstation ran Windows Vista Business 32-bit whereas the other three workstations ran Windows XP.

A hashdb instance was created for each drive. A hashdb instance was also created for a clean hard drive with only a Windows operating system (XP and 7). The subtract command in hashdb was used to remove Windows operating system sectors from the hashdb instance associated with each employee. These are referred to as "slimmed" hashdb instances. A imaginary drive was created by randomly choosing five random slimmed hashdb instances from among all the slimmed hashdb instances.

An imaginary hashdb instance I_S_Charlie.hdb was created from Charlie's Nov-11, Nov-20, Nov-30, Dec-04 and Dec-10 slimmed hashdb instances. This imaginary drive corresponded to a cluster of drives against which the similarity of a target drive would be assessed. A Jaccard index value was computed for each target drive hashdb instance against I_S_Charlie.hdb. When the target drive and cluster drives are from different categories, the similarity values would be expected to be much lower. Imaginary cluster drives were also created for the other three employees and the Jaccard index values were computed.

Figure 3 shows the JIWF results. Each sub-figure in Figure 3 shows the similarity values between the target drives of the four employees and the imaginary cluster drive created from an employee's daily images. Note that the daily images (along the x-axis) used to generate the imaginary drive associated with an employee are marked with @ symbols. Figure 3(a) shows the similarity values between the target drives of the four employees and Charlie's imaginary cluster drive. As days go by, the similarity values of Charlie's daily hard drives to Charlie's imaginary drive are higher than those of the other employees. Similar patterns are seen for Jo, Pat and Terry in Figures 3(b), 3(c) and 3(d), respectively. In the case of Figure 3(d), all the similarity values are lower compared with the similarity values in other three figures because Terry's hard drive was much larger than the hard drives of the other three employees.

6.4 JINF Computation

The JINF results shown in Figure 4 also involve the 2009 M57-Patents dataset. After creating a hashdb instance for each day for each employee, the subtract command was used to remove operating system blocks from each hashdb instance. An imaginary source drive was created for

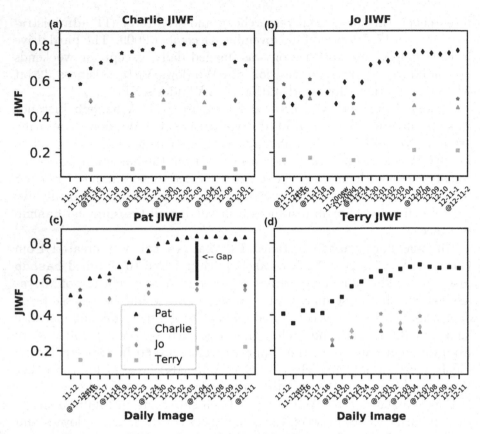

Figure 3.   JIWF results for the 2009 M57-Patents Scenario dataset.

each employee by combining five random `hashdb` instances from the employee's daily drive image list. The daily images used to generate the imaginary drive associated with each employee are marked with @ symbols.

As expected, the target drives of the employees have higher similarity values when they are compared against their own imaginary source drives. In general, the similarity values of each employee's daily target drives against his/her own imaginary drive increase steadily for the first ten days, stabilize and then drop during the last few days. This is because the similarity values increase each successive day until a certain usage level is reached, after which the similarity values during successive days are about the same. The similarity values drop during the last few days because files were deleted and sector contents were overwritten, reducing the number of sectors that matched the static imaginary drives.

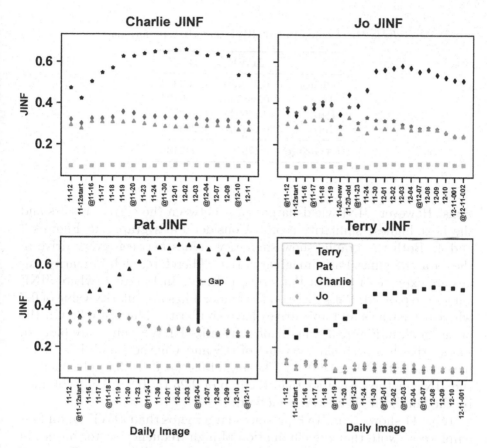

Figure 4. JINF results for the 2009 M57-Patents Scenario dataset.

In this test, a total of 305 hard drive images were compared against four imaginary drive images. Except for the first five target images belonging to Jo in Figure 4(b), all the other images yielded correct results, which is greater than 98% accuracy. The five incorrect results are for images that were taken before the images in the imaginary cluster drive; even so, they are still near the top candidates on the same day.

The experiments used a personal computer with an Intel(R) Core i7 2.30 GHz CPU and 2 TB SSD memory. It took an average of 90 minutes to compute the JINF value for a daily 40-gigabyte hard drive image.

6.5   JIWF and JINF Comparison

The JIWF and JINF methods applied to the 2009 M57-Patents Scenario dataset produce accurate results that could support triage deci-

Table 11.   Comparison of JIWF and JINF performance.

	JIWF	JINF
Charlie	0.229789	0.265333
Jo	0.085746	0.139794
Pat	0.146044	0.279771
Terry	0.244807	0.283844
Average	0.176597	0.242186

sions. However, JINF yields larger gaps between the correct results and the next highest similarity score. Consider Pat's graphs in Figures 3 and 4. Both the graphs show similarity values between every drive in the dataset against Pat's imaginary drive. Therefore, high similarity values are expected for all of Pat's target drives. In Figure 4, where JINF values are plotted, Pat's drive on December 4 has a similarity value of 0.7 whereas Charlie's and Jo's drives have similarity values of 0.3. On the other hand, in Figure 3, where non-normalized JIWF values are plotted, Pat's drive has a similarity value of 0.8 and Charlie's and Jo's drives have similarity values of 0.55. The gap of 0.4 (= 0.7 − 0.3) obtained by the JINF method is larger than the gap of 0.25 (= 0.8 − 0.55) obtained by the non-normalized JIWF method.

Table 11 shows that JINF produces larger gaps than JIWF for all four employees. Note that the elimination of high frequency sector hashes in the JINF method yielded higher similarity values. As the cut-off value of high frequency sector hashes was gradually lowered from 5,000 to 50, the similarity values increased accordingly, which is to be expected. In other words, lowering the sector hash frequency cutoff reduces "noise" hashes and concentrates the computations on the most significant matches.

7.   Conclusions

The digital media similarity measure presented in this chapter is based on a modified Jaccard index using sector hash values. The three modifications to the basic Jaccard index computation are the exclusion of a whitelist of low-entropy sectors, the incorporation of a hash frequency weight to account for content uniqueness (JIWF similarity) and the inclusion of a normalization factor to allow for accurate comparisons of media of different sizes (JINF similarity). The methodology was validated using drive images with known similarity and the highest accuracy and discrimination were obtained using the full JINF computation. The results also reveal that sector content comparisons, when appropriately computed, can provide accurate and rapid measures of digital media similarity that support digital image triage decisions and link discovery across sources and entities.

Future research will employ a larger validation dataset to confirm the utility of the normalization factor. Additionally, it will evaluate statistical sampling instead of processing all the sectors of digital media sources to help strike the right balance between accuracy and speed. Other refinements include giving more weight to important feature sectors and considering the relative positions of matching sectors. Future work will also consider using matching sectors to direct practitioners to specific files or file remnants on digital media.

References

[1] R. Beverly, S. Garfinkel and G. Cardwell, Forensic carving of network packets and associated data structures, *Digital Investigation*, vol. 8(S), pp. S78–S89, 2011.

[2] P. Bjelland, K. Franke and A. Arnes, Practical use of approximate hash-based matching in digital investigations, *Digital Investigation*, vol. 11(S1), pp. S18–S26, 2014.

[3] B. Bloom, Space/time trade-offs in hash coding with allowable errors, *Communications of the ACM*, vol. 13, pp. 422–426, 1970.

[4] F. Breitinger and H. Baier, Performance issues about context-triggered piecewise hashing, *Proceedings of the International Conference on Digital Forensics and Cyber Crime*, pp. 141–155, 2012.

[5] F. Breitinger, B. Guttman, M. McCarrin, V. Roussev and D. White, Approximate Matching: Definition and Terminology, NIST Special Publication 800-168, National Institute of Standards and Technologies, Gaithersburg, Maryland, 2014.

[6] S. Bunting and W. Wei, *EnCase Computer Forensics: The Official EnCE: EnCase Certified Examiner Study Guide*, Wiley Publishing, Indianapolis, Indiana, 2006.

[7] H. Chu, Lightning Memory-Mapped Database Manager (LMDB), Symas Corporation, Grand Junction, Colorado (`www.lmdb.tech/doc`), 2011.

[8] Digital Corpora, `hashdb 3.1.0` Users Manual (`downloads.digitalcorpora.org/downloads/hashdb/hashdb_um.pdf`), 2017.

[9] Digital Corpora, 2009 M57-Patents Scenario (`digitalcorpora.org/corpora/scenarios/m57-patents-scenario`), 2019.

[10] Digital Corpora, Real Data Corpus (`digitalcorpora.org/corpora/disk-images/real-data-corpus`), 2019.

[11] S. Garfinkel, Forensic feature extraction and cross-drive analysis, *Digital Investigation*, vol. 3(S), pp. S71–S81, 2006.

[12] S. Garfinkel, Digital media triage with bulk data analysis and `bulk_extractor`, *Computers and Security*, vol. 32, pp. 56–72, 2013.

[13] S. Garfinkel, P. Farrell, V. Roussev and G. Dinolt, Bringing science to digital forensics with standardized forensic corpora, *Digital Investigation*, vol. 6(S), pp. S2–S11, 2009.

[14] S. Garfinkel and M. McCarrin, Hash-based carving: Searching media for complete files and file fragments with sector hashing and `hashdb`, *Digital Investigation*, vol. 14(S1), pp. S95–S105, 2015.

[15] S. Garfinkel, A. Nelson, D. White and R. Roussev, Using purpose-built functions and block hashes to enable small block and sub-file forensics, *Digital Investigation*, vol. 7(S), pp. S13–S23, 2010.

[16] J. Kornblum, Identifying almost identical files using context-triggered piecewise hashing, *Digital Investigation*, vol. 3(S), pp. 91–97, 2006.

[17] V. Moia and M. Henriques, A comparative analysis about similarity search strategies for digital forensic investigations, *Proceedings of the Thirty-Fifth Brazilian Symposium on Telecommunications and Signal Processing*, pp. 462–466, 2017.

[18] National Institute of Standards and Technology, National Software Reference Library (NSRL), Gaithersburg, Maryland (`www.nsrl.nist.gov`), 2019.

[19] J. Oliver, C. Cheng and Y. Chen, TLSH – A locality sensitive hash, *Proceedings of the Fourth Cybercrime and Trustworthy Computing Workshop*, pp. 7–13, 2013.

[20] J. Oliver, S. Forman and C. Cheng, Using randomization to attack similarity digests, *Proceedings of the International Conference on Applications and Techniques in Information Security*, pp. 199–210, 2014.

[21] H. Parsonage, Computer Forensics Case Assessment and Triage – Some Ideas for Discussion (`computerforensics.parsonage.co.uk/triage/ComputerForensicsCaseAssessmentANDTriageDiscussionPaper.pdf`), 2009.

[22] P. Penrose, W. Buchanan and R. Macfarlane, Fast contraband detection in large capacity disk drives, *Digital Investigation*, vol. 12(S1), pp. S22–S29, 2015.

[23] RCFL National Program Office, Regional Computer Forensics Laboratory Annual Report for Fiscal Year 2017, Quantico, Virginia (`www.rcfl.gov/file-repository/09-rcfl-annual-2017-190130-print-1.pdf/view`), 2017.

[24] R. Real and J. Vargas, The probability basis of Jaccard's index of similarity, *Systematic Biology*, vol. 45(30), pp. 380–385, 1996.

[25] V. Roussev, Building a better similarity trap with statistically improbable features, *Proceedings of the Forty-Second Hawaii International Conference on System Sciences*, 2009.

[26] V. Roussev, Data fingerprinting with similarity digests, in *Advances in Digital Forensics VI*, K. Chow and S. Shenoi (Eds.), Springer, Berlin Heidelberg, Germany, pp. 207–226, 2010.

[27] V. Roussev, Y. Chen, T. Bourg and G. Richard, `md5bloom`: Forensic filesystem hashing revisited, *Digital Investigation*, vol. 3(S), pp. S82–S90, 2006.

[28] W. Stallings and L. Brown, *Computer Security: Principles and Practice*, Pearson Education, Upper Saddle River, New Jersey, 2015.

[29] J. Taguchi, Optimal Sector Sampling for Drive Triage, M.S. Thesis, Department of Computer Science, Naval Postgraduate School, Monterey, California, 2013.

[30] A. Tridgell, `spamsum` (`samba.org/ftp/unpacked/junkcode/spamsum/README`), 2002.

[31] R. Walls, E. Learned-Miller and B. Levine, Forensic triage for mobile phones with DECoDE, *Proceedings of the Twentieth USENIX Security Symposium*, 2011.

[32] J. Young, K. Foster, S. Garfinkel and K. Fairbanks, Distinct sector hashes for target file detection, *IEEE Computer*, vol. 45(12), pp. 28–35, 2012.

Chapter 8

RESIDENT DATA PATTERN ANALYSIS USING SECTOR CLUSTERING FOR STORAGE DRIVE FORENSICS

Nitesh Bharadwaj, Upasna Singh and Gaurav Gupta

Abstract   Storage drives are huge reservoirs of digital evidence. The acquisition and examination of storage drives for evidentiary artifacts require enormous amounts of manual effort and computing resources, leading to huge case backlogs. This chapter describes a forensic triage methodology that leverages random sampling and unsupervised clustering to provide insights about the regions of interest on a storage drive. The number of sector samples to be evaluated during triage for legitimate inferences to be drawn about drive content is also discussed. Experiments involving storage drives of various capacities illustrate the effectiveness and utility of the extracted patterns for rapid drive triage.

Keywords: Large storage drives, random sector sampling, unsupervised clustering

1.   Introduction

The rapid growth of storage capacity in computers and electronic devices has severely affected the timeliness of digital forensic investigations. The volume of data encountered in investigations is relentlessly advancing beyond the processing capabilities of digital forensic practitioners and traditional forensic tools [17]. As a result, huge backlogs of cases exist in forensic laboratories around the world. The immediate solution is not to modify well-defined digital forensic procedures, but to make evidence processing strategies more efficient and effective.

This research leverages random sector sampling and unsupervised clustering in the first step of a forensic examination, namely triage, to render evidence processing more efficient and effective. The idea is to perform a quick forensic survey that provides insights about resident data and data patterns on storage media. The data patterns assist in

© IFIP International Federation for Information Processing 2020
Published by Springer Nature Switzerland AG 2020
G. Peterson and S. Shenoi (Eds.): Advances in Digital Forensics XVI, IFIP AICT 589, pp. 137–157, 2020.
https://doi.org/10.1007/978-3-030-56223-6_8

rapidly identifying forensically-significant and insignificant regions on the media. A region is a collection of similar types of contiguous sectors on a storage drive, which can be broadly classified based on their non-null (significant) or null (insignificant) content. The significant regions include human-readable, executable, compressed and encrypted content, as well as non-null sectors, all of which are important in investigations. The insignificant regions include negligibly-important null, empty and unallocated sectors. Clearly, the identification, preservation and examination of significant regions and the elimination of insignificant regions from further processing can save enormous amounts of resources.

This chapter describes a forensic triage methodology that leverages random sector sampling and unsupervised clustering to provide insights about the regions of interest on a storage drive. The methodology rapidly explores media for resident data patterns, identifies forensically-significant and insignificant regions and makes inferences about the resident data content. The number of sector samples that need to be evaluated to make legitimate inferences about drive content is discussed. Experiments involving storage drives of various capacities illustrate the effectiveness and utility of the extracted patterns for rapid drive triage.

2.   Background and Related Work

Richard and Roussev [15] have discussed the difficulties involved in processing large volumes of digital evidence. They highlighted the need for novel techniques for evidence acquisition and analysis. Garfinkel [7] notes that the massive capacity of storage devices, diversity of hardware interfaces, operating systems and file formats, large quantities of devices per case, use of anti-forensic strategies, proliferation of remote cloud storage and legal challenges are contributing to a "coming digital forensic crisis." He also discusses research directions that could help mitigate the coming crisis.

Beebe [1] emphasizes the need to address data volume and scalability issues in digital forensics using selective acquisition and effective computational and analytical approaches (e.g., data-mining-based search, file classification and graphical processing units). Quick and Choo [13] have identified the need to leverage data reduction, data mining and intelligence analysis to advance digital forensic capabilities.

Bharadwaj and Singh [3] have highlighted the key challenges and gaps (e.g., evidence examination delays, resource constraints, data heterogeneity, preservation costs, and methods and tool development) that impact digital forensics. It is imperative to develop advanced forensically-sound techniques and tools that can support the rapid and efficient processing of large volumes of digital evidence.

2.1 Triage

Triage refers to a partial forensic examination conducted under limited time and resource constraints [17].

Garfinkel [8] has advocated the use of random sector sampling in a triage method to achieve fast drive analysis. He demonstrated its effectiveness at identifying digital media content and detecting whether or not a drive was wiped properly. Random sampling has been utilized very effectively by the New South Wales Police Force in discovery processes involving child abuse material; the application of random sampling significantly reduced case backlogs [10].

Random sampling has been used to rapidly assess storage media and identify 4 KiB blocks identical to target data [5, 21]. Taguchi [21] has developed a confidence model to handle situations where no traces of target data are identified using a sector sampling approach. Canceill [5] has provided insights on how sector sampling can assist in storage drive analysis. He demonstrates that random sampling is an adaptive and scalable method for fast drive analysis. Since the selected 4 KiB blocks were evaluated in an overlapping manner, most of the sectors (512 bytes) had to be processed multiple times. Additional sector processing introduces computational loads that result in evidence processing delays.

Bharadwaj and Singh [3] have identified the number of sector samples that needs to be analyzed on an entire drive or in regions of storage to identify sectors with content identical to the target data. In these and other triaging methodologies, information about the desired target files must be available. However, the methodology proposed in this chapter does not have this constraint. The methodology leverages random sector sampling and clustering to gain insights about the regions of interest on a drive. Prioritizing the consideration of significant regions realizes substantial savings in evidence processing resources.

2.2 Data Reduction

An alternative approach to triage is data reduction. Roussev and Quates [16] have employed similarity digests for forensic triage. They show that the scope of an investigation can be narrowed by ignoring known excludable files during the acquisition and examination phases. Quick and Choo [14] have presented an approach that enhances the traditional forensic process by imaging a selection of key files such as registry, Internet history, log, picture and video files.

Digital forensic practitioners typically have complete access to suspects' data during investigations. However, Verma et al. [22, 23] argue that privacy preservation and completeness of investigations are incompatible with each other. They proposed a method for finding the most relevant pieces of evidence while preserving data privacy in a manner that increases investigative efficiency without negatively impacting evidence integrity and admissibility.

Beebe and Clark [2] discuss the benefits of applying data mining in digital forensic investigations. However, limited published work incorporates data mining and other techniques to reduce the effort involved in preserving and examining large volumes of digital evidence [12].

In contrast, the methodology proposed in this chapter does not rely on the collection of essential files; instead, regions of interest are identified by intelligently evaluating randomly-selected sector samples from a drive. The evaluation draws on clustering techniques that determine the significant regions based on the features selected for each random sector. These significant regions are targeted for selective acquisition and examination instead of processing all the drive sectors.

2.3   Clustering

Clustering has been employed in data mining and unsupervised learning applications to identify and understand data patterns in unlabeled, high-dimensional data. Clustering groups data using similarity measures based on centroid, hierarchical, expectation maximization and density techniques. Each clustering technique has its own advantages and disadvantages in terms of cluster quality, efficiency in handling noisy data and computational complexity. The efficiency and effectiveness of clustering techniques are dependent on the features selected for evaluation. This work employs simple centroid and density based clustering techniques to determine forensically-significant regions on evidentiary drives.

Centroid-Based Clustering.   The k-means clustering technique computes the centroid of a cluster as the mean of the feature vectors assigned to the cluster. The technique requires the number of clusters to be specified in advance. It divides W samples into k disjoint clusters such that a distance function computed as the sum of squares of the intra-cluster distances to the centroid of the cluster is minimized. The distance function is given by:

$$Distance\ Function\ = \sum_{j=1}^{k} \sum_{i=1}^{W} \|w_i^{(j)} - c_j\|^2 \qquad (1)$$

where c_j is the centroid of cluster j and $w_i \in W$.

In this work, the distinction between the significant and insignificant regions on a drive is formulated by considering three clusters ($k = 3$) that broadly represent three distinct types of data.

Density-Based Clustering. The density-based spatial clustering of applications with noise (DBSCAN) technique considers a cluster to be an area of high density separated by low-density samples. The clusters identified using this technique can be of any shape (non-linear boundaries), yielding different results compared with k-means and other linear clustering algorithms.

Two user-defined parameters *minimum_samples* and *eps* determine the density of samples needed to form a cluster. Higher *minimum_samples* and lower *eps* values indicate higher densities while lower *minimum_samples* and higher *eps* values indicate lower densities.

A sample in a dataset is called a core sample when other neighboring samples (*minimum_samples*) exist within a radius or distance of *eps*. Thus, prior information about the number of clusters is not required. The number of clusters is estimated based on the *minimum_samples* and *eps* parameter values.

2.4 Extracted Features

Extracted features or metrics can provide valuable insights about digital evidence. In this work, insights about forensically-significant regions on storage media are obtained using two derived metrics: (i) ASCII score; and (ii) entropy value.

ASCII Score. The greater the amount of text or human-readable ASCII bytes contained in a data unit, the greater the probability of it containing directly understandable information [19]. A sector is considered to be the smallest data unit on a drive. It is recommended that small sectors or blocks (e.g., 512 bytes) be considered because file blocks should efficiently map to drive sectors [24]. Hence, the standard size of a data unit (sector) considered in this research is 512 bytes.

Traditionally, the ASCII score is the ratio of the number of ASCII bytes to the total number of bytes in a file [19]. However, in this work, the ASCII score is evaluated for every randomly-selected sector instead of a specific file. This may assist a digital forensic practitioner in examining even minute details instantaneously from the drive, such as keywords, credit card details, email, phone numbers and other information that can be directly recorded and understood by the practitioner. Moreover, the ASCII score can help exclude sectors containing little or no human-readable information. If an investigative scenario requires the analysis of plaintext or directly-readable information, then sectors with high ASCII scores should be analyzed first (highest priority) because it becomes much easier to extract useful information that could provide important leads when dealing with a large volume of data.

Entropy Value. Entropy specifies the amount of uncertainty of an unknown or random quantity. It is computed by summing the frequency of each observed byte value in a fixed-length data block and then computing an entropy value. Lyda and Hamrock [11] compute the entropy value based on bytes (00 to FF) in a file using `bintropy`, a binary-file entropy analysis tool that enables practitioners to conveniently and quickly identify encrypted and packed malware.

In this work, an entropy value is computed for bytes in every randomly-selected sector on a drive. The entropy value is low for sectors that are less compressed (e.g., text files) and high for compressed file fragments [19]. Encrypted data also has a high entropy value.

The entropy value $E(s$ of a randomly-selected sector s is given by:

$$E(s) = -\sum_{b=1}^{m} P(b) \log_2 P(b) \qquad (2)$$

where $P(b)$ is the probability of the frequency of the bth byte information in sector s that consists of a series of m bytes. Alternatively, the entropy value can be viewed as considering all the values that a byte b in a sector s can take, and $P(b)$ is the probability of the frequency of each occurring byte in the randomly-selected sector s.

Randomly-selected sectors are easily classified as null or non-null sectors based on their content [4]. In this work, the entropy metric is used to identify sectors with human-readable, multimedia (images, audio and video), encoded, compressed, encrypted or executable content. Hence, the entropy value is used in addition to the ASCII score in sector evaluations.

A sector that contains only zero or null bytes is referred to as a null-sector. A null-sector has the lowest entropy value of zero. The ASCII score for a null-sector would be high. However, in this work, a null sector is considered to have an ASCII score of zero due to the absence of relevant information. A sector that contains information other than null bytes is referred to as a non-null sector. Non-null sectors have plaintext (direct human readable), multimedia, encoded, compressed, encrypted or executable content.

Table 1. Random sector categories based on the ASCII scores and entropy values.

Range of ASCII Score (x)	Range of Entropy Value (y)	Assumed Sector Category
0	0	Null data
$0.6 \leq x \leq 1.0$	$0 < y \leq 4.8$	Plaintext data
$0 < x < 0.6$	$4.8 < y \leq 8.0$	Compressed/encrypted data

Lyda and Hamrock [11] statistically evaluated a large set of packed and encrypted malware files based on the entropy of their bytes. They classified them into four categories of files: (i) plaintext; (ii) native; (iii) packed; and (iv) encrypted executable.

2.5 Assumptions

The proposed methodology assumes that three categories of data exist: (i) null data; (ii) plaintext data; and (iii) compressed/encrypted data. In general, it is easy to discriminate between null and non-null sectors. However, it is difficult to differentiate between resident and deleted data in the absence of the original filesystem or prior information.

The proposed methodology employs two metrics, ASCII score and entropy value, to determine forensically-significant regions on storage media. Storage media is considered to correspond to a bulk data volume, possibly without a legitimate filesystem and metadata, as in the case of deleted, altered or corrupted filesystem information or a formatted drive. The methodology is also applicable to forensic images with raw formats such as DD, IMG and RAW.

Table 1 shows how ASCII scores and entropy values are used to categorize randomly-selected sectors as containing null, plaintext and compressed/encrypted (encoded) data [11, 19]. As mentioned above, null data has an ASCII score of zero and an entropy value of zero. Since readable (plaintext) file fragments always have high ASCII scores and low entropy values, the ranges for this category are set to [0.6, 1.0] and (0, 4.8], respectively. Finally, the ASCII score and entropy value ranges for compressed/encrypted data are set to (0.0, 0.6) and (4.8, 8.0], respectively.

Many clustering algorithms, including k-means, require the number of clusters to be known *a priori*. Therefore, the proposed methodology assumes that the maximum number of clusters is three. DBSCAN clustering is highly dependent on the *minimum_samples* and *eps* parameter

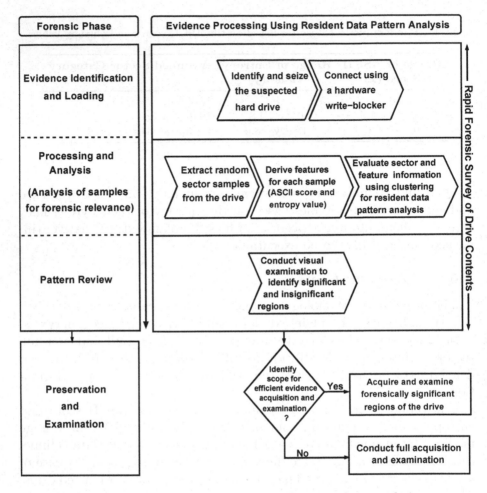

Figure 1. Proposed methodology for efficient evidence analysis.

values. The proposed methodology typically uses *minimum_samples* = 10 and *eps* = 0.5. However, explicit mentions are made when different values of these parameters are employed.

3.   Proposed Methodology

Figure 1 presents the proposed methodology for efficient evidence analysis. The storage media drive is assumed to be mounted on the investigator's computer.

The process begins with the random extraction of a specified number of sector samples from across the drive. Important features such as the ASCII score, entropy value and sector category are computed and recorded for each extracted sample. The sector versus feature map is examined using k-means and DBSCAN clustering to gain insights about the significant and insignificant regions on the drive. Although fewer sector samples are examined, it is still possible to obtain a good idea of the distribution and characteristics of data on the drive. When a reasonable quantity of insignificant sectors exist on the drive, their elimination from consideration reduces the subsequent analysis effort. When the drive data patterns reveal that the number of significant sectors is large or the drive is completely filled with data, it is advisable to proceed with a full forensic acquisition followed by the exhaustive examination of artifacts.

The random sector samples are selected based on the accessible sector count. This information can be obtained using utilities such as `fdisk` and `hdparm`. In random sampling, an arbitrary number between the first and last sector number is generated, which is then recorded for further evaluation. During analysis, care is taken care to ensure that the random samples are fetched without replacement. Specifically, no sector should be selected multiple times; this is accomplished by maintaining a record of the previously-selected sectors. When a previously-selected sector is identified, it is dropped in favor of a new sector despite an increase in the evaluation load. Therefore, it is important to determine the sample size that provides good outcomes in a timely manner while eliminating the need to conduct an exhaustive examination of the drive.

Sampling theory is engaged to determine the number of sector samples for random extraction. Specifically, random sector sampling without replacement is employed.

Sample Size Determination. Bharadwaj and Singh [3] have specified the numbers of random samples that need to be evaluated to identify sectors that are identical to target file fragments on storage media with different probabilities, regardless of the presence or absence of filesystem metadata. However, when the target data of interest is not known, it is difficult to determine the number of random samples that need to be examined.

The determination of the number of sector samples that can provide adequate insights about the resident sectors on a drive resembles the problem of determining the adequate sample size for a finite population [9]. Four parameters are needed to determine the sample size: (i) population size (total number of accessible sectors on a drive); (ii) precision (user-specified); (iii) confidence level (user-specified); and (iv) degree of variability (user-specified).

Precision (sampling error) is the range in which the true value of a population is estimated to reside [9]. Precision has an inverse relationship with the number of samples – the lower the specified precision, the greater the number of samples required [20]. In general, precision is expressed as a percentage (e.g., ±3%, ±5%, ±10%). For example, if 60% of the sector samples were determined to be unallocated with a precision of ±3%, then between 57% and 63% of the sectors on the drive are actually unallocated.

The confidence level, which originates from the central limit theorem, provides the probability that the sample contains the value being estimated. It is expressed as a percentage (e.g., 90%, 95%, 99%). The confidence level generally corresponds to the standard (constant) z-score value [20]. Different z-scores based on different confidence levels must be employed when deriving the sample size.

Finally, the degree of variability expresses the distribution of attributes in a population. A more heterogeneous population requires a larger number of samples whereas a more homogeneous population requires fewer samples. A safe decision is to use 0.5 (50%) as the degree of variability because it balances a large sample size against maximal population variability.

According to Cochran [6], the following equation can be used to obtain a representative sample size n_0 as a proportion of a population:

$$n_0 = \frac{Z^2 pq}{e^2} \tag{3}$$

where Z^2 is the abscissa of the normal curve that cuts off the area of the desired confidence level, e is the desired precision or sampling error, p is the estimated proportion of attributes present in the population and $q = (1 - p)$.

When the population is finite, the desired sample size n is given by:

$$n = \frac{n_0}{1 + \frac{(n_0 - 1)}{N}} \tag{4}$$

where N is the population size.

Equations 3 and (4) are used to determine the number of sector samples that need to be processed in order to estimate the characteristics of the sectors residing on storage media.

4.   Experiments and Analysis

Experiments were conducted to evaluate the efficacy of the proposed significant region identification methodology for drive triage. A generic

Table 2. Minimum sample sizes for various drive capacities.

Confidence	Precision	Drive Capacity				Sample Size
		4 GB	8 GB	16 GB	1 TB	
	±1%	16,558	16,574	16,582	16,590	**17,000**
	±2%	4,146	4,147	4,148	4,148	**4,500**
99%	±3%	1,844	1,844	1,844	1,844	**2,000**
	±5%	664	664	664	664	**700**
	±10%	166	166	166	166	**200**
	±1%	9,594	9,599	9,602	9,604	**10,000**
	±2%	2,401	2,401	2,401	2,401	**2,500**
95%	±3%	1,068	1,068	1,068	1,068	**1,100**
	±5%	385	385	385	385	**400**
	±10%	97	97	97	97	**100**
	±1%	6,761	6,764	6,765	6,766	**7,000**
	±2%	1,692	1,692	1,692	1,692	**1,800**
90%	±3%	752	752	752	752	**800**
	±5%	271	271	271	271	**300**
	±10%	68	68	68	68	**80**

eight-core computing system with 4 GB RAM running Kali Linux 2.0 was employed in the experiments. The implementation is available at GitHub (`github.com/niteshdiat2014/Resident_Data_Pattern_Analysis`).

The experiments were conducted on four storage drives, D_1, D_2, D_3 and D_4, with capacities, 4 GB, 8 GB, 16 GB and 1 TB, respectively. Drive D_1 was completely filled with data whereas D_2, D_3 and D_4 were partially filled with data. The analysis was performed using a custom Python 2.7 script. Clustering was implemented as described in the scikit-learn documentation [18].

4.1 Sector Sample Size

Equations (3) and (4) were used to estimate the numbers of samples necessary for drive analyses. Table 2 shows the numbers of sector samples for various drive capacities at precision (sampling error) values of ±1%, ±2%, ±3%, ±5% and ±10%, where the estimated proportion of attributes present in the population $p = 0.5$. The sample sizes in the last column of the table are the upper bounds on the sample sizes used to analyze evidence.

The computed sample sizes are valid for the considered scenario; however, the sample sizes would vary when Equations (3) and (4) are computed with different parameter values depending on the scenario requirements. The sample size does not change much for populations larger than 20,000, which implies that the total number of samples should be considered at least during data pattern analysis. Similarly, the computed sample sizes are not very different for different storage media with different numbers of sectors for a particular precision and confidence level.

The computed sample size should guarantee well-distributed sectors from a drive. However, forensic practitioners may use arbitrarily large numbers of samples according to their investigative needs. Obviously, the larger the sample size, the better the ability to make precise decisions about a drive, but this comes with increased analysis effort.

4.2   Significant Region Analysis

In order to identify the important regions on the drives, features were recorded for every randomly-selected sector in the retrieved sample set. The features, ASCII score and entropy value, were clustered separately using k-means and DBSCAN. This enabled the sectors with similar feature values to be segregated from sector groups with completely distinct feature values. Finally, the sector samples were mapped based on the computed cluster labels to make inferences about the important regions on the drives.

It was observed that the resident data patterns obtained using the two clustering approaches were very similar. In general, k-means provided better results when drives had fewer null sectors. However, k-means sometimes misclassified sectors because it produces clusters with linear structures; this was mitigated by DBSCAN clustering that handles clusters of arbitrary (non-linear) shapes.

In order to measure the efficacy of the proposed methodology, analysis was performed using the computed number of sector samples (e.g., 17,000 with 99% confidence and $\pm 1\%$ precision).

The k-means clustering technique was first used to segregate the sample set into three clusters. Figure 2 shows the clusters obtained by k-means on the 16 GB drive based on the ASCII scores and entropy values. The three clusters correspond to the different types of data on the drive: (i) null sectors with ASCII scores and entropy values of zero; (ii) sectors with moderate ASCII scores and high entropy values; and (iii) sectors with high ASCII scores and medium entropy values.

The cluster labels were utilized to map the sector numbers with their corresponding feature values from the sample set. Figures 3(a) and 3(b) show the resident data pattern analysis using k-means clustering on the 16 GB drive. Figure 3(a) shows the feature maps based on sector samples and ASCII scores. Figure 3(b) shows the feature map based on

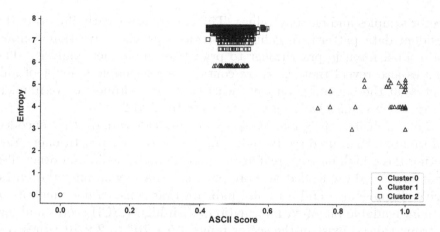

Figure 2. Clusters obtained using *k*-means clustering (16 GB drive).

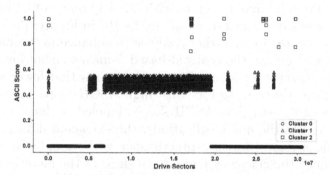

(a) Feature map based on sector numbers and ASCII scores.

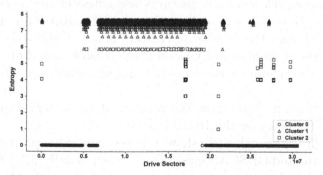

(b) Feature map based on sector samples and entropy values.

Figure 3. Resident data pattern analysis using *k*-means clustering (16 GB drive).

sector samples and entropy values. The two figures clearly illustrate the resident data pattern, revealing the regions on the drive that contain data for a forensic practitioner to prioritize for further analysis. The figures also reveal that the drive contains a reasonable amount of null sectors at the beginning and end whereas a large proportion of implicit information resides between sectors 0.4×10^7 and 2×10^7.

The implicit sectors may contain images, videos and other encoded information that are directly understood by a forensic practitioner. Targeting these high entropy regions to analyze multimedia and other files that are usually encoded is more effective than examining the entire drive. Figures 3(a) and 3(b) also indicate that considerable amounts of human-readable plaintext information (with high ASCII scores and low entropy values) exist in the sector range 1.5×10^7 to 2×10^7; these regions can be directly interpreted by a forensic practitioner. Selective file carving and recovery approaches can be used to improve the overall efficiency. On the other hand, regions with large amounts of null data, such as those in the sector range 1.5×10^7 to 2×10^7 in Figures 3(a) and 3(b), should be excluded from further analysis to enhance performance.

As discussed above, the centroid-based k-means clustering technique causes some misclassifications. Figure 3(a) shows that fewer sectors are labeled incorrectly (e.g., sectors with high ASCII scores labeled as null data and sectors with low ASCII scores labeled as human-readable). However, despite the misclassifications, the extracted data pattern can still provide a digital forensic practitioner with valuable insights that would enhance the efficiency and effectiveness of the analysis.

Figure 4 shows the clusters obtained by DBSCAN on the 16 GB drive based on the ASCII scores and entropy values. The clustering is based on the densities (closeness) of features regardless of the mean values of the clusters. Note that the sectors with similar features are in the same clusters. Although the number of clusters is not required for DBSCAN clustering, the technique still yielded three clusters based on the feature values and the related parameters ($minimum\_samples = 10$ and $eps = 0.5$).

Figures 5(a) and 5(b) show the resident data pattern analysis using DBSCAN clustering on the 16 GB drive.

Figures 6(a) through 6(d) show the resident data pattern analyses using k-means and DBSCAN clustering on the partially-filled 8 GB drive. A total of 8,000 random samples were selected. Note that different DBSCAN parameter values $minimum\_samples = 8$ and $eps = 0.18$ were employed for the 8 GB drive.

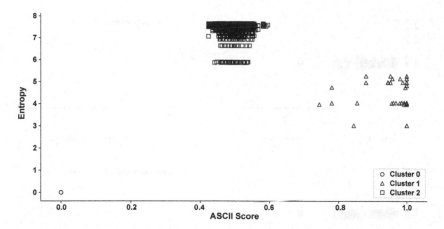

Figure 4. Clusters obtained using DBSCAN clustering (16 GB drive).

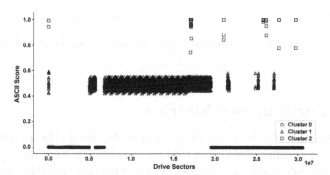

(a) Feature map based on sector numbers and ASCII scores.

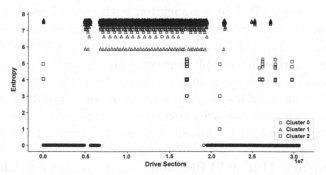

(b) Feature map based on sector samples and entropy values.

Figure 5. Resident data pattern analysis using DBSCAN clustering (16 GB drive).

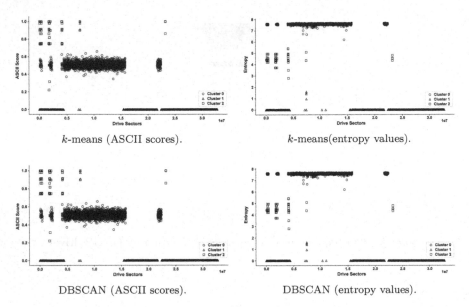

k-means (ASCII scores).   k-means(entropy values).

DBSCAN (ASCII scores).   DBSCAN (entropy values).

Figure 6.   Resident data pattern analyses using k-means and DBSCAN (8 GB drive).

4.3   Performance Metrics

It is important for forensic practitioners to assess the performance of the proposed methodology to satisfy the scientific testing criterion [7]. The performance measures employed are the true positive rate (TPR) and false positive rate (FPR), along with the receiver operating characteristic (ROC) curve.

The TPR and FPR values associated with each clustering technique were computed by comparing the actual labels against the observed outcomes for arbitrary numbers of samples (e.g., 1,000, 5,000, 10,000, 50,000 and 100,000). Arbitrary sample sizes were chosen to evaluate the efficacy of the proposed methodology in situations where it is needed to evaluate a range of sector samples (few samples to a considerably large number of samples). The sample sizes cover the minimum number of samples (up to 17,000) required to provide a general pattern of the contents of an entire drive.

The computed TPR and FPR values obtained with k-means and DB-SCAN clustering on drives D_1, D_2, D_3 and D_4 are plotted as ROC curves in Figure 7. Since drive D_1 (4 GB) was completely filled, the assumed number of clusters and the *minimum_samples* and *eps* values do not provide satisfactory outcomes (low TPR and high FPR values). This is due to the very small number of unallocated or null sectors on

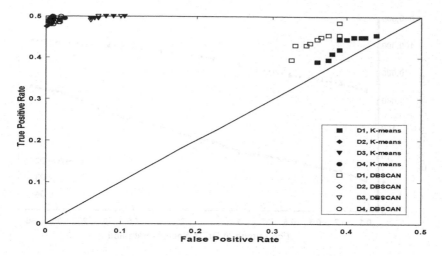

Figure 7. ROC plots for *k*-means and DBSCAN based pattern analyses.

the drive. However, acceptable results – high TPR and low FPR values – are obtained for drives D_2 (8 GB), D_3 (16 GB) and D_4 (1 TB) because they were partially filled with data.

4.4   Evaluation Delay

Increasing the sample size increases the evaluation delay. The evaluation delay is also affected by the input/output performance of the storage media and computing system, efficiency of feature value derivation and computational effort associated with the clustering techniques. Increasing the number of features also increases the computational effort.

Figure 8 shows the evaluation delays for various proportions of random sector samples. Increasing the number of random samples increases the evaluation delay. In contrast, the input/output rate is platform centric, implying that different outcomes are expected for different scenarios and computing environments. A small number of samples can be examined at a high input/output rate whereas a large number of samples significantly reduces the input/output rate.

4.5   Error Rate

Although random sector sampling is effective for rapid drive analysis, it is difficult to ignore its associated error rate (i.e., evaluation of repeated sectors) in the absence of a perfect random number generator. In order to assess the error rate related to significant region determination and resident pattern analysis, different proportions (0.1% to 50%) of random

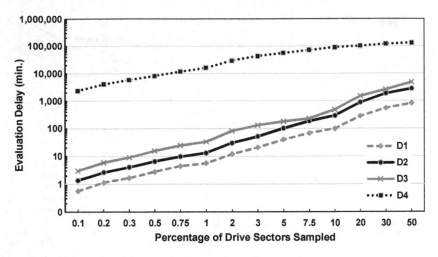

Figure 8. Evaluation delays for various proportions of random sector samples.

samples from the four drives were analyzed to measure the extent of repeated sector evaluation.

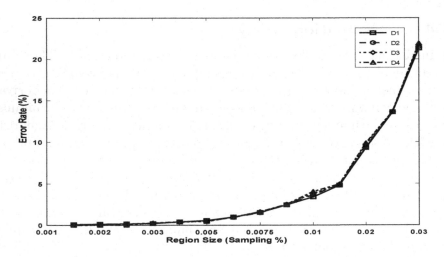

Figure 9. Error rates for various proportions of random sector samples.

Figure 9 presents the error rates for various proportions of random sector samples. The error rate increases at an average rate of approximately 20% as the proportion of random sectors increases. The error rate can be managed by keeping track of previously-generated sector samples.

If a previously-generated sector sample is selected, it is dropped from consideration and a new random sector sample is selected in its place.

5. Conclusions

The proposed triage methodology assists digital forensic practitioners in rapidly evaluating resident data patterns on storage media to narrow the scope of evidence acquisition and examination to forensically-relevant data. It leverages random sector sampling and unsupervised clustering to provide insights about the regions of interest on storage media. The proposed methodology is applicable when metadata information or resident data content are not readily available, for example, when filesystem metadata is corrupted, altered, deleted or overwritten, or when drives are formatted, deleted or overwritten. Without the methodology, the only alternative in these situations would be to exhaustively examine every sector for evidentiary artifacts. The methodology is not intended to replace full evidence examination. Instead, it is most effective for conducting visual examinations of drive content layout, intelligence analyses, resident data pattern analyses, rapid reviews, quick forensic surveys, pre-seizure media analyses, drive triage, and partial or selective evidence processing.

Experiments involving storage drives of various capacities illustrate the effectiveness and usability of the extracted patterns for rapid drive triage. However, the performance degrades when large numbers of random sector samples have to be evaluated when processing large-capacity storage media. The methodology is designed to handle three types of clusters corresponding to null, plaintext and compressed/encrypted data; however, the results are negatively impacted when insufficient data is associated with the clusters. The methodology is unable to handle completely encrypted drives where sectors have low ASCII scores and high entropy values; in such cases, it is necessary to decrypt the storage media before applying the methodology. Additionally, the methodology cannot handle advanced and compressed file formats such as the Advanced Forensic Format (AFF) and Encase image file format (E01).

Future research will focus on extending the types of data that can be handled. Also, it will focus on enhancing the efficiency of the methodology and reducing error rates.

References

[1] N. Beebe, Digital forensic research: The good, the bad and the unaddressed, in *Advances in Digital Forensics V*, G. Peterson and S. Shenoi (Eds.), Springer, Heidelberg, Germany, pp. 17–36, 2009.

[2] N. Beebe and J. Clark, Dealing with terabyte data sets in digital investigations, in *Advances in Digital Forensics*, M. Pollitt and S. Shenoi (Eds.), Springer, Boston, Massachusetts, pp. 3–16, 2006.

[3] N. Bharadwaj and U. Singh, Efficiently searching for target data traces in storage devices with region-based random sector sampling, *Digital Investigation*, vol. 24, pp. 128–141, 2018.

[4] N. Bharadwaj and U. Singh, Significant data region identification and analysis using k-means in large storage drive forensics, *Security and Privacy*, vol. 1(4), paper no. e40, 2018.

[5] N. Canceill, Random Sampling Applied to Rapid Disk Analysis, Master's Research Project Report, Department of System and Network Engineering, University of Amsterdam, Amsterdam, The Netherlands, 2013.

[6] W. Cochran, *Sampling Techniques*, John Wiley and Sons, New York, 1977.

[7] S. Garfinkel, Digital forensics research: The next 10 years, *Digital Investigation*, vol. 7(S), pp. S64–S73, 2010.

[8] S. Garfinkel, Fast disk analysis with random sampling, presented at the *Annual CENIC Conference*, 2010.

[9] G. Israel, Determining Sample Size, Fact Sheet PEOD-6, Florida Cooperative Extension Service, University of Florida, Gainesville, Florida, 1992.

[10] B. Jones, S. Pleno and M. Wilkinson, The use of random sampling in investigations involving child abuse material, *Digital Investigation*, vol. 9(S), pp. S99–S107, 2012.

[11] R. Lyda and J. Hamrock, Using entropy analysis to find encrypted and packed malware, *IEEE Security and Privacy*, vol. 5(2), pp. 40–45, 2007.

[12] D. Quick and K. Choo, Data reduction and data mining framework for digital forensic evidence: Storage, intelligence, review and archival, *Trends and Issues in Crime and Criminal Justice*, no. 480, 2014.

[13] D. Quick and K. Choo, Impacts of the increasing volume of digital forensic data: A survey and future research challenges, *Digital Investigation*, vol. 11(4), pp. 273–294, 2014.

[14] D. Quick and K. Choo, Big forensic data reduction: Digital forensic images and electronic evidence, *Cluster Computing*, vol. 19(2), pp. 723–740, 2016.

[15] G. Richard and V. Roussev, Next-generation digital forensics, *Communications of the ACM*, vol. 49(2), pp. 76–80, 2006.

[16] V. Roussev and C. Quates, Content triage with similarity digests: The M57 case study, *Digital Investigation*, vol. 9(S), pp. S60–S68, 2012.

[17] V. Roussev, C. Quates and R. Martell, Real-time digital forensics and triage, *Digital Investigation*, vol. 10(2), pp. 158–167, 2013.

[18] scikit-learn, Machine learning in Python (scikit-learn.org), 2019.

[19] M. Shannon, Forensic relative strength scoring: ASCII and entropy scoring, *International Journal of Digital Evidence*, vol. 2(4), 2004.

[20] A. Singh and M Masuku, Sampling techniques and determination of sample size in applied statistics research: An overview, *International Journal of Economics, Commerce and Management*, vol. II(11), 2014.

[21] J. Taguchi, Optimal Sector Sampling for Drive Triage, M.S. Thesis, Department of Computer Science, Naval Postgraduate School, Monterey, California, 2013.

[22] R. Verma, J. Govindaraj and G. Gupta, Data privacy perceptions about digital forensic investigations in India, in *Advances in Digital Forensics XII*, G. Peterson and S. Shenoi (Eds.), Springer, Cham, Switzerland, pp. 25–45, 2016.

[23] R. Verma, J. Govindaraj and G. Gupta, DF 2.0: Designing an automated, privacy preserving and efficient digital forensic framework, *Proceedings of the Annual ADFSL Conference on Digital Forensics, Security and Law*, pp. 127–150, 2018.

[24] J. Young, K. Foster, S. Garfinkel and K. Fairbanks, Distinct sector hashes for target file detection, *IEEE Computer*, vol. 45(12), pp. 28–35, 2012.

IV

CLOUD FORENSICS

Chapter 9

FORENSIC ANALYSIS OF ADVANCED PERSISTENT THREAT ATTACKS IN CLOUD ENVIRONMENTS

Changwei Liu, Anoop Singhal and Duminda Wijesekera

Abstract   Cloud forensic investigations involve large volumes of diverse devices and data. Investigations involving advanced persistent threat attacks involve filtering noisy data and using expert knowledge to identify the missing steps in the attacks that typically have long time spans. Under such circumstances, obtaining timely and credible forensic results is a challenge.

This chapter engages a case study to demonstrate how MITRE's ATT&CK knowledge base and Lockheed Martin's Cyber Kill Chain methodology can be used in conjunction to perform forensic analyses of advanced persistent threat attacks in cloud environments. ATT&CK is a globally-accessible knowledge base of adversary tactics and techniques developed from real-world observations of attacks. The Cyber Kill Chain methodology describes a series of steps that trace a cyber attack from its early reconnaissance stage to the later data exfiltration stage. Because advanced persistent threat attacks on cloud systems involve the key Cyber Kill Chain phases of reconnaissance, command and control communications, privilege escalation, lateral movement through a network and exfiltration of confidential information, it is beneficial to combine the ATT&CK knowledge base and Cyber Kill Chain methodology to identify and aggregate evidence, and automate the construction of the attack steps.

Keywords: Cloud forensics, advanced persistent threat, ATT&CK, Cyber Kill Chain

1.   Introduction

Digital forensics is the application of scientific theories and methodologies to the identification, collection, examination and analysis of evidentiary data while preserving its integrity and maintaining a strict

© IFIP International Federation for Information Processing 2020
Published by Springer Nature Switzerland AG 2020
G. Peterson and S. Shenoi (Eds.): Advances in Digital Forensics XVI, IFIP AICT 589, pp. 161–180, 2020.
https://doi.org/10.1007/978-3-030-56223-6_9

chain of custody [8]. Due to the volume and diversity of cyber activities and devices in a cloud environment, the scope of post-attack cloud forensic investigations has expanded in two dimensions. The first is the attack surfaces of cloud devices that may not have undergone rigorous security checks. The second is the analysis of diverse data. A key concern is that servers running on virtual machines (VMs) in the cloud are monitored by hypervisors that lack warnings, procedures and tools for forensic investigations. Current computer forensic techniques are not designed for cloud environments and it is challenging to use existing tools to perform forensic analyses of cloud environments. Moreover, in the case of advanced persistent threat (APT) attacks that stretch over long periods of time (e.g., one year or more), the timestamps of evidence from different sources may not be indicators of a single attack. Investigating cloud environment attacks involves filtering noisy data and using expert knowledge and experience to speculate about the attack steps. These tasks are challenging and make it difficult to obtain credible forensic results.

Several researchers have proposed methodologies for collecting evidence from multiple sources and correlating them during forensic analyses of cloud attacks. These include collecting data from hypervisors and virtual machines [9, 12], and leveraging graphical frameworks to reconstruct cloud attack scenarios [10, 13]. However, the research is based on strong assumptions that the forensic data can be manually aggregated and pre-processed to produce evidence representing pre-attack conditions and post-attack conditions, and the forensic investigator can construct the attack steps when the associated evidence is incomplete or compromised.

The Adversarial Tactics and Common Knowledge Base (ATT&CK) developed by MITRE [16] is a globally-accessible knowledge base of adversary tactics and techniques based on real-world observations that assists in emulating cyber attacks. It has been used in recent years to create a taxonomy of attacks on enterprise information technology environments that enable defenders to understand which attacks are being used in the wild and to apply methods for detecting the attacks, including certain APT attacks.

Lockheed Martin's Intrusion Kill Chain (also called Cyber Kill Chain) methodology considers seven distinct phases that include reconnaissance, weaponization, delivery, exploitation, installation, command and control, and actions on objectives. Because most APT attacks involve successful reconnaissance, command and control communications, privilege escalation, lateral movement in a network and exfiltration of sensitive information, the Cyber Kill Chain has been used to analyze security logs, develop attack detection and defense systems, and aggregate evidence in analyses of APT attacks [1, 15].

Inspired by these works, the research described in this chapter leverages the ATT&CK knowledge base and Cyber Kill Chain methodology to identify evidence of cloud APT attacks from various sources, aggregate the evidence and subsequently correlate the evidence to construct the attack steps. The research advances previous work on cloud forensics [10, 13] that relies on digital forensic investigators' knowledge and experience to identify evidence and construct attack steps when the associated evidence is incomplete or compromised. Although researchers have used ATT&CK and the Cyber Kill Chain independently to detect cyber attacks and aggregate/correlate evidence [1, 3, 15, 18], no published work combines the two frameworks for attack evidence identification and correlation, which is the main contribution of this research. Sample advanced persistent threat attacks on an experimental cloud environment are employed to demonstrate how the combined frameworks can be used to identify forensic data in a cloud environment and convert it to pre-attack and post-attack conditions, which are processed by a Prolog-based forensic tool to automatically construct the attack steps.

2. Background and Related Work

This section describes MITRE's ATT&CK knowledge base, Lockheed Martin's Cyber Kill Chain methodology and related work.

2.1 ATT&CK Knowledge Base

MITRE's well-known Adversarial Tactics and Common Knowledge Base (ATT&CK) is a behavioral model that is based on real-world observations [16, 18]. Unlike other threat models that were constructed by analyzing available threat/vulnerability reports, ATT&CK describes the behaviors of real adversaries. All the attack techniques in ATT&CK correspond to real-world examples employed by malware and red teams. In addition, ATT&CK has public descriptions of attack techniques, how they are leveraged and why cyber defenders should pay attention to them. Therefore, it is useful for cyber defenders and forensic investigators to decide what should be monitored and investigated, respectively, in order to construct the attack steps and mitigate the risks.

2.2 Cyber Kill Chain Methodology

Figure 1 shows the seven attack phases in Lockheed Martin's Kill Chain methodology, which cover all the steps involved in a successful cyber attack. In the first "reconnaissance" phase, the adversary iden-

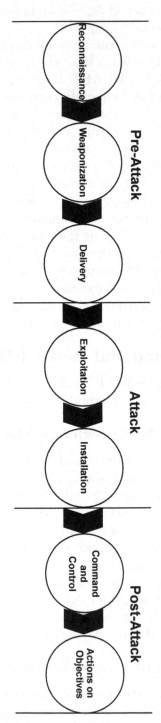

Figure 1. Cyber Kill Chain methodology.

tifies the targets by researching which targets can meet the attack objectives and collects information needed to launch the attack. In the second "weaponization" phase, the adversary prepares for the operation by coupling malware and exploits in a deliverable payload, and selecting backdoors/implants and an appropriate command and control infrastructure for the cyber operation. In the third "delivery" phase, the adversary conveys the malware to the target to launch the attack. In the fourth "exploitation" phase, the adversary triggers exploits to gain access to the target. In the fifth "installation" phase, the adversary installs a persistent backdoor or an implant in the target to maintain access for an extended period of time. In the sixth "command and control" phase, the adversary remotely controls a backdoor or implant to open a command channel so that the adversary can control the target. In the seventh and final "actions on objectives" phase, the adversary achieves the attack objectives, which include collecting user credentials, escalating privileges, destroying the system and overwriting, corrupting or modifying data [14]. According to Milajerdi at el. [15], most APT attacks are accomplished via steps that conform to the Cyber Kill Chain methodology and have the goal of obtaining and exfiltrating highly confidential information.

Cyber Reboot [2] has reexamined the seven phases and argued that there are three fundamental phases to most cyber attacks: (i) pre-attack; (ii) attack; and (iii) post-attack (Figure 1). During the pre-attack phase, the attacker is tasked with the attack objectives and performs reconnaissance of the target. During the attack phase, the attack is executed, enabling the attacker to break through the target's defense and set up communications with the target. During the post-attack phase, further exploitation and access of the target occur, which enable the attacker to escalate his/her privileges, destroy the victim system, steal confidential information, etc.

2.3   Related Work

Techniques such as remote data acquisition, management plane acquisition, live forensics and snapshot analysis have been proposed to collect evidence from cloud environments [17]. Dykstra and Sherman [5] have retrieved volatile and non-volatile data from an active Amazon EC2 cloud user instance platform using traditional forensic tools such as EnCase and FTK. In order to validate the integrity of the collected data, they subsequently developed the FROST toolkit that can be integrated in OpenStack to collect logs from an operating system that runs virtual machines [6]; however, this technique assumes that the cloud provider is trustworthy. Zawoad and Hasan [19] recently eliminated this assumption by designing a forensics-enabled cloud.

Hay and Nance [7] have conducted live digital forensic analyses of cloud environments with virtual introspection, a process that enables the hypervisor or any other virtual machine to observe the state of a chosen virtual machine. Dolan-Gavitt et al. [4] have bridged the semantic gap between high-level state information and low-level sources such as physical memory and CPU registers, and have developed a suite of virtual introspection tools for Xen and KVM. Several hypervisors, including Xen, VMware, ESX and Hyper-V, support snapshot features that can be used to obtain information about the running states of virtual machines.

In order to reduce the time and effort involved in forensic investigations, researchers have automated evidence correlation and attack reconstruction by leveraging rule-based tools and business process diagrams [13]. However, these approaches rely on forensic experts when the evidence is missing, disjointed or compromised. To help investigate attacks in a methodical manner and detect real-time APT attacks, the Cyber Kill Chain methodology has been modified to facilitate data aggregation in a relational database [1, 15].

3.   Experimental Cloud Environment Attacks

This section describes an experimental cloud environment that was targeted by conventional and cloud cyber attacks. The experimental environment and attacks are used to demonstrate how the ATT&CK knowledge base and Cyber Kill Chain methodology can be used together to advance cloud forensic investigations.

Based on the types of vulnerabilities and attacker capabilities, attacks on cloud environments can be categorized into two groups [10, 12]: (i) attacks from the Internet that exploit conventional cyber vulnerabilities to attack a virtual machine connected to the Internet; and (ii) attacks from a virtual machine that exploit vulnerabilities in shared cloud management resources to launch attacks on other virtual machines on the same hypervisor. The attacks include denial of service, information leakage, privilege escalation and arbitrary code execution, among others.

Figure 2 shows the experimental cloud environment and sample attacks. The environment comprised two Linux (Ubuntu 14.04) virtual machines, VM1 and VM2, configured on the same hypervisor (Xen 4.6). Additionally, a Windows machine was configured as a web server from which a web application could use SQL queries to retrieve database data stored in VM2, a file server that hosted a database and other files.

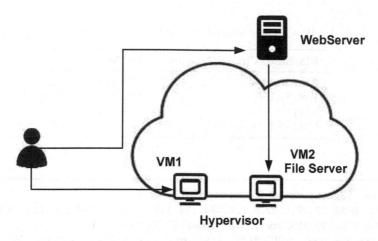

Figure 2. Experimental cloud environment and sample attacks.

Two attacks were launched at VM2. One was a conventional SQL injection attack that exploited the web application vulnerability that does not sanitize user inputs. The other one was a virtual machine escape attack, which could be a type of APT attack. The virtual machine escape attack exploited the CVE-2017-7228 vulnerability in VM1, which enabled VM1 to control Xen's privileged domain (domain 0) and then VM2, so that it could perform local operations such as deleting a file in VM2.

3.1 Forensic Data Obtained via Forensic Tools

Forensic data was collected by logging web server accesses, deploying the Snort intrusion detection system to monitor network traffic to the web server and file server, and installing the LibVMI virtual machine introspection tool on Xen Dom0 to capture events and running processes on the guest virtual machines VM1 and VM2. LibVMI is a C library that can be used to monitor the low-level details of a running Xen virtual machine by viewing its memory, trapping hardware events and accessing vCPU registers.

The IP addresses and forensic data captured using the methods/tools mentioned above are shown in Table 1 and Figures 3, 4 and 5, respectively. According to Table 1, the Snort alert in Figure 3 shows that the attacker at IP address 129.174.124.122 attempted to launch an SQL injection attack using the web application deployed on the web server at IP address 129.174.125.35 (port number 8080).

Table 1. IP addresses of machines and virtual machines in Figure 2.

Machine/Virtual Machine	IP Address
Attacker	129.174.124.122
Web Server	129.174.125.35
VM1	129.174.124.184
VM2 (File Server)	129.174.124.137

```
[**] SQL Injection Attempt --1=1 [**]
08/08-14:37:27.818279 129.174.124.122:1715 -> 129.174.124.35:8080
TCP TTL:128 TOS:0x0 ID:380 IpLen:20 DgmLen:48 DF
******S* Seq: 0xDEDBEABF  Ack: 0x0  Win: 0xFFFF  TcpLen: 28
TCP Options (4) => MSS: 1460 NOP NOP SackOK
...
```

Figure 3. Sample Snort alert.

```
129.174.124.122 - - [08/Aug/2019:14:35:34 -0400] "GET /lab/Test
                HTTP/1.1" 200 368
129.174.124.122 - - [08/Aug/2019:14:35:39 -0400] "POST /lab/Test
                HTTP/1.1" 200 981
...
```

Figure 4. Sample access log from the web server.

The web access history on the web server in Figure 4 shows that the attacker machine accessed the web application just before the Snort alert shown in Figure 3.

Figure 5 shows the SQL database log with the SQL injection query (40 Query select * from profiles where name='Alice' AND password ='alice' or '1'='1') that resulted in the information leakage.

Figure 6 shows the forensic data obtained by running LibVMI on the attacker virtual machine. The data includes the running processes (Figure 6(a)), injected Linux modules (Figure 6(b)) and CPU (CR3) register values corresponding to the running processes (Figure 6(c)). Note that the process identifiers (PIDs) were used to find the process names.

```
130808 14:37:29
   40 Query SET NAMES latin1
   40 Query SET character_set_results = NULL
   40 Query SET autocommit=1
   40 Query SET GLOBAL general_log = 'ON'
   40 Query select * from profiles where name='Alice' AND
            password='alice' or '1'='1'
   40 Quit
```

Figure 5. Sample SQL database log.

```
[  630] agetty (struct addr:ffff880003c8e200)
[  669] systemd (struct addr:ffff880076060000)
[  674] (sd-pam) (struct addr:ffff880076104600)
[  677] bash (struct addr:ffff880003c8aa00)
[  703] sudo (struct addr:ffff880004341c00)
[  704] attack (struct addr:ffff880004343800)
```

(a) Running processes.

```
test
intel_rapl
x86_pkg_temp_thermal
coretemp
...
```

(b) Injected Linux modules.

```
Waiting for events...
PID 0 with CR3=77130000 executing on vcpu 1. Previous CR3=788d1000
Waiting for events...
PID 1246 with CR3=788d1000 executing on vcpu 1. Previous CR3=77130000
```

(c) CPU register values.

Figure 6. VM2 processes, injected Linux modules and CPU register values.

4. Forensic Investigation

This section shows how ATT&CK and the Cyber Kill Chain methodology are used to assist the forensic investigation.

4.1   Identifying Forensic Data

MITRE's ATT&CK includes a knowledge base of 11 tactics and hundreds of techniques that an attacker could leverage when compromising an enterprise environment. A tactic in ATT&CK is a high-level description of certain types of attack behavior whereas a technique provides a detailed description of every type of behavior within a tactic class. The tactics in ATT&CK are not followed in a linear order as in the case of Lockheed's Cyber Kill Chain methodology. Additionally, an attacker may bounce between tactics in order to achieve the final goal.

Forensic data is mapped to the ATT&CK matrix [16] in order to help identify the evidence in a cloud forensic investigation. The matrix model covers the phases of the attack lifecycle: "initial access," "execution," "persistence," "privilege escalation," "defense evasion," "credential access," "discovery," "lateral movement," "collection," "command and control," "exfiltration" and "impact" (first column). Each phase involves the application of various techniques listed in the matrix (second and third columns). The following are the general descriptions of the phases:

- **Initial Access:** This phase involves the application of techniques that use entry vectors to gain an initial foothold in a network, which may provide the attacker with continued access to external remote services.

- **Execution:** This phase involves the application of techniques that cause attacker-controlled code to execute on a local or remote system, which can achieve broader goals such as exploring a network or stealing data by pairing the techniques with other techniques. Note that this phase may not leave any evidence.

- **Persistence:** This phase involves the application of techniques that enable an attacker to maintain a foothold on a system, even after system interruptions cut off attacker access.

- **Privilege Escalation:** This phase involves the application of techniques that enable an attacker to gain higher-level privileges in a system or network. Common approaches involve exploiting system weaknesses, misconfigurations and vulnerabilities.

- **Defense Evasion:** This phase involves the application of techniques that uninstall or disable security software, or obfuscate or encrypt data and scripts used by an attacker to avoid detection over the entire attack lifecycle.

- **Credential Access:** This phase involves the application of techniques that enable an attacker to steal credentials to gain system or network access, providing the opportunity to create multiple accounts to achieve the attack goals.

- **Discovery:** This phase involves the application of techniques that enable an attacker to gain knowledge about the system and network. During this phase, the attacker explores what can be controlled and obtains knowledge that could advance the post-compromise information-gathering goals.

- **Lateral Movement:** This phase involves the application of techniques that enable an attacker to enter and control systems in a network. An attacker might install custom remote access tools to accomplish lateral movement or use legitimate credentials with the help of native network and operating system tools.

- **Collection:** This phase involves the application of techniques that enable an attacker to gather sensitive information. Having obtained the information, the attacker may proceed to exfiltrate (steal) the information.

- **Command and Control:** This phase involves the application of techniques that enable an attacker to communicate with and control systems in the targeted network.

- **Exfiltration:** This phase involves the application of techniques that enable an attacker to steal sensitive information from the targeted network. The attacker often compresses or encrypts the information to avoid detection. The channels used for exfiltration typically include the attacker's command and control channel or an alternate channel with limited bandwidth.

- **Impact:** This phase involves the application of techniques that enable an attacker to disrupt availability or compromise integrity by manipulating business and operational processes, including destroying or tampering with data.

In the experimental cloud environment, evidence of the SQL injection attack was provided by the Snort alert (Figure 3) along with the SQL query (Figure 5), which clearly identified it as an SQL injection attack.

In the case of the virtual machine escape attack that exploited the CVE-2017-7228 vulnerability, although the attack was observed (deletion of a file in VM2), it was difficult to construct the attack from the data obtained using LibVMI (Figure 6). This is because there was no obvious logged data that could help identify the attack. Clearly, this step did not leave any evidence.

In such a situation, ATT&CK could be used to narrow the scope of the search and help find evidence. According to ATT&CK, the initial access techniques include "drive-by compromise, exploit public facing application, external remote services, hardware additions, replication through removable media, spear phishing attachment and trusted relationship."

In the experimental cloud environment, except for the facts that the database in VM2 could be queried by the web application on the web server and that VM2 shared the same hypervisor (and thus hardware) with VM1, it did not have any other connected media, remote services or running applications. Thus, the initial accesses could be narrowed to the tactics: "exploit public-facing application" from the web server and "hardware additions" from the hypervisor.

Because the observed attack activities on VM2 included the SQL injection alert and file deletion, according to ATT&CK, the attack execution techniques fall into two categories "exploitation for client execution" (corresponding to the web application on the web server) and "command-line interface" (corresponding to the hardware addition). Additionally, the techniques for "privilege escalation" could be narrowed down to "exploitation for privilege escalation" because the attacker obviously escalated his/her privileges over the Internet or from the other virtual machine remotely. Other techniques such as "access token manipulation" and "accessibility features" would not be applicable given the configuration of the cloud environment.

The SQL injection attack left obvious evidence as shown in Figures 3, 4 and 5. However, in the case of the virtual machine escape attack that resulted in the file deletion, the data in Figure 6 only show the running processes (including the normal Linux processes and a suspicious user process named **attack**) and injected modules (including normal Linux modules and a suspicious injected user module named **test**). No information was available about the attack process that exploited the shared hardware vulnerability.

Using the potential attack tactics from ATT&CK, a forensic practitioner could continue to investigate more forensic data related to successful exploitations of "hardware additions" and "command-line interface" that enabled the attacker to escalate privileges to the hypervisor level and proceed to delete the file in VM2. Previous papers by the authors of this chapter [10, 12] have revealed that system calls constitute good forensic evidence, so a snapshot of VM2 captured during the attack was used to retrieve the system calls and kernel messages of the suspicious process **attack** and suspicious module **test**.

```
 1. execve("./attack", ["./attack", "rm victim ~/samplefile.txt"],
    [/* 30 vars */]) = 0
 2. brk(NULL) = 0x8cd000
 3. mmap(NULL, 4096, PROT_READ|PROT_WRITE, MAP_PRIVATE|MAP_ANONYMOUS,
    -1, 0) = 0x7fa3a3022000
 4. access("/etc/ld.so.preload", R_OK) = -1 ENOENT (No such file or
    directory)
 5. open("/etc/ld.so.cache", O_RDONLY|O_CLOEXEC) = 3
... ...
25. open("test.ko", O_RDONLY) = 3
26. finit_module(3, "user_shellcmd_addr=1407334317317"..., 0) = 0
27. fstat(1, {st_mode=S_IFCHR|0620, st_rdev=makedev(136, 0), ...}) = 0
28. mmap(NULL, 4096, PROT_READ|PROT_WRITE, MAP_PRIVATE|MAP_ANONYMOUS,
    -1, 0) = 0x7fa3a3021000
29. mmap(0x600000000000, 4096, PROT_READ|PROT_WRITE, MAP_PRIVATE|
    MAP_FIXED|MAP_ANONYMOUS|MAP_LOCKED, -1, 0) = 0x600000000000
30. delete_module("test", O_NONBLOCK) = 0
31. exit_group(0) = ?
```

Figure 7. System calls obtained by tracing the `attack` process.

Figure 7 shows the system calls obtained by tracing the `attack` process. In fact, the arguments following the `execve` command in Line 1 clearly reveal that the attacker on VM1 used a command line to execute a program named `attack` and attempted to delete the file `samplefile.txt` located in the home folder of VM2 (named `victim` in the experimental network). Also, Line 25 clearly shows that the Linux module `test.ko` was injected into the Linux kernel of VM1 for some reason.

Figure 8 shows the VM2 kernel activities. The kernel messages between Lines 1 and 6 reveal that the attacker on VM1 wrote some bytes to memory after the address `ffff88007c723008`. The messages between Lines 8 and 19 show that the attacker controlled the page table in Xen to execute his/her shellcode by linking the physical memory address where the shellcode was held to the virtual memory address in the page table. This clearly shows the attacker used the shared memory to launch the attack.

Identifying an attack component is not a trivial task due to the nature of APTs. It requires detailed analysis such as looking at all the processes and process threads that could have altered the state of an object, even under enhanced super-user privileges. As shown in this example, identifying some of these missing steps may have to consider the system call logs. ATT&CK maintains tactics and techniques that

```
 1. [  127.408066] write_byte_hyper(ffff88007c723008, 0x7)
 2. [  127.436071] write_byte_hyper(ffff88007c723009, 0x90)
 3. [  127.460074] write_byte_hyper(ffff88007c72300a, 0xba)
 4. [  127.484055] write_byte_hyper(ffff88007c72300b, 0x26)
 5. [  127.512054] write_byte_hyper(ffff88007c72300c, 0x1)
 6. [  127.548083] write_byte_hyper(ffff88007c72300d, 0x0)
 7. [  127.628071] write_byte_hyper(ffff88007c723010, 0x0)
 8. [  127.660074] going to link PMD into target PUD
 9. [  127.668058] linked PMD into target PUD
10. [  127.676046] going to unlink mapping via userspace PUD
11. [  127.684077] mapping unlink done
12. [  127.692076] copying HV and user shellcode...
13. [  127.700077] copied HV and user shellcode
14. [  127.708066] int 0x85 returned 0x7331
15. [  127.716077] remapping paddr 0x21e8dd000 to vaddr
                   0xffff880079846800
16. [  127.724076] IDT entry for 0x80 should be at 0xffff83021e8dd800
17. [  127.732080] remapped IDT entry for 0x80 to 0xffff804000100800
18. [  127.740077] IDT entry for 0x80: addr=0xffff82d080229ef0,
                   selector=0xe008, ist=0x0, p=1, dpl=3, s=0, type=15
19. [  127.748085] int 0x85 returned 0x1337
```

Figure 8. Kernel message from the injected module.

are based on real-world observations, which makes them very helpful for identifying processes and system calls related to a sub-attack phase of an APT attack.

4.2   Mapping Log Entries to Attack Steps

After the evidence has been identified by leveraging ATT&CK, the Cyber Kill Chain model can be used to map the evidence to various attack phases in order to construct the attack steps.

The evidence shown in Figures 3, 4 and 5 pertain to the SQL injection attack because it is consistent with the timestamps and alerts. The data in Figures 3 and 4 reveal that the attacker at IP address 129.174.124.122 accessed the web server at IP address 129.174.124.35 using the SQL injection attempt ('1'='1'), which is considered to be "initial access" in ATT&CK. This is easily mapped to "weaponization" in pre-attack phase. The data in Figure 5 shows that, at the same time, the database was queried using select * from profiles where name='Alice' AND password='alice' or '1'='1', which is clearly an SQL injection attack on the database. Since the database did not have any security mechanisms, the implication is that the attack was successful. Therefore, the data in Figure 5 can be mapped to the "attack" phase in the Cyber Kill Chain.

The forensic data in Figure 6 was linked to the same attack by matching the process name `attack` and injected module name `test.ko`. Because the data in Figures 6(a) and 6(b) only show that the attacker from VM1 ran the process `attack` and module `test` to do some work (without any details), the data could be mapped to the "weaponization" phase that belongs to the pre-attack stage.

In addition, as described in Section 4.1, the data in Figures 7 and Figure 8 show that the attacker manipulated the shared memory in the same hypervisor to execute shellcode on the victim virtual machine, which can be mapped to the "exploitation" phase in the attack stage. Because the `samplefile.txt` file in the victim virtual machine was deleted, the attack succeeded and can be mapped to "actions on objectives" in the Cyber Kill Chain of the post-attack stage.

4.3 Correlating Attack Steps to APTs

In previous work by the authors [11], a Prolog-based tool was employed to generate attack steps using evidence (expressed as Prolog predicates) to instantiate rules with the predicates that represented attack pre-conditions and post-conditions. The rules, which simulated generic attack techniques, were written in the form: p :- p_1, p_2, $\cdots$, p_n, where the predicate p represents the post-conditions of an attack and predicates p_1, p_2, $\cdots$, p_n represent the pre-conditions of the attack. The post-conditions refer to the privileges that the attacker obtained after the attack and the pre-conditions include the attacker's initial privileges, location, system configuration and vulnerability exploited by the attack.

While the Prolog-based tool can be used to generate attack steps, it requires users to categorize evidence pertaining to the post-attack conditions, attack techniques and pre-attack conditions. The tool does not map predicates to the seven Cyber Kill Chain phases. Also, it does not have corresponding rules that correlate the evidence associated with the seven phases of the Cyber Kill Chain to pre-attack conditions and post-attack conditions.

The deficiencies are addressed by making the following changes:

1. Predicates Pr_r, Pr_w, Pr_d, A_e, A_i, Po_c and Po_a are used to represent the pre-attack "reconnaissance," "weaponization" and "delivery" phases, the attack "exploitation" and "installation" phases, and the post-attack "command and control" and "actions on objectives" phases, respectively.

Table 2.   Descriptions of the nodes in Figure 9.

Node	Description	Node	Description
1	ExecCode(VM2, read)	6	networkServiceInfo(database, httpd, tcp, 3660, user)
2	ExecCode(VM2, modify)	7	vulExists(webServer, 'CWE89,' httpd)
3	Through 3 (Remote exploit of server)	8	hasAccount(attacker, VM1, root)
4	Through 8 (Compromise of host via shared hardware)	9	vulExists(VM2, 'CVE-2017-7228,' sharedmemory)
5	attackerAccess(publicWebApp)	10	vulProperty('CVE-2017-7228,' localExploit, privEscalation)

2. Techniques in the ATT&CK matrix are converted to the corresponding predicates and mapped to the Cyber Kill Chain phases as follows: (i) predicates of "initial access" are mapped to Pr_r; (ii) predicates of "execution," "persistence," "privilege escalation," "defense evasion" and "credential access" are mapped to Pr_w; (iii) predicates of "discovery" are mapped to A_i; (iv) predicates of "lateral movement" are mapped to A_i; (v) predicates of "command and control" are mapped to Po_c; and (vi) predicates of "collection," "exfiltration" and "impact" are mapped to Po_a.

Note that symbols Pr_r, Pr_w, Pr_d, A_e, A_i, Po_c and Po_a are used to categorize predicates to pre-attack conditions, attack techniques and post-attack conditions, which are removed when the predicates are presented to show the constructed attack steps, as illustrated in Table 2. In the table, Nodes 5, 6, 7, 8, 9, 10 correspond to pre-attack conditions; Nodes 3, 4 correspond to attack techniques; and Nodes 1, 2 correspond to post-attack conditions.

The predicates have names and variables that depict facts such as system configuration, attacker privileges, network topology, operating system permissions and software vulnerability. The "exploit public-facing application" technique in "initial access" of the ATT&CK matrix is written to "Pr_r(attackerAccess(_host, _program))" and the "account manipulation" technique in "credential access" of the ATT&CK matrix is written to "Pr_w(hasAccount(_principal, _host, _account))," where the variables (e.g., _host, _program, _account) following the predicate names (e.g., "attackerAc-

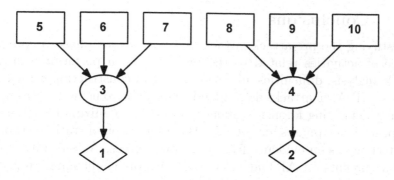

Figure 9. Constructed attack steps in the experimental cloud environment.

cess" and "hasAccount") are instantiated using concrete information during the execution of the Prolog tool.

3. Rules are added to use the Cyber Kill Chain to correlate the predicates corresponding to different phases to an attack step. The rules are of the form:

$$Po_c : -(Pr_r; Pr_w; Pr_d), (A_e; A_i).$$

and

$$Po_a : -(Pr_r; Pr_w; Pr_d), (A_e; A_i).$$

where ";" denotes logical OR and "," denotes logical AND.

These rules mean that, if there is evidence found in all the pre-attack, attack and post-attack phases, then an attack step is constructed.

After incorporating these changes in the Prolog-based tool, intuitive graphical attack steps were constructed for the two attacks as shown in Figure 9 (Table 2 provides the node descriptions). The left path shows that the attacker used a publicly-available web application to launch the SQL injection attack on the database in VM2. The right path shows the attacker exploited the vulnerability in the shared hardware to attack VM2 and then deleted a file in VM2.

Note that the miniature example provides an initial example of the ATT&CK rule model. Although some rules – e.g., lateral movement by the attacker and passing the hash attacks – are missing, the missing rules could be generated by machine learning algorithms and incorporated into the steps of the ATT&CK process.

5.   Conclusions

Justifying the pre-attack, attack and post-attack phases requires evidence of activities related to the phases. When performing an APT attack analysis, difficulties are encountered in constructing attack steps because: (i) APT attacks do not lend themselves to using time as indicators for identifying forensic evidence; and (ii) recognizing the pre-attack and post-attack phases may require the application of statistical correlation techniques on evidence from multiple sources. As a result, creating valid arguments for APT attacks becomes more challenging, in particular, assigning timestamps to APT attacks in a cloud environment.

The ATT&CK knowledge base is readily leveraged to identify the evidence and build the attack steps by mapping the available evidence to various phases in the Cyber Kill Chain methodology. The experimental cloud environment case study validates the benefits of combining the ATT&CK knowledge base and Cyber Kill Chain methodology to identify and aggregate evidence, and feed it to a Prolog-based tool that can automate the construction of the attack steps.

Future research will attempt to extend the relationships between the Cyber Kill Chain and the evidence gathering and attack-attribution tasks.

This chapter is not subject to copyright in the United States. Commercial products are identified in order to adequately specify certain procedures. In no case does such an identification imply a recommendation or endorsement by the National Institute of Standards and Technology, nor does it imply that the identified products are necessarily the best available for the purpose.

References

[1] B. Bryant and H. Saiedian, A novel kill-chain framework for remote security log analysis with SIEM software, *Computers and Security*, vol. 67, pp. 198–210, 2017.

[2] Cyber Reboot, The Cyber Attack Chain, In-Q-Tel, Menlo Park, California (www.cyberreboot.org), 2020.

[3] A. D'Amico and K. Whitley, The real work of computer network defense analysts, *Proceedings of the Workshop on Visualization for Computer Security*, pp. 19–37, 2007.

[4] B. Dolan-Gavitt, B. Payne and W. Lee, Leveraging Forensic Tools for Virtual Machine Introspection, Technical Report GT-CS-11-05, School of Computer Science, Georgia Institute of Technology, Atlanta, Georgia, 2011.

[5] J. Dykstra and A. Sherman, Acquiring forensic evidence from infrastructure-as-a-service cloud computing: Exploring and evaluating tools, trust and techniques, *Digital Investigation*, vol. 9(S), pp. S90–S98, 2012.

[6] J. Dykstra and A. Sherman, Design and implementation of FROST: Digital forensic tools for the OpenStack cloud computing platform, *Digital Investigation*, vol. 10(S), pp. S87–S95, 2013.

[7] B. Hay and K. Nance, Forensic examination of volatile system data using virtual introspection, *ACM SIGOPS Operating Systems Review*, vol. 42(3), pp. 74–82, 2008.

[8] K. Kent, S. Chevalier and T. Grance, Guide to Integrating Forensic Techniques into Incident Response, NIST Special Publication 800-86, National Institute of Standards and Technology, Gaithersburg, Maryland, 2006.

[9] LibVMI Community, LibVMI: LibVMI Virtual Machine Introspection, LibVMI (`libvmi.com`), 2020.

[10] C. Liu, A. Singhal, R. Chandramouli and D. Wijesekera, Determining forensic data requirements for detecting hypervisor attacks, in *Advances in Digital Forensics XV*, G. Peterson and S. Shenoi (Eds.), Springer, Cham, Switzerland, pp. 253–272, 2019.

[11] C. Liu, A. Singhal and D. Wijesekera, A probabilistic network forensic model for evidence analysis, in *Advances in Digital Forensics XII*, G. Peterson and S. Shenoi (Eds.), Springer, Cham, Switzerland, pp. 189–210, 2016.

[12] C. Liu, A. Singhal and D. Wijesekera, Identifying evidence for cloud forensic analysis, in *Advances in Digital Forensics XIII*, G. Peterson and S. Shenoi (Eds.), Springer, Cham, Switzerland, pp. 111–130, 2017.

[13] C. Liu, A. Singhal and D. Wijesekera, A layered graphical model for cloud forensic mission attack impact analysis, in *Advances in Digital Forensics XIV*, G. Peterson and S. Shenoi (Eds.), Springer, Cham, Switzerland, pp. 263–289, 2018.

[14] Lockheed Martin Corporation, Gaining the Advantage – Applying Cyber Kill Chain Methodology to Network Defense, Bethesda, Maryland, 2015.

[15] S. Milajerdi, R. Gjomemo, B. Eshete, R. Sekar and V. Venkatakrishnan, HOLMES: Real-time APT detection through correlation of suspicious information flows, *Proceedings of the IEEE Symposium on Security and Privacy*, pp. 1137–1152, 2018.

[16] MITRE Corporation, ATT&CK Matrix for Enterprise, Bedford, Massachusetts (attack.mitre.org), 2020.

[17] A. Pichan, M. Lazarescu and S. Soh, Cloud forensics: Technical challenges, solutions and comparative analysis, *Digital Investigation*, vol. 13, pp. 38–57, 2015.

[18] B. Strom, J. Battaglia, M. Kemmerer, W. Kupersanin, D. Miller, C. Wampler, S. Whitley and R. Wolf, Finding Cyber Threats with ATT&CK-Based Analytics, MITRE Technical Report MTR170202, MITRE Corporation, Annapolis Junction, Maryland, 2017.

[19] S. Zawoad and R. Hasan, A trustworthy cloud forensics environment, in *Advances in Digital Forensics XI*, G. Peterson and S. Shenoi (Eds.), Springer, Cham, Switzerland, pp. 271–285, 2015.

Chapter 10

A TAXONOMY OF HYPERVISOR FORENSIC TOOLS

Anand Kumar Mishra, Mahesh Govil and Emmanuel Pilli

Abstract   Cloud computing models are deployed on a compute server whose hardware resources are virtualized to enable multiple virtual machines to run on a single physical system. Several types of virtualization such as bare metal and hosted virtualization are available along with virtualization modes such as full, paravirtualized, hardware-assisted and paravirtualized-hardware-assisted virtualization. Virtual machines are inaccessible from each other when the physical server hardware is abstracted in the full virtualization mode. Physical information such as hard disk drives and server memory are made available in a virtualized environment as a virtual hard disk, vCPU and guest operating system state.

Hypervisor operations generate copious amounts of data that are of value in forensic investigations of virtualized cloud environments. This chapter presents a taxonomy of hypervisor forensic tools, which provides a searchable catalog for forensic practitioners to identify specific tools that fulfill their technical requirements. A case study involving a KVM hypervisor demonstrates the evidence that can be found in a virtual machine at the virtual machine manager and host system layers.

Keywords: Cloud computing, hypervisors, forensic tool taxonomy

1.   Introduction

In 2003, National Institute of Standards and Technology (NIST) [34] initiated the Computer Forensic Tool Testing (CFTT) Project to support the international digital forensics community. The project has classified computer forensic tools according to their specifications, test procedures, test criteria, test sets and test hardware. A similar taxonomy is required for cloud forensic tools.

© IFIP International Federation for Information Processing 2020
Published by Springer Nature Switzerland AG 2020
G. Peterson and S. Shenoi (Eds.): Advances in Digital Forensics XVI, IFIP AICT 589, pp. 181–199, 2020.
https://doi.org/10.1007/978-3-030-56223-6_10

Previous research has developed a taxonomy of cloud endpoint forensic tools [32]. This chapter extends the previous research by presenting a taxonomy for hypervisor forensic tools that considers the various layers of a hypervisor system. The chapter also discusses the potential data sources in virtual machines (VMs) and virtual machine managers (VMMs), and discusses the uses of the extracted data in forensic investigations. A case study using a KVM hypervisor demonstrates the valuable evidence that can be found in a virtual machine at the virtual machine manager and host system layers.

2.   Hypervisors

A hypervisor is a software system that abstracts the storage, operating system (OS), network and applications. The software layer is implemented on top of hardware to enable multiple virtual machines to be created in isolation. The virtual machines incorporate a processor, memory, secondary storage and networking. The hypervisor also controls the host processor and assets, dispensing resources to virtual machines and ensuring that they are isolated from each other.

A virtualized environment has multiple layers. The hardware layer comprises the processor for computation, network interface card, memory and secondary storage. The host operating system layer is situated between the hardware and hypervisor layers. Virtual machines are created on top of the hypervisor layer. A guest operating system is installed in each virtual machine for user interactions and running applications. The applications execute in a virtualized environment in the guest operating system.

A hypervisor is a software system that virtualizes hardware resources and manages the resources for virtual machines. There are two types of hypervisors. In a Type 1 or bare-metal or native-type hypervisor, the hypervisor software runs directly on the computer system hardware. Example Type 1 hypervisors include VMware ESX and ESXi, Microsoft Hyper-V, Citrix XenServer and Oracle VM (based on opensource Xen). In a Type 2 or hosted or application level hypervisor, the hypervisor software runs on a host operating system that provides virtualization services such as input/output device support and memory management. Example Type 2 hypervisors include VMware Workstation/Fusion/Player, VMware Server, Microsoft Virtual PC, Oracle VM VirtualBox, Red Hat Enterprise Virtualization and KVM.

Depending of their underlying technologies, several types of virtualization techniques have been deployed, including full virtualization, hardware-assisted virtualization and paravirtualization. In full virtual-

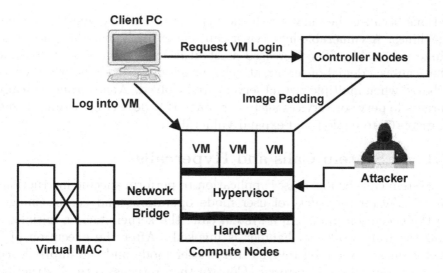

Figure 1. Attack on the hypervisor layer.

ization, a virtual machine runs in isolation; examples include VMware Workstation, VirtualBox (32-bit guests) and VMware Server. Hardware-assisted virtualization is a type of full virtualization that directly interrupts the hardware using virtualization technology, including processors such as Intel-VTx and AMD-V; examples include VMware ESXi/ESX, KVM, Hyper-V and Xen. Paravirtualization (operating system assisted virtualization) is installed on a physical server (host) and a guest operating system is installed in the environment. Unlike full virtualization, virtual guests are aware that they are virtualized; examples include Oracle VM for SPARC (LDOM) and Oracle VM for x86 (OVM).

3. Hypervisor Attacks and Vulnerabilities

Previous work [31] has discussed the top threats to cloud computing, including wrapping, malware-injection, flooding and browser attacks, insecure interfaces and APIs, malicious administrators, data theft and data leakage. Pearce et al. [37] have conducted a detailed study of virtualization techniques and the accompanying security threats.

When a cloud environment is attacked, the impacts can occur throughout the environment; this complicates evidence collection. Figure 1 shows an attack on the hypervisor layer of a private cloud. When a compute node is compromised, changes occur not only at the node, but also at the cloud controller node, hypervisor level and storage systems.

Forensic investigations of cloud environments are also challenging due to the movement of data within providers. Attacks on a hypervisor are serious because they may crash the hypervisor and the guest or virtual machines. A vulnerable hypervisor can render every installed guest machine vulnerable. The increased asset utilization by a virtual machine that causes a denial-of-service attack on a service provider server is exacerbated when multiple virtual servers are involved. An attacker typically targets hypervisor services such as `created()`, `delete()`, `clone()` and `migrate()` to exploit and expand vulnerabilities.

3.1   System Calls and Hypercalls

System calls enable a user application to perform specific instructions that maintain the safety of user mode operations and kernel changes to the execution mode. In a system call. the kernel stack is initialized and the framework call handler is invoked. After the execution of a user request, execution returns to the user mode and the unprivileged register connection is restored. Control then returns to the instruction after the system call. Because of the discriminating extension between user applications and the host operating system, system call disruptions are attractive to malicious entities that have access to cloud services.

Attackers often focus on the hypervisor layer and leverage hypercalls, which are software traps from a kernel of a guest virtual machine to the hypervisor. Milenkoski et al. [30] have listed vulnerabilities in several hypercalls: `memory_op`, `gnttab_op`, `set_debugreg`, `physdev_op` and `mmuext_op` (Table 1). Because cloud computing architectures are based on virtualization, these hypercall vulnerabilities can affect cloud services. Due to the ubiquity of cloud computing, forensic investigations of hypercall-based attacks are on the increase.

Perez-Botero et al. [38] have analyzed vulnerabilities in the Xen and KVM hypervisors. Their analysis covers hypervisor functionalities, which are mapped to vulnerabilities and attack vectors.

3.2   Virtual Machine Introspection

Virtual machine introspection (VMI) is used to investigate real-time events in a virtual machine and to ensure that the virtual system is running properly. Garfinkel and Rosenblum [11] originally defined virtual machine introspection as examining a virtual machine from the outside with the goal of dissecting the software running inside it.

Virtual machine introspection enables an investigation to be conducted without interrupting the monitored virtual machine. Virtual machine introspection assists in malware collection, malware analysis, intrusion detection, intrusion prevention, stealthy debugging, cloud security and mobile security [47].

Table 1. Hypercall vulnerabilities.

Vulnerability	Hypercall	Description	Post-Attack State
CVE-2012-3496, CVE-2012-5513	memory_op	Management of virtual machine memory	Hypervisor crash, overwritten memory
CVE-2012-4539, CVE-2012-5510, CVE-2013-1964	gnttab_op	Management of shared memory among virtual machines	Hypervisor crash, virtual machine hanging, operation disruption
CVE-2012-3494	set_debugreg	Register value management of CPU allocated to a guest virtual machine	Hypervisor crash
CVE-2012-3495	physdev_op	Management of component requests by a guest virtual machine	Hypervisor crash, overwritten memory
CVE-2012-5525	mmuext_op	Management of memory pages	Hypervisor crash, invalid page information

Figure 2 shows the virtual machine introspection components. The components are:

- **Virtual Machine Introspection API:** This library module serves as an interface between a virtual machine introspection application and the virtual machine monitor.

- **Virtual Machine Introspection Application:** This application observes the monitored guest virtual machine using the virtual machine introspection API functions, which support memory introspection, data streaming and storage performance evaluation.

- **Guest OS Symbol Table:** This virtual machine introspection component collects low-level information that is acquired externally. The low-level information includes the virtual address, system call table and interrupt descriptor table (IDT).

Several tools and utilities have been developed to support hypervisor forensics. These include LibVMI, file carving tools, disk image mounting

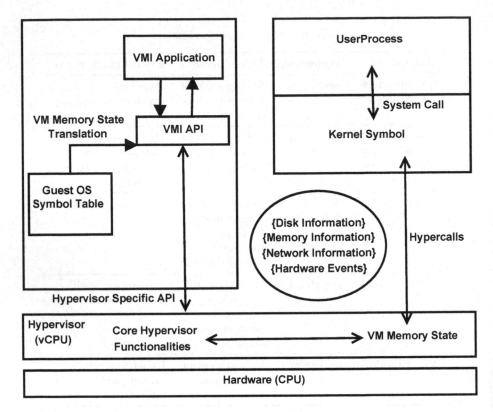

Figure 2. Virtual machine introspection components.

utilities, LiveView, Bitdefender Hypervisor Introspection and Volatility. Interested readers are referred to [16, 33] for details about virtual machine introspection techniques and their applications.

4. Taxonomy of Hypervisor Forensic Tools

Hypervisor forensics is the application of digital forensic techniques and tools to collect and analyze digital evidence for event construction, interpretation and reporting in order to prove hypervisor usability and exploitation. The primary goal of the hypervisor forensic tool taxonomy presented in this section is to provide a searchable catalog of digital forensic tools. Forensic practitioners can use the taxonomy to identify tools that meet the technical requirements of hypervisor investigations.

Figure 3 shows the taxonomy of hypervisor forensic tools. Evidentiary data can be extracted from five distinct layers or levels: (i) virtual machine layer; (ii) virtual machine manager layer; (iii) network layer; (iv) host operating system layer; and (v) hardware layer.

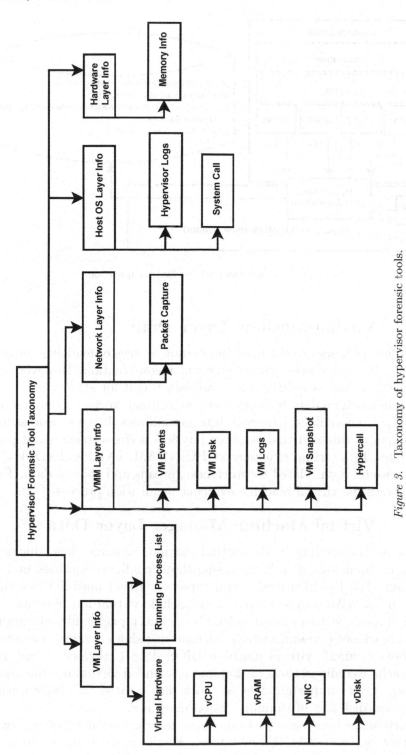

Figure 3. Taxonomy of hypervisor forensic tools.

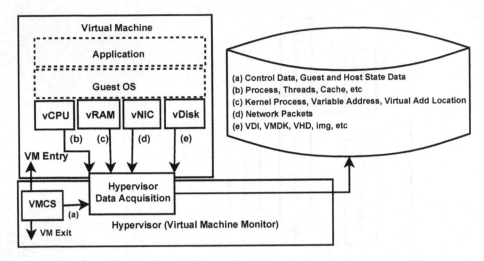

Figure 4. Virtual machine evidence acquisition.

4.1 Virtual Machine Layer Data

Virtual machines are the most important sources of evidence, including data that can support complete event reconstruction. However, virtual machine data is volatile and is an easy target for attackers.

Virtual machine data includes memory content, register contents, input/output device flags, Ethernet/Internet address changes, process list, kernel symbol table, virtual machine physical address space, guest page table, etc. In a virtual machine, vCPU, vRAM, vNIC and vDisk also provide useful data related to processes, threads and control data. Figure 4 shows the virtual machine evidence acquisition process.

4.2 Virtual Machine Manager Layer Data

Information residing in the virtual machine manager layer includes virtual machine logs, disk images, snapshots, configuration files, etc.

Shavers [41] has identified useful types of virtual machine files that reside in a VMWare hypervisor. These include virtual machine activity log files (.log), virtual machine disk files (.vmdk), paging files of running virtual machines (.vmem), virtual machine snapshots (.vmsn), metadata snapshots (.vmsd), virtual machine BIOS data (.nvram), stored virtual machine configurations (.vmx) and suspended virtual machine data (.vmss). Other important files are lock files created for configuration (.lck) and disk files of running virtual machines.

A virtual machine manager supports an interface similar to /dev/kmem that provides access to the monitored host's memory in the form of a flat file. This enables the capture of virtual machine layer events such as virtual machine rebooting or powering down. Hypercalls can also be monitored to enable the analysis of guest machine execution. Additionally, copies of virtual machine images can be preserved.

Forensic tools such as FTK Imager and OSForensics can be used to mount a virtual machine on an external drive. The virtual machine manager needs the virtual machine control structure (VMCS) that holds all the data pertaining to virtual machine configuration and the rules that must be obeyed. This control structure contains a shadow indicator, indicator, guest state area, host state area, virtual machine execution control fields, virtual machine exit control fields, virtual machine entry control fields and virtual machine exit information fields. These fields are very important because the values are stored in registers.

4.3 Network Layer Data

Network layer evidentiary data is crucial when a live acquisition is performed to investigate an active network intrusion. Network managers help analyze and manage overall network traffic and performance.

4.4 Host Machine Layer Data

Hypervisor logs, system calls and hypervisor events are maintained in the host machine layer. An image of a host machine should also be preserved because it contains all the details of the virtual machine and virtual machine manager. Files and folders associated with virtual machines should also collected from the host machine.

4.5 Hardware Layer Data

A RAM capture is one of the most important tasks in live acquisition. This is because the capture contains the footprints of running processes that can be analyzed further in the case of malicious events.

5. Related Work

This section summarizes key research in the areas of hypervisor introspection and forensic investigations. Most of the approaches employ virtual machine introspection techniques for malware detection and/or vulnerability detection.

Tables 2 through 4 list research published from 2003 to 2018. The first column presents author-year information, the second column presents the hypervisor (virtual machine manager) used and the third column the forensic method or methods used. The fourth and fifth columns list

Table 2. Hypervisor introspection and forensic investigation research.

Authors	Hypervisor	Forensic Method	Layer	Extracted Data	Objective
Garfinkel et al., 2003 [11]	VMware Workstation	VMI	VMM to VM, VM to VM	Guest OS metadata	Intrusion detection
Joshi et al., 2005 [21]	User mode Linux	VMI	Host OS to VM	Guest OS processes, kernel processes	Vuln. detection
King et al., 2006 [22]	VMware Workstation Windows XP, Linux	VM-based rootkit, VM detection	VMM to VM	Keystrokes, packets, disk state, memory	Malware detection
Kourai et al., 2005 [24]	Persona OS FreeBSD	VM monitoring mechanisms	VMM to VM	Processes, packets, disk state	Intrusion detection
Quynh et al., 2007 [39]	Xen	Filesystem integrity tools	VMM to VM, VM to VM	System calls, log files	Intrusion detection, system monitoring
Jones et al., 2008 [20]	Xen v3.0.3	Cross-view validation	VMM to VM	Guest OS processes	Hidden
Gu et al., 2011 [13]	KVM Ubuntu 10.04	VMI	VMM to VM, inside VM	Process list	Malware tracing in VM
Dolan-Gavitt et al., 2011 [6]	QEMU	Trace logging, preproc., merging	VMM to VM, VM to VM	Process IDs, process list	Secure VMI
Thorpe et al., 2011 [42]; 2012 [44]	VMware ESXi	Log synch.	Inside VM	VM networks	Event reconstrn.
Harrison et al., 2012 [14]	Xen	Forensic VM and VM	VM to VM via hypervisor	Processes	Malicious behavior
Lim et al., 2012 [28]	VMware Workstation	Direct VM image	Inside VM	VM and vDisk config., VM	VM and VM state
Kourai et al., 2012 [23]	Xen	Packet filtering at VMM recovery	VMM to VM	Attack source, log info. log, etc.	Outbound attack detection, recovery

Table 3. Hypervisor introspection and forensic investigation research (continued).

Authors	Hypervisor	Forensic Method	Layer	Extracted Data	Objective
Alarifi et al., 2012 [1]	KVM	VM host system call analysis	Inside VM	VMM system calls	Anomaly detection
Deng et al., 2012 [5]	KVM	User level library call tracing	VM	Log files	Dynamic malware analysis
Fu et al., 2012 [8]	QEMU v0.15.50	OS level, binary code reuse	VMM to VM, VM to VM	VM logs, system calls	VMI
Wang et al., 2012 [45]	Xen	VMI	VMM to VM	Process list	Virus detection
Jin et al., 2013 [19]	Xen	Network packet capture	VM to VM	Packets	Anomaly detection, file integrity
Fu et al., 2013 [9]	QEMU v0.15.50	OS kernel code	VMM to VM	VM details	VMI
Fu et al., 2013 [10]	QEMU v1.0	Exterior data acq.	VMM to VM	VM details	VMI
Thorpe et al., 2013 [43]	VMware ESXi	VM log auditing	VMM, VM	VM events, hypervisor logs, kernel logs	VM log auditing
Graziano et al., 2013 [12]	HyperDbg, KVM, Xen, VirtualBox, VMware	VM control structure	VMM	Hypervisor RAM data	Memory acq. and analysis
Lamps et al., 2014 [26]	Xen	WinWizard	VMM to VM, VM to VM	VM data, VM layer info.	VMI
Kumara et al., 2015 [25]	Xen	System call tracing, LibVMI	VMM to VM, VM to VM	VM data	Malicious process detection
Xiao et al., 2016 [46]	QEMU	Hyperlink	VMM to VM, VM to VM	VM data	VMI

Table 4. Hypervisor introspection and forensic investigation research (continued).

Authors	Hypervisor	Forensic Method	Layer	Extracted Data	Objective
Jia et al., 2017 [17]	KVM	Trusted VMI model	VMM to VM, VM to VM	VM data	VMI
Riaz et al., 2018 [40]	VMware	VM data acquisition	VMM to VM	VM log files and snapshot	VMI

the layer or layers containing data and the extracted data, respectively. The sixth column provides the objective or objectives of the research.

Other research focusing on virtual machines and introspection methods include ReVirt [7], network attack detection using Collapsar [18], trustworthy intrusion detection using Psyco-Virt [4], virtual machine monitoring with XenAccess [35, 36], direct kernel structure manipulation attack analysis using virtual machine introspection [3], live digital forensic analysis using the Xen VIX tool [15], rootkit detection in Xen using Patagonix [29], peer-to-peer network monitoring using virtual machine introspection [2], and virtual machine privacy and integrity protection using CloudVisor [49] and CryptVMI [48].

6.   KVM Hypervisor Forensics

In the KVM hypervisor forensics case study, LibVMI [27] was installed in a QEMU-KVM hypervisor v2.0.0 on a Linux Ubuntu 14.04.1 operating system (64-bit, v3.13.0-32 generic kernel). The KVM made it possible to spin up multiple virtual machines running unmodified Linux or Windows operating systems with private virtualized hardware, a network card, disk, graphics adapter, etc.

Figure 5 shows virtual machine data acquisition using hypervisor introspection. In the scenario, an attacker targets the virtualized environment containing the compute nodes C1, C2 and C3.

The LibVMI C language library provides low-level information about running virtual machines such as memory, process lists and process IDs. Using LibVMI, it is possible to examine process records, kernel module records, system call observations and memory page information. The core function of virtual machine introspection, specifically vmi_read(), makes it possible to read the virtual machine memory that supports translation, caching and hypervisor access. The translation of the kernel virtual address to the physical address is performed by vmi_translate_kv2p.

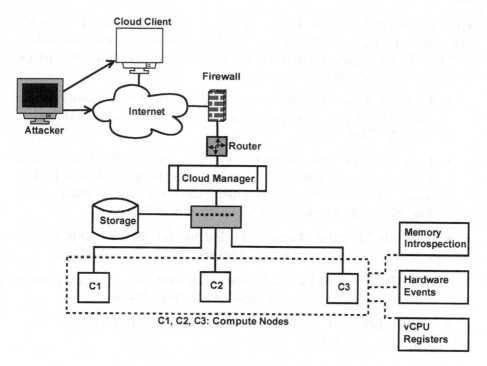

Figure 5. Virtual machine data acquisition.

```
def main(argv):
vmi = pyvmi.init(argv[1], "complete")
print vmi
print vmi.get_name()
print vmi.get_vmid()
print vmi.get_ostype()
print vmi.get_memsize()
for pid,x in list_processes(vmi):
print pid
print x
try:
print vmi.pid_to_dtb(pid)
```

Figure 6. Process ID to directory table base code snippet.

The code snippet in Figure 6 shows that, if the process ID (PID) is known, then the vmi_pid_to_dtb function returns the virtual address of the directory table base (DTB) for the process address space. This address is effectively in the CR3 control register while the process is executing. The CR3 register, which indicates the page directory base, holds the physical address of the initial structure used for address translation.

The following data related to the KVM hypervisor and its virtual machines was obtained:

- **Process List:** The list of running processes was extracted via LibVMI using the command: `$sudo ./process-list VIRTUAL_MACHINE_NAME`.

- **Disk Images and Formats:** Virtual machine disk images with format `qcow2` at `/var/lib/libvirt/images` were obtained. The image format can be converted using the command: `$ sudo qemu-img convert -O qcow2 vm1.img vm1.qcow2`.

- **Virtual Machine Logs:** The log file for each running virtual machine at `/var/log/libvirt/qemu/VM.log` was obtained.

- **SSH Login:** SSH login information at `/var/log/auth.log` along with the IP addresses and login times were obtained.

- **Audit Logs:** Hypervisor audit logs at `/var/log/audit/audit.log` were obtained.

7.   Conclusions

Hypervisor operations generate considerable data that is of evidentiary value in forensic investigations of virtualized environments. The evidence may be extracted from multiple layers – virtual machine layer, virtual machine manager layer, host operating system layer, network layer and hardware layer. As such, there is a need for forensic tools that can extract hypervisor-based native artifacts from virtualized environments with minimum effort and time. The taxonomy of hypervisor forensic tools provides a searchable catalog that assists forensic practitioners in identifying specific tools that fulfill their technical requirements. Additionally, the taxonomy could play a vital role in steering the development of standard forensic tools for virtualized environments.

Future research will enhance the tool taxonomy by incorporating features that cover the entire hypervisor forensic process, including acquisition and analysis.

References

[1] S. Alarifi and S. Wolthusen, Detecting anomalies in IaaS environments through virtual machine host system call analysis, *Proceedings of the International Conference on Internet Technology and Secured Transactions*, pp. 211–218, 2012.

[2] R. Ando, Y. Kadobayashi and Y. Shinoda, Blink: Large-scale P2P network monitoring and visualization system using VM introspection, *Proceedings of the Sixth International Conference on Networked Computing and Advanced Information Management*, pp. 351–358, 2010.

[3] S. Bahram, X. Jiang, Z. Wang, M. Grace, J. Li, D. Srinivasan, J. Rhee and D. Xu, DKSM: Subverting virtual machine introspection for fun and profit, *Proceedings of the Twenty-Ninth IEEE Symposium on Reliable Distributed Systems*, pp. 82–91, 2010.

[4] F. Baiardi and D. Sgandurra, Building trustworthy intrusion detection through VM introspection, *Proceedings of the Third International Symposium on Information Assurance and Security*, pp. 209–214, 2007.

[5] Z. Deng, D. Xu, X. Zhang and X. Jiang, IntroLib: Efficient and transparent library call introspection for malware forensics, *Digital Investigation*, vol. 9(S), pp. S13–S23, 2012.

[6] B. Dolan-Gavitt, T. Leek, M. Zhivich, J. Giffin and W. Lee, Virtuoso: Narrowing the semantic gap in virtual machine introspection, *Proceedings of the IEEE Symposium on Security and Privacy*, pp. 297–312, 2011.

[7] G. Dunlap, S. King, S. Cinar, M. Basrai and P. Chen, ReVirt: Enabling intrusion analysis through virtual-machine logging and replay, *ACM SIGOPS Operating Systems Review*, vol. 36(SI), pp. 211–224, 2002.

[8] Y. Fu and Z. Lin, Space traveling across VM: Automatically bridging the semantic gap in virtual machine introspection via online kernel data redirection, *Proceedings of the IEEE Symposium on Security and Privacy*, pp. 586–600, 2012.

[9] Y. Fu and Z. Lin, Bridging the semantic gap in virtual machine introspection via online kernel data redirection, *ACM Transactions on Information and System Security*, vol. 16(2), article no. 7, 2013.

[10] Y. Fu and Z. Lin, EXTERIOR: Using a dual-VM based external shell for guest OS introspection, configuration and recovery, *ACM SIGPLAN Notices*, vol. 48(7), pp. 97–110, 2013.

[11] T. Garfinkel and M. Rosenblum, A virtual machine introspection based architecture for intrusion detection, *Proceedings of the Network and Distributed Systems Security Symposium*, pp. 191–206, 2003.

[12] M. Graziano, A. Lanzi and D. Balzarotti, Hypervisor memory forensics, *Proceedings of the Sixteenth International Workshop on Recent Advances in Intrusion Detection*, pp. 21–40, 2013.

[13] Z. Gu, Z. Deng, D. Xu and X. Jiang, Process implanting: A new active introspection framework for virtualization, *Proceedings of the Thirtieth IEEE International Symposium on Reliable Distributed Systems*, pp. 147–156, 2011.

[14] K. Harrison, B. Bordbar, S. Ali, C. Dalton and A. Norman, A framework for detecting malware in the cloud by identifying symptoms, *Proceedings of the Sixteenth IEEE International Enterprise Distributed Object Computing Conference*, pp. 164–172, 2012.

[15] B. Hay and K. Nance, Forensic examination of volatile system data using virtual introspection, *ACM SIGOPS Operating Systems Review*, vol. 42(3), pp. 74–82, 2008.

[16] Y. Hebbal, S. Laniepce and J. Menaud, Virtual machine introspection: Techniques and applications, *Proceedings of the Tenth International Conference on Availability, Reliability and Security*, pp. 676–685, 2015.

[17] L. Jia, M. Zhu and B. Tu, T-VMI: Trusted virtual machine introspection in cloud environments, *Proceedings of the Seventeenth IEEE/ACM International Symposium on Cluster, Cloud and Grid Computing*, pp. 478–487, 2017.

[18] X. Jiang and D. Xu, Collapsar: A VM-based architecture for a network attack detention center, *Proceedings of the Thirteenth USENIX Security Symposium*, pp. 15–28, 2004.

[19] H. Jin, G. Xiang, D. Zou, S. Wu, F. Zhao, M. Li and W. Zheng, A VMM-based intrusion prevention system in a cloud computing environment, *Journal of Supercomputing*, vol. 66(3), pp. 1133–1151, 2013.

[20] S. Jones, A. Arpaci-Dusseau and R. Arpaci-Dusseau, VMM-based hidden process detection and identification using Lycosid, *Proceedings of the Fourth ACM SIGPLAN/SIGOPS International Conference on Virtual Execution Environments*, pp. 91–100, 2008.

[21] A. Joshi, S. King, G. Dunlap and P. Chen, Detecting past and present intrusions through vulnerability-specific predicates, *Proceedings of the Twentieth ACM Symposium on Operating Systems Principles*, pp. 91–104, 2005.

[22] S. King and P. Chen, SubVirt: Implementing malware with virtual machines, *Proceedings of the IEEE Symposium on Security and Privacy*, pp. 314–327, 2006.

[23] K. Kourai, T. Azumi and S. Chiba, A self-protection mechanism against stepping-stone attacks for IaaS clouds, *Proceedings of the Ninth International Conference on Ubiquitous Intelligence and the Ninth International Conference on Autonomic and Trusted Computing*, pp. 539–546, 2012.

[24] K. Kourai and S. Chiba, HyperSpector: Virtual distributed monitoring environments for secure intrusion detection, *Proceedings of the First ACM/USENIX International Conference on Virtual Execution Environments*, pp. 197–207, 2005.

[25] M. Kumara and C. Jaidhar, Virtual machine introspection based spurious process detection in virtualized cloud computing environments, *Proceedings of the International Conference on Futuristic Trends in Computational Analysis and Knowledge Management*, pp. 309–315, 2015.

[26] J. Lamps, I. Palmer and R. Sprabery, WinWizard: Expanding Xen with a LibVMI intrusion detection tool, *Proceedings of the Seventh IEEE International Conference on Cloud Computing*, pp. 849–856, 2014.

[27] LibVMI Community, LibVMI: LibVMI Virtual Machine Introspection, LibVMI (`libvmi.com`), 2020.

[28] S. Lim, B. Yoo, J. Park, K. Byun and S. Lee, A research on the investigation method of digital forensics for a VMware Workstation virtual machine, *Mathematical and Computer Modeling*, vol. 55(1-2), pp. 151–160, 2012.

[29] L. Litty, H. Lagar-Cavilla and D. Lie, Hypervisor support for identifying covertly executing binaries, *Proceedings of the Seventeenth USENIX Security Symposium*, pp. 243–258, 2008.

[30] A. Milenkoski, M. Vieira, B. Payne, N. Antunes and S. Kounev, Technical Information on Vulnerabilities of Hypercall Handlers, *arXiv:* 1410.1158v1, 2014.

[31] A. Mishra, P. Matta, E. Pilli and R. Joshi, Cloud forensics: State-of-the-art and research challenges, *Proceedings of the International Symposium on Cloud and Services Computing*, pp. 164–170, 2012.

[32] A. Mishra, E. Pilli and M. Govil, A taxonomy of cloud endpoint forensic tools, in *Advances in Digital Forensics XIV*, G. Peterson and S. Shenoi (Eds.), Springer, Cham, Switzerland, pp. 243–261, 2018.

[33] A. More and S. Tapaswi, Virtual machine introspection: Towards bridging the semantic gap, *Journal of Cloud Computing*, vol. 3, article no. 16, 2014.

[34] National Institute of Standards and Technology, Computer Forensic Tools and Techniques Catalog, Gaithersburg, Maryland (`tool catalog.nist.gov`), 2019.

[35] B. Payne, M. Carbone and W. Lee, Secure and flexible monitoring of virtual machines, *Proceedings of the Twenty-Third Annual Computer Security Applications Conference*, pp. 385–397, 2007.

[36] B. Payne, M. Carbone, M. Sharif and W. Lee, Lares: An architecture for secure active monitoring using virtualization, *Proceedings of the IEEE Symposium on Security and Privacy*, pp. 233–247, 2008.

[37] M. Pearce, S. Zeadally and R. Hunt, Virtualization: Issues, security threats and solutions, *ACM Computing Surveys*, vol. 45(2), article no. 17, 2013.

[38] D. Perez-Botero, J. Szefer and R. Lee, Characterizing hypervisor vulnerabilities in cloud computing servers, *Proceedings of the International Workshop on Security in Cloud Computing*, pp. 3–10, 2013.

[39] N. Quynh and Y. Takefuji, A novel approach for a filesystem integrity monitor tool for a Xen virtual machine, *Proceedings of the Second ACM Symposium on Information, Computer and Communications Security*, pp. 194–202, 2007.

[40] H. Riaz and M. Tahir, Analysis of VMware virtual machine in forensics and anti-forensics paradigms, *Proceedings of the Sixth International Symposium on Digital Forensics and Security*, 2018.

[41] B. Shavers, A Discussion of Virtual Machines Related to Forensic Analysis, *Forensic Focus*, November 2008.

[42] S. Thorpe, I. Ray and T. Grandison, A synchronized log cloud forensic framework, presented at the *International Conference on Cybercrime, Security and Digital Forensics*, 2011.

[43] S. Thorpe, I. Ray, T. Grandison, A. Barbir and R. France, Hypervisor event logs as a source of consistent virtual machine evidence for forensic cloud investigations, *Proceedings of the Twenty-Seventh Annual IFIP WG 11.3 Working Conference on Data and Applications Security and Privacy*, pp. 97–112, 2013.

[44] S. Thorpe, I. Ray, I. Ray, T. Grandison, A. Barbir and R. France, Formal parameterization of log synchronization events within a distributed forensic compute cloud database environment, *Proceedings of the Third International ICST Conference on Digital Forensics and Cyber Crime*, pp. 156–171, 2012.

[45] L. Wang, Y. Peng, W. Liu and H. Gao, VMSecurexec: Transparent on-access virus detection for virtual machine in the cloud, *Proceedings of the Symposium on ICT and Energy Efficiency and Workshop on Information Theory and Security*, pp. 116–121, 2012.

[46] J. Xiao, L. Lu, H. Wang and X. Zhu, HyperLink: Virtual machine introspection and memory forensic analysis without kernel source code, *Proceedings of the IEEE International Conference on Autonomic Computing*, pp. 127–136, 2016.

[47] H. Xiong, Z. Liu, W. Xu and S. Jiao, LibVMI: A library for bridging the semantic gap between guest OS and VMM, *Proceedings of the Twelfth IEEE International Conference on Computer and Information Technology*, pp. 549–556, 2012.

[48] F. Yao, R. Sprabery and R. Campbell, CryptVMI: A flexible and encrypted virtual machine introspection system in the cloud, *Proceedings of the Second International Workshop on Security in Cloud Computing*, pp. 11–18, 2014.

[49] F. Zhang, J. Chen, H. Chen and B. Zang, CloudVisor: Retrofitting protection of virtual machines in a multi-tenant cloud with nested virtualization, *Proceedings of the Twenty-Third ACM Symposium on Operating Systems Principles*, pp. 203–216, 2011.

V

SOCIAL MEDIA FORENSICS

Chapter 11

PUBLIC OPINION MONITORING FOR PROACTIVE CRIME DETECTION USING NAMED ENTITY RECOGNITION

Wencan Wu, Kam-Pui Chow, Yonghao Mai and Jun Zhang

Abstract   Public opinion monitoring has been well studied in sociology and informatics. Considerable amounts of crime-related information are available on social media platforms every day. Current methods for monitoring public opinion are typically based on rule matching and manual searching instead of automated processing and analysis. However, the extraction of useful information from large volumes of social media data is a major challenge in public opinion monitoring.

This chapter describes a methodology for extracting key information from a large volume of Chinese text using named entity recognition based on the LSTM-CRF model. Since traditional named entity recognition datasets are small and only contain a few types, a custom crime-related corpus was created for training. The results demonstrate that the methodology can automatically extract key attributes such as person, location, organization and crime type with a precision of 87.58%, recall of 83.22% and F1 score of 85.24%.

Keywords: Public opinion monitoring, named entity recognition, crime alerts

1.   Introduction

Public opinion monitoring – or social listening – is a promising approach for alerting law enforcement about crimes before they occur, because some crimes are planned using social media [8]. Several such cases were encountered during the protests against the Hong Kong extradition bill of 2019. The demonstrations against the bill began in March and April 2019 and escalated significantly in June 2019 [1]. A significant number of criminal activities occurred during the protests, including intimidation, beatings and looting that seriously impacted public safety

© IFIP International Federation for Information Processing 2020
Published by Springer Nature Switzerland AG 2020
G. Peterson and S. Shenoi (Eds.): Advances in Digital Forensics XVI, IFIP AICT 589, pp. 203–214, 2020.
https://doi.org/10.1007/978-3-030-56223-6_11

and social order. Many of these activities were planned and coordinated using social media platforms and online discussion groups.

Unfortunately, discovering potential crimes is difficult because of the need to sift through large volumes of data and interpret the slang terms used by criminal entities. Current approaches for recognizing criminal activities, which employ simple rule matching or manual processing, are inefficient and error-prone.

Named entity recognition is a fundamental component of many natural language processing applications such as relation extraction, event extraction, knowledge graphs and question-answering systems. It can classify specific and useful entities into appropriate semantic classes such as persons, locations, organizations, dates and times [5].

This chapter describes a named entity recognition methodology for monitoring public opinion in Chinese language posts and extracting crime-related features. Specifically, the LSTM-CRF model, an artificial recurrent neural network [3], is employed to extract key information from a large volume of Chinese text. Since traditional named entity recognition datasets are small and contain few types, a custom crime-related corpus was created for training. Experiments reveal that the trained LSTM-CRF model was able to recognize special features that did not exist in the training dataset. The methodology automatically extracted key attributes such as person, location, organization and crime type with a precision of 87.58%, recall of 83.22% and F1 score of 85.24%.

2.   Named Entity Recognition

Named entity recognition, also known as sequence labeling, is used to identify special entities in structured or unstructured text. Conventional named entity recognition methods fall in two categories, one based on rules or dictionaries and the other based on statistics [2].

Named entity recognition methods based on rules typically employ finite-state machines to match specific language models. However, the rule maker needs to have sufficient knowledge of the language to construct the finite-state machine. Methods based on dictionaries rely on previously-created dictionaries of persons, locations and organizations. Thus, the methods based on rules and dictionaries require large amounts of time and resources to prepare the supporting materials. Additionally, the methods have high error rates.

Statistics-based named entity recognition methods were developed to address the disadvantages of rule and dictionary based methods. These methods employ n-gram, hidden Markov, maximum entropy, conditional random field, support vector machine or decision tree models. All these

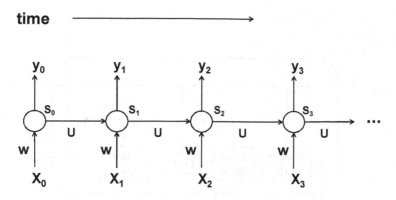

Figure 1. Recurrent neural network structure.

models require training datasets. While creating the datasets is not difficult, model performance depends significantly on the quality and quantity of the datasets [15].

The proposed methodology processes large amounts of text using deep learning and transfer learning. The first step is to create the training and testing datasets. Since no public corpora containing crime-related words exist, a custom criminal corpus was created. BIO labels were added to each word and the resulting corpus was divided into a training dataset (90% of the data) and a testing dataset (10% of the data).

3. LSTM-CRF Model

A long short-term memory and conditional random field (LSTM-CRF) model combines a long short-term memory (LSTM) model and a conditional random field (CRF) model. The LSTM model is a special type of recurrent neural network that processes long-term dependence better than conventional recurrent neural networks. The CRF model is effective at labeling and segmenting serialized data.

A traditional neural network has an input layer, a hidden layer and an output layer, where all the nodes in each layer are fully connected to nodes in the next layer. The output values of each layer, which are computed from the input values of the layer, are passed as input values to the next layer. Each input value is processed independently and the process has no memory. For input data that is sequential, such as a sentence, it is necessary to process the data in sequence, one element at a time. A recurrent neural network is a special type of neural network that is geared for processing sequential data. Specifically, it iterates through the data in sequence and maintains state information while processing. Figure 1 shows the structure of a recurrent neural network.

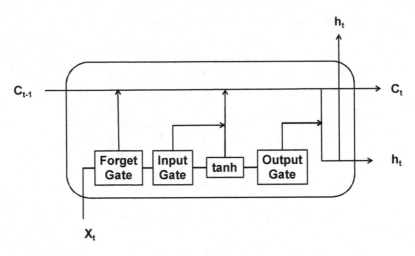

Figure 2. LSTM memory cell.

The LSTM model is a special type of recurrent neural network where the neurons are replaced by memory cells, each with input gates, forget gates and output gates. This special structure makes the LSTM model better at processing long-term dependence than a recurrent neural network; also, it avoids gradient disappearance and gradient expansion problems [13].

Figure 2 shows an LSTM memory cell. Note that C_{t-1} and X_t are the input values at time t, tanh is a neural layer, h_t is the state at time t and C_t is the output value at time t.

The CRF model is a statistical name entity recognition technique. A conditional random field defines when a random variable Y, conditioned on a set of observations X, $\text{Prob}(Y \mid X)$, obeys the Markov property. In this work, X is a set of words and Y is the corresponding label. The CRF model can then be used to learn the relationship between labels. For example, when a word is labeled as B-PER, the label of the next word is strongly believed to be I-PER. Compared with a conventional labeling model, the CRF model is better at using sentence-level label (tag) information and is able to model the transition behavior of different tags. Also, with CRF, the labeling of one character considers the labels of neighboring characters to determine the final label [4, 7].

The proposed LSTM-CRF model combines the LSTM and CRF models. Figure 3 shows the structural graph of the LSTM-CRF model. It comprises three layers. The first layer is the word embedding layer, which transforms each word into a corresponding vector so that the entire sentence can be represented as an embedding matrix. The second layer is the LSTM layer, which uses forward propagation and backward

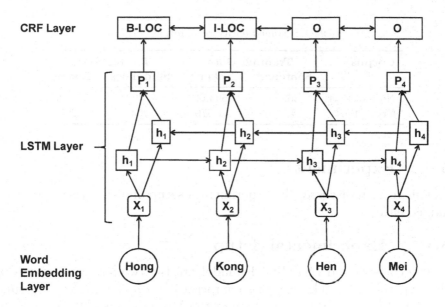

Figure 3. LSTM-CRF model.

propagation to extract features automatically. The third layer is the CRF layer, which uses the output of the second layer to label words with maximum probability.

4. Related Work

As mentioned above, a significant number of criminal activities occurred during the protests against the Hong Kong extradition bill of 2019, including intimidation, beatings and looting that impacted public safety and social order. Since many of these activities were planned and coordinated using social media platforms and online discussion groups, Hong Kong government authorities were interested in monitoring public opinion to identify potential crimes and work proactively to mitigate the hazards. However, very limited research has been done on applying deep learning techniques to detect potential criminal events by analyzing Chinese text in social media and online discussion groups.

Wang et al. [12] have employed machine learning for sentimental entity recognition with a precision of 89%. Kleinberg et al. [6] have developed an automated verbal deception detection system that employs the spaCy and Stanford NER tools. Motivated by these efforts, the research described in this chapter extracts information from large volumes of Chinese text using named entity recognition based on the LSTM-CRF model.

Table 1.   Named entity recognition corpora.

Corpus	Training Data		Testing Data	
	Sentences	Tokens	Sentences	Tokens
Normal Part	36,657	1,595,064	4,360	177,231
Crime Part	4,726	11,670	224	1,295

5.   Experiments

This section discusses the experimental setup and the classification of named entities.

5.1   Experimental Setup

The corpora and LSTM-CRF model are the two key components in the experiments. The corpora comprise a normal part and a crime part. The normal part is a portion of the MSRA corpus [9] whereas the crime part comprising three Chinese dictionaries specializing in crime was downloaded from the Sougou platform [11].

Table 1 shows the distribution of data in the named entity recognition corpora. One corpus is the normal part, which contains four types of entities, i.e., person, location, organization and not a named entity (non-named entity). The other corpus is the crime part, which only contains the criminal entity type.

Each entry (sentence) in the corpora was processed to extract a set of tokens (Chinese characters). The BIO tagging style employed for labeling uses O, B-PER, I-PER, B-LOC, I-LOC, B-ORG, I-ORG, B-CRM and I-CRM, where (i) O means that the word is not a named entity; (ii) B-X means that the word is the beginning of X (e.g., B-PER means that the word is the beginning of person); and (iii) I-X means that the word is inside word X. Figure 4 shows examples that use the BIO tagging style [10].

5.2   Classification of Named Entities

The classification of named entities involves two steps:

- **Step 1: Data Processing:** Based on the corpus, each word is labeled with a corresponding tag. Next, the corpus is serialized and a dictionary containing non-replicative words is constructed. The dictionary has the form: { "first word": [id1, counts], "second word": [id2, counts], ... }, where a raw word is in quotes and the square brackets contain the identification number of the word and

调 O 查 O 范 O 围 O 涉 O 及 O 故 B-LOC 宫 I-LOC 、 O 历 B-LOC 博 I-LOC 、 O 古 B-ORG 研 I-ORG 所 I-ORG 、 O 北 B-LOC 大 I-LOC 清 I-LOC 华 I-LOC 图 B-LOC 书 I-LOC 馆 I-LOC 、 O 北 B-LOC 图 I-LOC 、 O 日 B-LOC 伪 O 资 O 料 O 库 O 等 O 二 O 十 O 几 O 家 O,O 言 O 及 O 文 O 物 O 二 O 十 O 万 O 件 O 以 O 上 O,O 洋 O 洋 O 三 O 万 O 余 O 言 O,O 是 O 珍 O 贵 O 的 O 北 B-LOC 京 I-LOC 史 O 料 O 。	The survey covers the Forbidden City, Libo, Institute of antiquity, Tsinghua University Library, beitu, Japanese and puppet databases and more than 200,000 cultural relics and 30,000 foreign words, which are precious historical materials of Beijing.
微 B-CRM 信 I-CRM 催 B-CRM 眠 I-CRM 水 I-CRM 催 B-CRM 情 I-CRM 粉 I-CRM 催 B-CRM 情 I-CRM 药 I-CRM 催 B-CRM 情 I-CRM 藥 I-CRM 挫 B-CRM 仓 I-CRM 毕 B-CRM 业 I-CRM 证 I-CRM 答 B-CRM 案 I-CRM 包 I-CRM 答 B-CRM 案 I-CRM 提 I-CRM 供 I-CRM 发 B-CRM 票 I-CRM 出 I-CRM 发 B-CRM 票 I-CRM 代 I-CRM 发 B-CRM 票 I-CRM 销 I-CRM 發 B-CRM 票 I-CRM 蒙 B-CRM 汗 I-CRM 药 I-CRM 迷 B-CRM 幻 I-CRM 型 I-CRM 迷 B-CRM 幻 I-CRM 药 I-CRM 迷 B-CRM 幻 I-CRM 藥 I-CRM 迷 B-CRM 昏 I-CRM 口 I-CRM 迷 B-CRM 昏 I-CRM 药 I-CRM	Wechat hypnotic water, aphrodisiac powder, aphrodisiac drug, Tulun graduation certificate, answer package, provide invoice, replace invoice, sell Invoice, Mongolian sweat drug, psychedelic drug, psychedelic drug, aphrodisiac drug

Figure 4. BIO tagging style.

the number of occurrences. Based on the counts, words with low frequencies are eliminated from the dictionary. Figure 5 shows the data processing step.

- **Step 2: Model Setup:** The LSTM-CRF model was employed in the experiments – the LSTM layer is located at the bottom whereas the CRF layer is located on top. The softmax function was used to compute the probabilities of each target class over all possible target classes.

The hyper-parameters used in the experiments are shown in Table 2. The batch size was set to 64, meaning that 64 samples were trained in each epoch. The epoch value was set to 10, meaning that each sample was trained ten times over the experiment. The dimension of the hidden

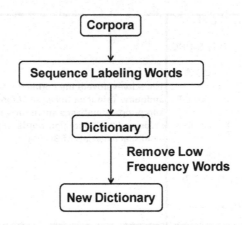

Figure 5.   Data processing.

Table 2.   Hyper-parameter values.

Parameter	Value	Parameter	Value
batch_size	64	clip	5
epoch	10	dropout	0.5
hidden_dim	300	update_embedding	TRUE
optimizer	Adam	embedding_dim	300
lr	0.001	pretrain_embedding	random

state (hidden_dim) was 300, the optimizer was Adam, the learning rate (lr) was 0.001 and the gradient clipping (clip) was 5.

Table 3.   Dataset proportions.

Corpus	Training Dataset	Testing Dataset
Normal Part	1,595,064	177,231
Crime Part	11,670	1,295
Total Number	1,606,734	178,526
Proportion	90%	10%

Table 3 shows the proportions of the training dataset and testing dataset. The amount of training data was set to 1,606,734 and the amount of testing data was set to 178,526, corresponding to proportions of 90% and 10%, respectively. In the experiment, the extracted tokens were used as the basic unit of processing. After each epoch, the loss function value, global step, precision, recall and F1 score were recorded.

	据警方報導示威者準備去中環站打警察	The police said demonstrators will set fire and beat cops at the central station
Example 1	PERSON: ['示威者'] LOCATION: ['中環站'] ORGANIZATION: ['警方'] CRIM: ['打警察']	PERSON: ['demonstrators'] LOCATION: ['central station'] ORGANIZATION: ['The police'] CRIM: ['beat cops']
Example 2	如果警方想/引你們暴亂，令(全球)怪罪你們，你們便全敗！他們脫罪！明未？😡官方中有秦會和高球，死的只會是岳家軍和水浒軍！😡😡😡聰明些吧！必須(立即)停暴！你們才能勝！你們影响民生時，人民只會放棄你們而(不會)幫你們迫政府的！要勝必須停！！！	If the police want to / lead you to riot and blame you all over the world, you will all be defeated! They get away with it! Do you understand? There are Qin Hui and Gao Qiu in the official, only Yue Jiajun and Shui hujun will die! Be smart! The violence must be stopped (immediately)! You can win! When you influence people's livelihood, the people will only give up on you and (will not) help you to force the government! To win must stop!!!
	PERSON: ['秦會', '高球'] LOCATION: ['全球'] ORGANIZATION: ['警方', '岳家軍', '水浒军', '人民', '政府'] CRIM: ['暴亂', '脫罪', '停暴']	PERSON: ['Qin Hui', 'Gao Qiu'] LOCATION: ['all over the world'] ORGANIZATION: ['the police', 'Yue Jiajun', 'Shui Hujun', 'the people', 'the government'] CRIM: ['riot', 'get away with it', 'The violence must be stopped']

Figure 6. Two experimental examples.

6. Experimental Results and Discussion

After being trained, the LSTM-CRF model was able to identify the four entities in a sentence. Figure 6 shows the input sentence: "The police said demonstrators will set fire and beat cops at the central station." The model was able to recognize person as demonstrators, location as the central station, organization as the police and the crime as set fire and beat cops.

In the second example in Figure 6, the model was able to identify person as Qin Hui and Gao Qiu, location as the world, organization as the police, Yue Jiajun, Shui Hujun, the people and the government, and crime as riot, get away with it and the violence must be stopped.

Table 4 compares the LSTM-CRF and LSTM models. The LSTM-CRF model produces better results. The LSTM model is good at learning the sequential relationships of entities (i.e., words in this study) automatically, but it ignores the sequential relationships of labels. On the other hand, the CRF model is good at learning the sequential relationships of labels. Since the CRF model addresses the LSTM model deficiencies, the LSTM-CRF model performs better than the basic LSTM model.

As shown in Table 4, when the crime part is eliminated, higher values for precision of 90.37%, recall of 86.27% and F1 score of 88.27% are

Table 4.   LSTM and LSTM-CRF model evaluation.

Models	Precision	Recall	F1 Score
LSTM	84.16%	82.07%	83.11%
LSTM-CRF	87.58%	83.22%	85.24%
LSTM-CRF (Without Crime Part)	90.37%	86.27%	88.27%

obtained. This is because the other three parts (person, location and organization) have been studied in public datasets by other researchers, but only this research contains the crime part. Also, since the corpus was created for crimes, it is more difficult to train the model to recognize crime-related entities.

As expected, the models produce different results. The named entity recognition technique is limited in that it only extracts key entities from text, but does not analyze the entities. As a consequence, the investigator has to analyze the extracted entities and make manual decisions.

7.   Conclusions

Automated monitoring of social media platforms and online discussion groups can provide insights into potential criminal events, enabling law enforcement to work proactively to mitigate the hazards. The combined LSTM-CRF model described in this chapter is able to extract key information from large volumes of Chinese text using named entity recognition. Experiments indicate that the automated extraction of key attributes such as person, location, organization and crime is accomplished with a maximum precision of 87.58%, recall of 83.22% and F1 score of 85.24%. These results demonstrate that the methodology is effective at discovering potential criminal events.

Due to the absence of crime-related corpora, custom corpora had to be created for training and testing. Future research will focus on developing richer and larger corpora with criminal events. Training the model using these corpora would improve the overall performance.

A limitation of the methodology is that, while it identifies key entities, it cannot analyze them. Yang and Chow [14] have employed statistical methods to create relationships between entities. Future research will pursue this line of inquiry and also focus on relation extraction and emotional analysis using deep learning techniques.

References

[1] H. Chan, In pictures: 12,000 Hongkongers march in protest against "evil" China extradition law, organizers say, *Hong Kong Free Press*, March 31, 2019.

[2] N. Greenberg, T. Bansal, P. Verga and A. McCallum, Marginal likelihood training of BiLSTM-CRF for biomedical named entity recognition from disjoint label sets, *Proceedings of the 2018 Conference on Empirical Methods in Natural Language Processing*, pp. 2824–2829, 2018.

[3] S. Hochreiter and J. Schmidhuber, Long short-term memory, *Neural Computation*, vol. 9(8), pp. 1735–1780, 1997.

[4] Z. Huang, W. Xu and K. Yu, Bidirectional LSTM-CRF Models for Sequence Tagging, arXiv: 1508.01991v1, 2015.

[5] A. Katiyar and C. Cardie, Nested named entity recognition revisited, *Proceedings of the 2018 Conference of the North American Chapter of the Association for Computational Linguistics: Human Language Technologies*, vol. 1 (Long Papers), pp. 861–871, 2018.

[6] B. Kleinberg, M. Mozes and A. Arntz, Using named entities for computer-automated verbal deception detection, *Journal of Forensic Sciences*, vol. 63(3), pp. 714–723, 2018.

[7] G. Lample, M. Ballesteros, S. Subramanian, K. Kawakami and C. Dyer, Neural architectures for named entity recognition, *Proceedings of the 2016 Conference of the North American Chapter of the Association for Computational Linguistics: Human Language Technologies*, pp. 260–270, 2016.

[8] C. Marcum, *Cyber Crime*, Wolters Kluwer, Frederick, Maryland, 2014.

[9] Pudn, MSRA (www.pudn.com/Download/item/id/2435241.html), 2020.

[10] C. Santos and V. Guimaraes, Boosting Named Entity Recognition with Neural Character Embeddings, *arXiv:* 1505.05008v2, 2015.

[11] Sougou, Sougou Corpus (pinyin.sougou.com), 2020.

[12] Z. Wang, X. Cui, L. Gao, Q. Yin, L. Ke and S. Zhang, A hybrid model of sentimental entity recognition on mobile social media, *EURASIP Journal on Wireless Communications and Networking*, vol. 2016, article no. 253, 2016.

[13] D. Xu, R. Ge and Z Niu, Forward-looking element recognition based on the LSTM-CRF model with the integrity algorithm, *Future Internet*, vol. 11(1), article no. 17, 2019.

[14] M. Yang and K. Chow, An information extraction framework for digital forensic investigations, in *Advances in Digital Forensics XI*, G. Peterson and S. Shenoi (Eds.), Springer, Cham, Switzerland, pp. 61–76, 2015.

[15] J. Zhang and X. Liu, Research on Chinese named entity recognition based on deep learning, *Proceedings of the Fourth IEEE International Conference on Computer and Communications*, pp. 2142–2147, 2018.

Chapter 12

RETRIEVING E-DATING APPLICATION ARTIFACTS FROM iPHONE BACKUPS

Ranul Thantilage and Nhien-An Le-Khac

Abstract   Criminal activities are widely facilitated by online means; so are sex crimes. Online dating, also referred to as e-dating, enables people to get in touch with potential romantic partners through digital means. Unfortunately, sex criminals also exploit online dating platforms to find victims.

Several e-dating applications have been developed for computers and mobile phones, but few, if any, efforts have focused on retrieving evidence from e-dating applications. This chapter describes forensic methods for retrieving evidence from two popular e-dating applications – Tinder and Coffee Meets Bagel – by examining iPhone backups created via iTunes on Windows and Macintosh personal computers.

Keywords: iPhone forensics, evidence retrieval, e-dating applications

1.   Introduction

Many crimes, including sex crimes, are facilitated by online activities. Online dating applications, also referred to as e-dating applications, enable people to interact with potential romantic partners via digital means. Unfortunately, sex criminals also exploit online dating applications to find victims.

One such application is Tinder, which is widely used by young individuals. Tinder's terms of use forbid users below the age of 18 from using the application [21]. However, it is common for young teens to register with the application by faking their ages. This makes them vulnerable to sexual predators.

According to a 2016 report by the National Crime Agency of the United Kingdom [15], online-dating-related rape increased 450% during the previous six years. Meanwhile, the number of e-dating application

© IFIP International Federation for Information Processing 2020
Published by Springer Nature Switzerland AG 2020
G. Peterson and S. Shenoi (Eds.): Advances in Digital Forensics XVI, IFIP AICT 589, pp. 215–230, 2020.
https://doi.org/10.1007/978-3-030-56223-6_12

users has increased significantly. According to 2020 usage statistics [13], Tinder has more than 57 million registered users and processes approximately 1.6 billion swipes every day.

Another e-dating application, Coffee Meets Bagel, has more than seven million installs [19]. The app received international coverage on Valentine's Day 2019 after it suffered a data breach affecting around six million users [6]. The stolen data was offered on the dark web for $20,000 in Bitcoin [17].

Millennials and post-millennials use smart devices more than any other population age group, with iPhones being the most popular devices. Therefore, this research focuses on iPhone-based usage of Tinder and Coffee Meets Bagel. iPhone forensics is a well-established area of digital forensics, but little work has concentrated on extracting evidence from iPhone backups. This is a key gap because investigators may not have access to the smart devices of criminals and/or victims; in fact, they may only know the names of the individuals.

Since it is common to backup iPhone data on Windows and Macintosh computers, investigators could access these computers at the criminals' and/or victims' homes, and proceed to examine the backups to find evidence of criminal activity. Indeed, iPhone backups on personal computers contain considerable amounts of data related to e-dating application usage.

This research concentrates on evidence retrieval from iPhone backups created by iTunes. The main contributions are forensic acquisition and analysis of artifacts from Tinder and Coffee Meets Bagel apps in iPhone backups on personal computers.

2.   Related Work

As Internet usage increases around the globe, so does online dating. A 2002 research study reported that 1,458 of 1,836 (79.4%) of surveyed Internet users in Sweden used the Internet for sexual purposes [5]. A factor analysis study in 2010 revealed that online dating application users were primarily interested in seeking partners and accessing erotica [4].

Van Voorst et al. [22] have discussed the risks associated with using mobile apps to meet potential partners. They also described the forensic acquisition and analysis of evidence from an Instant Messaging within a Virtual Universe (IMVU) 3D application, which has been exploited by criminal entities to commit a variety of offenses.

Newett et al. [16] researched the intimate lives of Australians aged 18 to 30 years. They also studied how the Tinder platform contributed to intimate outcomes. Full 91.92% of the respondents were frequent Tinder users. While sex was the least motivating factor for female respondents, it was the third most important factor for male respondents. Ranzini and Lutz [18] noted that women use Tinder more for friendship and self-validation whereas men use it hooking up/sex, traveling and forming relationships.

Feltz [11] researched the security of Tinder and demonstrated that it has significant vulnerabilities as a geosocial mobile app. In particular, attackers can use methods such as trilateration to pinpoint the exact physical locations of users. Other security researchers have found vulnerabilities in Tinder; many of the vulnerabilities have been addressed, but some persist.

Farnden et al. [10] have conducted a study of geosocial apps. They analyzed popular proximity-based dating applications to determine the types of data that can be recovered. An important result was that 50% of the apps supported the forensic recovery of chat messages.

Heffernen [12] has described a forensic analysis of an early version of the Tinder app (version 2.1.0) on an iPhone 4S running iOS 6.1.3. The iPhone Analyzer tool was used to extract Tinder's SQLite database file. Analysis of the database tables revealed that very few artifacts were present.

Several researchers have focused on mobile device forensics and its important role in investigations [1, 9]. However, the vast majority of work has concentrated on extracting data from devices. For example, Cheema et al. [3] have analyzed the iOS filesystem to identify directories and files that could be relevant to traditional criminal investigations. Likewise, the iOS forensics work by Drish [7] deals mainly with data acquisition from devices. Epifani and Stirparo [8] discuss forensic analyses of iOS messaging apps; they showed how application data is separated from its bundles, and also investigated the directory structure and deleted data.

Baggili et al. [2] have developed a tool named LiFE that conducts forensic analyses of iOS backups. The tool analyzes device information, call history, voice messages, GPS locations, conversations, notes, images, address books, calendar entries, SMS messages, Facebook data and email.

A review of the literature reveals that research has largely concentrated on independent platforms and applications. Very little research has focused on iPhone backup forensics and what has been done involves general applications, not e-dating applications. Moreover, research on e-dating applications has studied vulnerabilities and usage statistics. In contrast, the research described in this chapter concentrates on the retrieval of Tinder and Coffee Meets Bagel artifacts from iPhone backups created by iTunes on Windows and Macintosh personal computers. This is important because investigators often do not have access to the physical iPhones, but they could access personal computers at the criminals' and/or victims' homes, and conduct forensic analyses of iTunes backups to find evidence of criminal activity.

3.   Challenges

Mobile devices are routinely encountered in criminal investigations. Lutes and Mislan [14] identify several challenges related to mobile device forensics. These include diverse carriers and manufacturers, data preservation, power and data connectors, operating systems, communications protocols and security mechanisms.

Compared with other mobile device platforms, iOS device forensics is more challenging because iOS devices employ full drive encryption as well as protections such as per-file keys and backup encryption (if enabled). Furthermore, iOS is a proprietary encrypted operating system.

4.   Evidence Extraction Methods

This section presents the methods used to extract e-dating application artifacts from iPhone backups on Windows and Macintosh personal computers.

iTunes is used to create iPhone backups on personal computers. Backups are stored at different locations depending on the operating systems on the personal computers. For example, the Windows 10 operating system stores the backup at:

```
%systempartition%\Users\%username%\AppData\Roaming\
       AppleComputer\Mobilesync\Backup\
```

In the case of a Macintosh operating system, the backup is stored as:

```
Users/%username%/Library/applicationsupport/
       MobileSync/backup
```

The backup folder is identified by a 40-digit SHA-1 hash value that is created from the unique device identifier (UID) of the iPhone. The file name is also encoded using a SHA-1 hash of the file path and file name.

The key to analyzing an iPhone backup is to identify the hash value of the required file. This requires the forensic practitioner to know the file name and file path (domain). Note that AppDomain is used for applications that are downloaded from the Apple App Store.

21	fa148e80e46580784ed1907d71b4cedfe5071a21	AppDomain-com.cardify.tinder	Libra
22	bd881d082294367de00a97791cbf3741481c3466	AppDomain-com.cardify.tinder	Libra
23	b50ed9ebfae9076641965008111c90ea5bfc56c0	AppDomain-com.cardify.tinder	Libra

(a) SHA-1 hash value in the `Manifest.db` file.

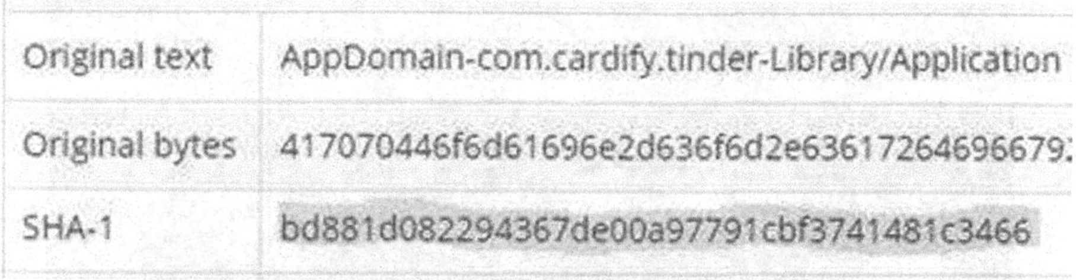

Original text	AppDomain-com.cardify.tinder-Library/Application
Original bytes	417070446f6d61696e2d636f6d2e63617264696679
SHA-1	bd881d082294367de00a97791cbf3741481c3466

(b) Computed SHA-1 hash value.

Figure 1. Verification of Tinder database SHA-1 hash values.

4.1 Tinder

Evidence related to Tinder is stored in an SQLite database. The database file is located at:

> AppDomain-com.cardify.tinder-Library/
> ApplicationSupport/Tinder/Tinder2.sqlite

The hash value of the SQLite database file can be obtained by going through the `Manifest.db` file available in the root of the backup or by computing it using a SHA-1 hash generator.

Figures 1(a) and 1(b) confirm that the hash value for the file is:

> bd881d082294367de00a97791cbf3741481c3466

Searching for the hash value in the backup folder enables a forensic practitioner to identify and extract the SQLite file. Note that, at first glance, the file does not show an extension. However, the file type can be checked using `file tool/command` in Linux.

Figures 2(a) and 2(b) show the SQLite files retrieved using the hash values from Windows and Macintosh iTunes backups, respectively.

The hash values of the files are the same for each application. Therefore, a forensic practitioner should record the file hash values needed in investigations to save time by not repeating the steps.

The Tinder database contains more than 30 tables, many of which could provide important evidence in an investigation. The tables of spe-

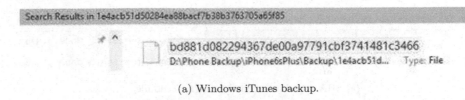

(a) Windows iTunes backup.

(b) Macintosh iTunes backup.

Figure 2.   Searching for the Tinder `SQLite.db` using the hash value.

cial interest are: ZMATCH, ZMESSAGE, ZPHOTO, ZPROCESSED-PHOTO, ZPROCESSEDVIDEO and ZUSER. Each table is linked using a database key (i.e., primary key). By writing appropriate queries, a forensic practitioner can link the tables to each other and gather a vast amount of data.

Table 1 shows the evidentiary data that can be retrieved from the Tinder SQLite database.

4.2   Coffee Meets Bagel

The method for retrieving evidentiary data from Coffee Meets Bagel (CMB) is similar to that used for Tinder. Coffee Meets Bagel also stores data in a SQLite database.

The database file is located at:

> `AppDomainGroup-group.com.coffeemeetsbagel.mainapp-`
> `CMBMobile.sqlite`

The hash value of the SQLite database file can be obtained by going through the `Manifest.db` file available in the root of the backup or by computing it using a SHA-1 hash generator.

Table 1. Evidentiary data in the Tinder SQLite database.

Table	Evidence
ZMATCH	Match Timestamp Last Activity Timestamp User ID Match ID
ZMESSAGE	Match ID Timestamps From User ID Message ID Message Text
ZPHOTO	User ID Photo ID Image URL
ZPROCESSEDPHOTO	Photo ID Image URL
ZVIDEO	Photo ID Video URL
ZUSER	Match ID Birthdate Distance in Miles Tinder Bio First Name User ID Liked

Figures 3(a) and 3(b) confirm that the hash value of the database file is:

18e36628c588925c485480d0440bbdad0dc2af3d

Figure 4 shows that the hash value can be searched in the backup folder in Windows to retrieve the SQLite.db file.

The Coffee Meets Bagel database contains more than 10 tables, many of which could provide important evidence in an investigation. The tables of special interest are: ZBAGEL, ZCHATMESSAGECACHE and ZPROFILE. Each table is linked using a database key (i.e., primary key). By writing appropriate queries, a forensic practitioner can link the tables to each other and gather a vast amount of data.

Table 2 shows the evidentiary data that can be retrieved from the Coffee Meets Bagel SQLite database.

40	4a25e81d43afd2213ebf8e5684ca98dca7ca39e6	AppDomainGroup-group.com.coffeemee
41	567aef44cb04c38d9b6ef1a331b42e9d76f98ea6	AppDomainGroup-group.com.coffeemee
42	18e36628c588925c485480d0440bbdad0dc2af3d	AppDomainGroup-group.com.coffeemee

(a) SHA-1 hash value in the `Manifest.db` file.

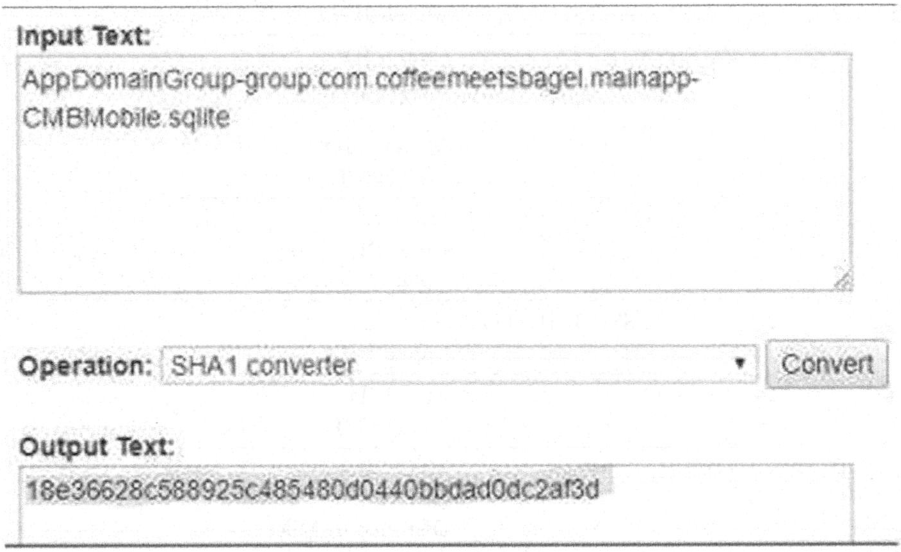

Input Text:

AppDomainGroup-group.com.coffeemeetsbagel.mainapp-
CMBMobile.sqlite

Operation: SHA1 converter   ▾   Convert

Output Text:

18e36628c588925c485480d0440bbdad0dc2af3d

(b) Computed SHA-1 hash value.

Figure 3.   Verification of Coffee Meets Bagel database SHA-1 hash values.

f50284ea88bacf7b38b3763705a65f85   ⌄ ↻   25c485

18e36628c588925c485480d0440bbdad0dc2af3d   Date modified: 9/5/2
D:\Phone Backup\iPhone6sPlus\Backup\1e4acb51d...   Type: File   Size: 200 KB

Figure 4.   Searching for the Coffee Meets Bagel `SQLite.db` using the hash value.

Tables 1 and 2 demonstrate that timestamps and dates are retrieved in several instances. The timestamps are stored in the Apple Cocoa Core Data timestamp format, which corresponds to the number of seconds elapsed since 00:00, January 1, 2001 GMT. These timestamps should be converted to a local time format.

Table 2. Evidentiary data in the Coffee Meets Bagel SQLite database.

Table	Evidence
ZBAGEL	Profile ID Created Timestamp Last Updated Timestamp
ZCHATMESSAGECACHE	Timestamp ID XMPP Message
ZPROFILE	User Age Personal Details (e.g., height) User Birthdate Last Updated Timestamp User Geolocation User City User Country User Bio User Employment Details User Ethnicity User Religion User First Name

5. Experimental Evaluation

The proposed methods were tested using several iPhone models and iOS versions to create Windows and Macintosh backup files. The following are the specifications of the iPhones used in the experimental evaluation:

- **Device 1:** iPhone 6S Plus, iOS 11.4, 64 GB capacity.

- **Device 2:** iPhone 6, iOS 11.4, 16 GB capacity.

- **Device 3:** iPhone XS Max, iOS 12.3, 64 GB capacity.

The following iTunes software versions were employed:

- **iTunes Version 1 (Windows):** Version 12.6.1.25.

- **iTunes Version 2 (Windows):** Version 12.9.2.6.

- **iTunes Version 3 (Macintosh):** Version 12.9.2.5.

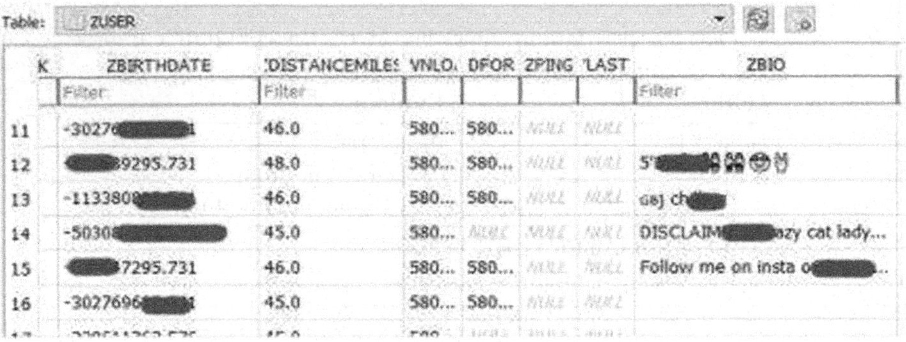

(a) User birthdate and bio information.

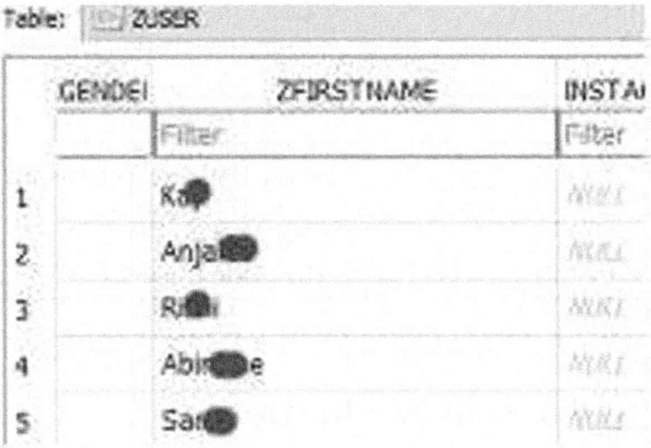

(b) User first name information.

Figure 5. User information extracted from the ZUSER table.

5.1 Tinder Evidence

Table 1 shows that considerable data pertaining to the Tinder application is stored in an iPhone backup. Therefore, a forensic practitioner can examine the personal computer of a suspect or victim to obtain evidence about online dating activities. This section discusses the evidentiary data that can be retrieved from the Tinder application.

Figure 5 shows the user birthdates, bios and first names that were extracted from the ZUSER table.

Figure 6 shows the message IDs and texts associated with matched users that were extracted from the ZMESSAGE table.

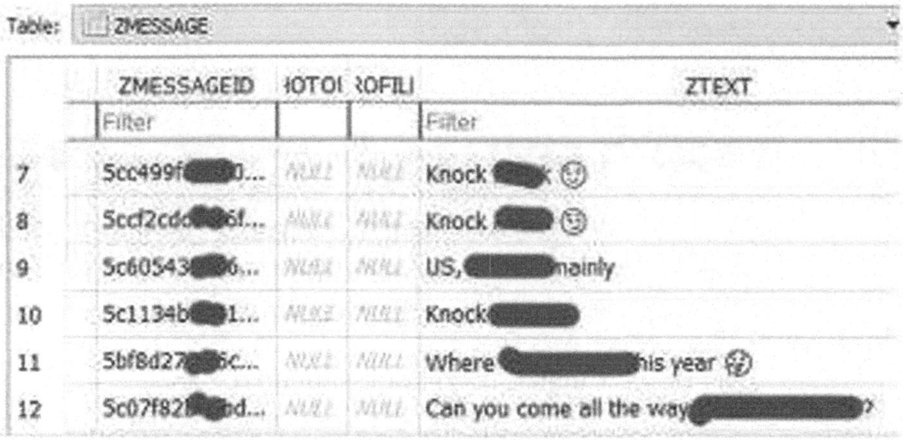

Figure 6. Message IDs and texts extracted from the ZMESSAGE table.

Figure 7 shows how the URLs of photographs can be retrieved from the ZPROCESSEDPHOTO table, along with a sample photograph. Note that portions of the images are covered or pixelated to preserve privacy.

5.2 Coffee Meets Bagel Evidence

Table 2 shows that considerable data pertaining to the Coffee Meets Bagel application is stored in an iPhone backup. An important feature of Coffee Meets Bagel is that geolocation information pertaining to users of the application can be extracted easily.

Figure 8 shows the personal information of users, including name, birthday, ethnicity, religion and geolocation data, that was extracted from the Coffee Meets Bagel backup file.

Figure 9 shows the exact location of a user obtained from geolocation data in the ZPROFILE table. Once again, portions of the screenshots are obfuscated for privacy reasons.

6. Conclusions

iPhone forensics is a well-established area of digital forensics, but little work has concentrated on extracting evidence from iPhone backups. This chapter has described forensic methods for retrieving evidence related to two popular e-dating applications – Tinder and Coffee Meets Bagel – by examining iPhone backups created via iTunes on Windows and Macintosh personal computers. Since it is common to backup iPhone data on Windows and Macintosh computers, investigators who

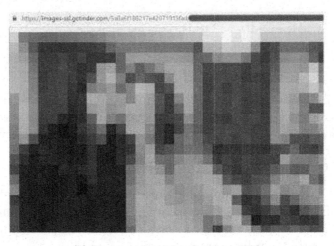

(a) Photograph URLs in the ZPROCESSEDPHOTO table.

(b) Photograph retrieved using a URL.

Figure 7. Photograph extracted using data in the ZPROCESSEDPHOTO table.

do not have access to user's iPhones could examine the backups to find evidence of criminal activity.

The experiments demonstrate that iPhone backups on personal computers contain considerable amounts of data related to e-dating application usage. By carefully analyzing the SQLite database of the backup folder, a digital forensic practitioner can obtain valuable information about interpersonal interactions conducted via the e-dating application. The recoverable evidence includes personal information, photographs, timestamps and conversation history from the Tinder and Coffee Meets Bagel apps, and, in the case of Coffee Meets Bagel, valuable geolocation data about app users as well.

ZCITY	ZCOUNTRY	A_E	ERIA_GE	UA_R	ZEMPLOYER	ZETHNICITY
Filter	Filter		Filter	...	Filter	Filter
Pannipitiya	LK		f			
Sri Jayawarde...	LK	*NULL*	m	*NULL*	Firm	Asian
Sri Jayawarde...	LK	*NULL*	m	*NULL*		South Asian
Colombo	LK	*NULL*	m	*NULL*	Bund Wien	White/Caucas...
Colombo	LK	*NULL*	m	*NULL*	Government	South Asian
Colombo	LK	*NULL*	m	*NULL*	Apcco Dairy	Asian

(a) User city, country, employer and ethnicity information.

ZPROFILE				⌄
GIVETAK	ZBIRTHDAY	ZLAST_UPDATED	ZLATITUDE	ZLONGITUDE
	Filter	Filter	Filter	Filter
	-3261	589374603	6.870887	79.94830
	-3156	589372286	6.869999	79.91000
	-3472	587562831	6.869999	79.940002
	-3786	491766908	6.909999	79.860000

(b) User birthday and geolocation information.

Buddhist	*NULL*	Western Province	*NULL*	*NULL*	Charm
	NULL	Western Province	*NULL*	*NULL*	Dilmini
Christian	*NULL*	Western Province	*NULL*	*NULL*	Julia
Buddhist	*NULL*	Western Province	*NULL*	*NULL*	Madhu
Catholic	*NULL*	Western Province	*NULL*	*NULL*	Sashika
Hindu	*NULL*	Western Province	*NULL*	*NULL*	Shakthi
Christian	*NULL*	Western Province	*NULL*	*NULL*	Jeuel

(c) User first name and religion information.

Figure 8.   User information obtained from the ZPROFILE table.

Although they are very popular, Tinder and Coffee Meets Bagel are by no means the only e-dating applications encountered in investigations. Future research will employ a new framework [20] to support evidence retrieval from other e-dating platforms on iPhones and Android devices.

Figure 9. Screenshot of user location obtained from data in the ZPROFILE table.

References

[1] L. Aouad, T. Kechadi, J. Trentesaux and N. Le-Khac, An open framework for smartphone evidence acquisition, in *Advances in Digital Forensics VIII*, G. Peterson and S. Shenoi (Eds.), Springer, Berlin Heidelberg, Germany, pp. 159–166, 2012.

[2] I. Baggili, S. Al Awawdeh and J. Moore, LiFE (Logical iOS Forensics Examiner): An open source iOS backup forensic examination tool, *Proceedings of the Conference on Digital Forensics, Security and Law*, pp. 41–52, 2014.

[3] A. Cheema, M. Iqbal and W. Ali, An open source toolkit for iOS filesystem forensics, in *Advances in Digital Forensics X*, G. Peterson and S. Shenoi (Eds.), Springer, Berlin Heidelberg, Germany, pp. 227–235, 2014.

[4] A. Cooper, S. Mansson, K. Daneback, R. Tikkanen and M. Ross, Predicting the future of Internet sex: Online sexual activities in Sweden, *Sexual and Relationship Therapy*, vol. 18(3), pp. 277–291, 2003.

[5] K. Daneback, S. Mansson and M. Ross, Using the Internet to find offline sex partners, *CyberPsychology and Behavior*, vol. 10(1), pp. 100–107, 2007.

[6] C. de Looper, Happy Valentine's Day! Coffee Meets Bagel dating app may have been breached, *Digital Trends*, Portland, Oregon, February 14, 2019.

[7] L. Drish, iOS Device Forensics, Graduate Project, Department of Computer Science, Governors State University, University Park, Illinois, 2014.

[8] M. Epifani and P. Stirparo, *Learning iOS Forensics*, Packt Publishing, Birmingham, United Kingdom, 2015.

[9] F. Faheem, N. Le-Khac and T. Kechadi, Smartphone forensic analysis: A case study of obtaining root access of an Android Samsung S3 device and analyzing the image without an expensive commercial tool, *Journal of Information Security*, vol. 5(3), pp. 83–90, 2014.

[10] J. Farnden, B. Martini and K. Choo, Privacy risks in mobile dating apps, *Proceedings of the Twenty-First Americas Conference on Information Systems*, 2015.

[11] M. Feltz, The Security of Tinder: A mobile app that may be more intimate than we thought, Report, Department of Computer Science, Tufts University, Medford, Massachusetts (`www.cs.tufts.edu/comp/116/archive/fall2015/mfeltz.pdf`), 2015.

[12] N. Heffernen, Analysis of Forensically Significant Artifacts of Tinder App on iPhones, M.Sc. Dissertation, School of Computer Science and Informatics, University College Dublin, Dublin, Ireland, 2013.

[13] M. Iqbal, Tinder revenue and usage statistics (2020), *Business of Apps*, Staines-upon-Thames, United Kingdom, April 24, 2020.

[14] K. Lutes and R. Mislan, Challenges in mobile phone forensics, *Proceedings of the Fifth International Conference on Cybernetics and Information Technologies, Systems and Applications*, pp. 348–352, 2008.

[15] National Crime Agency, Online first date rapes increase, London, United Kingdom, February 8, 2016.

[16] L. Newett, B. Churchill and B. Robards, Forming connections in the digital era: Tinder, a new tool in young Australian intimate life, *Journal of Sociology*, vol. 54(3), pp. 346–361, 2017.

[17] P. Paganini, Coffee Meets Bagel dating app confirms data breach, *Security Affairs*, February 15, 2019.

[18] G. Ranzini and C. Lutz, Love at first swipe? Explaining Tinder self-presentation and motives, *Mobile Media and Communication*, vol. 5(1), pp. 80–101, 2017.

[19] K. Seal, Coffee Meets Bagel users get hacked on Valentine's Day, *Dating Sites Reviews* (www.datingsitesreviews.com/article.php?story=coffee-meets-bagel-users-get-hacked-on-valentine-s-day), March 4, 2019.

[20] R. Thantilage and N. Le-Khac, Framework for the retrieval of social media and instant messaging evidence from volatile memory, *Proceedings of the Eighteenth IEEE International Conference on Trust, Security and Privacy in Computing and Communications and Thirteenth IEEE International Conference on Big Data Science and Engineering*, pp. 476–482, 2019.

[21] Tinder, Terms of Use, Match Group, Dallas, Texas (policies.tinder.com/terms/us/en), 2020.

[22] R van Voorst, T. Kechadi and N. Le-Khac, Forensic acquisition of IMVU: A case study, *Journal of Digital Forensics, Security and Law*, vol. 10(4), pp. 69–78, 2015.

VI

MULTIMEDIA FORENSICS

Chapter 13

TARGET IDENTITY ATTACKS ON FACIAL RECOGNITION SYSTEMS

Saheb Chhabra, Naman Banati, Gaurav Gupta and Garima Gupta

Abstract   Advancements in digital technology have significantly increased the number of cases involving the counterfeiting of identity documents. One example is exam fraud, where a counterfeiter creates a composite morphed photograph of the real candidate and an imposter, and attaches it to the examination admit card. Automated facial recognition systems are beginning to be deployed at examination centers to match candidates' faces against their official facial images. While the need to perform manual matches is eliminated, the vulnerabilities of these automated systems are a major concern.

This chapter evaluates the vulnerability of an automated facial recognition system to input image manipulation via a target identity attack. The attack manipulates a facial image so that it looks similar to the real candidate, but outputs the identity feature representation of the imposter. This chapter also evaluates the performance of facial recognition models with regard to impersonator recognition. Experiments using image databases demonstrate the effectiveness of target identity attacks.

Keywords: Counterfeiting, facial recognition, target identity attacks

1.   Introduction

Counterfeiting of identity documents is one of the fastest-growing frauds worldwide. Advancements in digital technology enable counterfeiters to perpetrate sophisticated frauds by creating fake identity cards and other related documents. An example is exam fraud, where a counterfeiter morphs the photograph of a real candidate with that of an imposter, and creates a tampered examination admit card with the morphed photograph. The quality of the counterfeit admit card makes it very difficult for a human examiner to determine that the person who

© IFIP International Federation for Information Processing 2020
Published by Springer Nature Switzerland AG 2020
G. Peterson and S. Shenoi (Eds.): Advances in Digital Forensics XVI, IFIP AICT 589, pp. 233–252, 2020.
https://doi.org/10.1007/978-3-030-56223-6_13

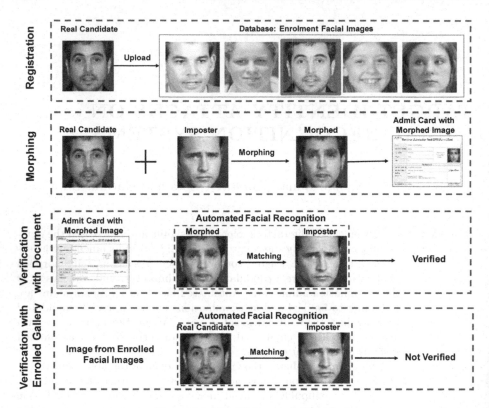

Figure 1. Identifying an imposter.

presents the card at an examination center is an imposter. The imposter then proceeds to take the exam on behalf of the real candidate.

Several instances of exam fraud involving the manipulation of facial images in admit cards have been reported by the international media. In 2018, law enforcement officers in Jodhpur, India arrested several members of a gang involved in a police examination cheating case [21]. The gang employed a team of 20 subject matter experts to take entry examinations on behalf of candidates who paid large sums of money. In another case [23], fifteen Chinese nationals were arrested for using counterfeit Chinese passports to take U.S. college entry tests such as the SAT, GRE and TOEFL.

Automated facial recognition systems are beginning to be deployed at examination centers to match candidates' faces against their official facial images. These systems perform a two-step verification procedure. The first step matches the facial image provided at the time of exam registration against the facial image of the supposed candidate who shows up at the examination center. The second step matches the photograph

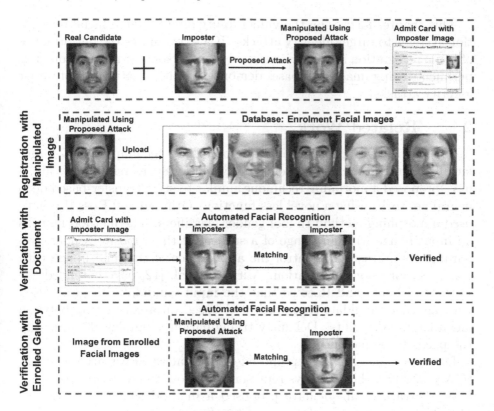

Figure 2. Successful target identity attack.

on the admit card against the facial image of the candidate that was provided at the time of exam registration.

Figure 1 shows how an automated facial recognition system identifies an imposter by comparing the photograph on the presented admit card against the facial image of the candidate that was provided at the time of exam registration.

The security of automated facial recognition systems is a major concern. Therefore, this research focuses on the vulnerability of an automated system to image manipulation using a novel target identity attack. This attack introduces perturbations in the facial image of the real candidate such that the manipulated image appears to be of the real candidate, but it outputs the identity features of an imposter (target). This manipulated image is submitted at the time of candidate registration. Thus, the imposter is able to masquerade as the real candidate and take the examination on his or her behalf. Figure 2 demonstrates a successful target identity attack.

This chapter focuses on the vulnerability of automated facial recognition systems to target identity attacks. It also evaluates the performance of facial recognition models with regard to impersonator recognition. Experiments using image databases demonstrate the effectiveness of target identity attacks.

2.   Related Work

Several researchers have proposed morphing techniques that target facial recognition and other biometric systems [18]. Korshunova et al. [7] have proposed a morphing technique similar to style-transfer-based deep neural networks using a novel loss function. Othman and Ross [14] have used a morphing method to fool gender classifiers. The method morphs an input image with an image of a subject of the opposite gender; two parameters are used to control the appearance of the final image with gender suppression information. Mirjalili et al. [12] have extended the work of Othman and Ross so that the input candidate image is fused with another candidate image selected based on a correlation between facial landmark points. Delaunay triangulation is employed to identify the pixels to be modified.

Damer et al. [3] have proposed a generative adversarial network (GAN) method that employs representation loss to create morphed images. Ferrara et al. [5] have proposed a method that creates double identity fingerprints; the features of two fingers are combined to yield a new fingerprint that fools fingerprint recognition systems. Rathgeb and Busch [16] have developed a stability-based bit substitution method that morphs two iris codes.

Several researchers have proposed methods for detecting morphed images. Raghavendra et al. [15] have proposed an approach that employs fine-tuned deep convolutional neural networks and a probabilistic collaborative representation classifier (P-CRC). The approach extracts features from fully-connected layers of VGG19 [20] and AlexNet [8] models, and concatenates them before sending them to the classifier. Seibold et al. [19] compare the morphing detection performance of pre-trained and trained-from-scratch AlexNet, GoogLeNet and VGG19 models. They created a database using the triangle and mesh warping techniques.

Wandzik et al. [22] have proposed a technique for distinguishing between original and morphed images. The technique employs features extracted from four facial recognition models and classifies them using a support vector machine (linear classifier). Batskos et al. [1] have developed a distance-based approach for detecting morphed images. Euclidean distances are computed for probe and morphed, morphed and e-pass, and probe and e-pass facial features, which yield 3D vectors. A support vector machine is used for linear classification.

Zhang et al. [24] have proposed a source identification scheme for detecting whether an image is *bona fide* or morphed. Scherhag et al. [17] have developed a technique for distinguishing morphed images using facial landmark points; the technique assumes that the intra-subject variance of landmarks extracted from *bona fide* images is less than the variance between landmarks of the morphed image and its contributing subjects. Debiasi et al. [4] have proposed a photo response non uniformity (PRNU) approach for detecting morphed images. Their approach assumes that the variance of PRNU signals increases across image cells when two images are morphed to create a single image.

Damer et al. [2] have employed two scenarios for morphing detection (i.e., with and without a probe). In the first scenario, facial landmarks are determined using an ensemble of regression trees, explicit shape regression and regressing local binary features; Euclidean distances are computed between the landmarks of live and previously-submitted images. In the second scenario, facial features are extracted using local binary pattern histograms and transferable deep convolutional neural networks.

Makrushin et al. [11] have proposed a morph detection algorithm, which assumes that some blocks in morphed images have undergone JPEG compression; however, blocks are not compressed in newly morphed images. The algorithm performs JPEG compression on a morphed image and determines nine Benford features that are used for classification. Finally, Neubert et al. [13] have employed frequency and spatial domain features for morph detection.

The review of the literature reveals that morphing methods have limitations that introduce ghosting artifacts and change the visual appearances. Figure 3 shows the images obtained using four morphing methods (from left to right): (i) Neubert et al. [13]; (ii) Batskos et al. [1]; (iii) Scherhag et al. [17]; and (iv) Damer et al. [2]. Note that the first and second rows show the original images whereas the third row shows the morphed composite images.

3. Target Identity Attacks

A target identity attack introduces adversarial perturbations in the facial image of the real candidate (source image) such that the manipulated image appears to be similar to the real candidate, but it outputs the identity features of the facial image of the imposter (target image). The manipulated image is submitted at the time of candidate registra-

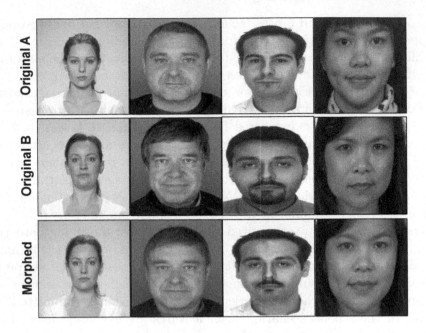

Figure 3.   Morphed images generated using four methods.

tion. Thus, the imposter can fool an automated facial recognition system and masquerade as the real candidate.

Figure 4 shows a block diagram of a target identity attack. The adversarial perturbation **N** is initialized as zero in the first iteration. In subsequent iterations, the perturbed image obtained by adding perturbations **N** to the source image **S**, and the target image **T** is provided an input to the facial recognition model. Optimization is performed over perturbations **N** until the stopping criterion is satisfied.

The detailed steps involved in the target identity attack are discussed below. In the following, the terms real candidate image and source candidate image are used interchangeably. Likewise, the imposter candidate image and target candidate image are used interchangeably.

The fundamental problem is to manipulate a source candidate image so that the manipulated image outputs the identity features of the target candidate image while appearing to be similar to the source candidate image.

Let **S** be the source candidate image and **T** be the target candidate image in the range [0, 1]. Let **P** be the manipulated or perturbed image generated by adding perturbation **N** to the source candidate image **S**. In order for the perturbed image to be valid, it should be in the range [0, 1]. Mathematically, this is written as:

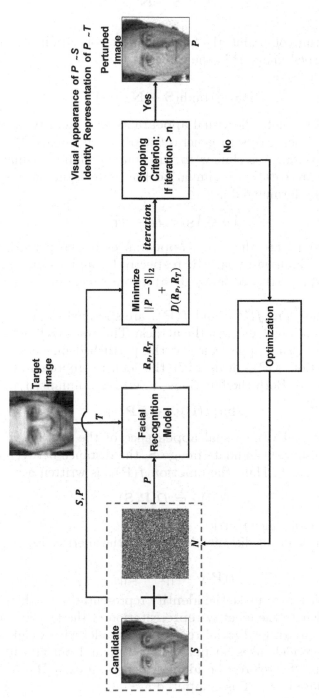

Figure 4. Target identity attack.

$$\mathbf{P} = \mathbf{S} + \mathbf{N} \tag{1}$$

where $\mathbf{P} \in [0, 1]$.

To satisfy this constraint, the following transformation is used to generate a perturbed image $\mathbf{P}$ in the range [0, 1]:

$$\mathbf{P} = \frac{1}{2}(\tanh(\mathbf{S} + \mathbf{N}) + 1) \tag{2}$$

Let V and I denote the visual appearance and identity of an image, respectively. The goal is to generate a perturbed image $\mathbf{P}$ such that its visual appearance is similar to the source candidate image $\mathbf{S}$ and its identity representation is similar to the target candidate $\mathbf{T}$. This is mathematically formulated as:

$$V_\mathbf{P} = V_\mathbf{S}; \quad I_\mathbf{P} = I_\mathbf{T} \tag{3}$$

where $V_\mathbf{P}$ and $V_\mathbf{S}$ are the visual appearances of the perturbed image $\mathbf{P}$ and source candidate image $\mathbf{S}$, respectively; and $I_\mathbf{P}$ and $I_\mathbf{T}$ are the identities of the perturbed image $\mathbf{P}$ and source candidate image $\mathbf{S}$, respectively.

Two loss functions $f(\mathbf{P})_V$ and $f(\mathbf{P})_I$ are specified to incorporate the constraints mentioned above in the attack. The first loss function $f(\mathbf{P})_V$ deals with the visual appearance of the perturbed image and the second loss function $f(\mathbf{P})_I$ deals with the identity representation of the perturbed image. Both the functions have to be minimized as follows:

$$\text{Min}\{f(\mathbf{P})_V + f(\mathbf{P})_I\} \tag{4}$$

In order to make the visual appearance of the perturbed image $\mathbf{P}$ similar to the source candidate image $\mathbf{S}$, the distance between $\mathbf{S}$ and $\mathbf{P}$ must be minimized. Thus, the function $f(\mathbf{P})_V$ is written as:

$$f(\mathbf{P})_V = D(\mathbf{P}, \mathbf{S}) \tag{5}$$

where D is the distance metric.

Since the Euclidean distance is used as the metric, Equation (5) is written as:

$$f(\mathbf{P})_V = ||\mathbf{P} - \mathbf{S}||_2 \tag{6}$$

The next task is to make the identity representation of the perturbed image P similar to the identity representation of the target image $\mathbf{T}$.

Let ϕ be a pre-trained facial recognition model with weights $\mathbf{W}$ and bias b. This model takes an image as input and outputs its identity representation. Therefore, the identity representation $\mathbf{R_T}$ of an input target candidate image $\mathbf{T}$ is computed as:

$$\mathbf{R_T} = \phi(\mathbf{WT} + b) \tag{7}$$

The corresponding identity representation $\mathbf{R_P}$ of the perturbed image $\mathbf{P}$ is computed as:

$$\mathbf{R_P} = \phi(\mathbf{WP} + b) \tag{8}$$

The next task is make the identity representation of the perturbed image $\mathbf{P}$ similar to the identity representation of the target candidate image $\mathbf{T}$. The distance between the identity representation of the perturbed image $\mathbf{P}$ and the target candidate image $\mathbf{T}$ is minimized. Thus, the function $f(\mathbf{P})_I$ is written as:

$$f(\mathbf{P})_I = D(\mathbf{R_P}, \mathbf{R_T}) \tag{9}$$

The Euclidean and cosine distance metrics are used to minimize the distance between the identity representations of the perturbed image $\mathbf{P}$ and target candidate image $\mathbf{T}$. Thus, the overall objective function is written as:

$$\mathrm{Min}\{||\mathbf{P} - \mathbf{S}||_2 + D(\mathbf{R_P}, \mathbf{R_T})\} \tag{10}$$

which is optimized over the perturbation variable $\mathbf{N}$.

4.   Experiments and Results

Experiments were performed to evaluate the effectiveness of target identity attacks. One set of experiments was performed under two scenarios, one involving white-box attacks and the other involving black-box attacks. Another set of experiments, involving impersonator recognition using pre-trained models, was performed to evaluate the performance of pre-trained facial recognition models in impersonator recognition.

The first set of experiments was performed on the Labeled Faces in the Wild (LFW) dataset [6]. The second set of experiments was performed on the Disguised Faces in the Wild (DFW) dataset [9].

The following dataset details and evaluation protocols are pertinent:

- **Labeled Faces in the Wild (LFW) Dataset:** This dataset contains 13,233 facial images of 5,749 subjects. The evaluation of target identity attacks in the white-box and black-box scenarios employed View 2 of the LFW dataset, which comprises 6,000 pairs of images. Of the 6,000 pairs of images, 3,000 pairs are genuine images while the remaining 3,000 pairs are imposter images.

  The target identity attacks were performed by perturbing one image from each imposter pair so that its identity representation becomes similar to the other image in the imposter pair.

Table 1.   Summary of experiments.

Experiment	Dataset	Model	Distance Metric
Target Identity Attacks	LFW	VGGFace, ResNet50	Euclidean, Cosine
Impersonator Recognition with Pre-Trained Models	DFW	VGGFace, ResNet50, LCNN-29	Euclidean, Cosine

- **Disguised Faces in the Wild (DFW) Dataset:** This dataset contains 11,157 facial images of 1,000 subjects. Four types of images – normal, validation, disguised and impersonator – are included for each subject.

  The DFW dataset provides three protocols. This research employed Protocol 1 (impersonation) to evaluate facial recognition models. Specifically, Protocol 1 is used to distinguish impersonators from legitimate subjects. In the protocol, the combination of a normal image with a validation image of the same subject corresponds to a genuine pair. The combination of an impersonator image with the normal, validation and disguised images of the same subject corresponds to an imposter pair.

Table 1 provides details about the two sets of experiments. The first set of experiments employed the VGGFace facial recognition model (pre-trained with the VGGFace dataset) and the ResNet50 facial recognition model (pre-trained with the VGGFace2 dataset); target identity attacks on the two facial recognition models were evaluated using the LFW dataset. The second set of experiments employed the VGGFace, ResNet50 and LCNN-29 facial recognition models for impostor recognition; the DFW dataset was used in the evaluation.

4.1   Implementation Details

The experiments were performed on an NVIDIA Tesla P100 server with 96 GB RAM and 16 GB GPU memory. All the images were resized to 224 × 224 pixels.

The target identity attacks were performed by learning the perturbation corresponding to each image to be attacked. The attacks were implemented in Tensorflow v1.9.0. The learning rate was set to 0.1 during the training phase. The perturbations were adjusted over 15 iterations.

Table 2. Imposter mean distance scores for the white-box and black-box scenarios.

| | Euclidean Distance | | | | Cosine Distance | | | |
| | ResNet50 | | VGGFace | | ResNet50 | | VGGFace | |
	Before	After	Before	After	Before	After	Before	After
ResNet50	1.20	0.30	0.91	0.77	0.72	0.08	0.42	0.31
VGGFace	1.20	1.06	0.91	0.30	0.72	0.62	0.42	0.08

4.2   Attack Performance Evaluation

This section discusses the performance of target identity attacks. The Euclidean distance and cosine distance were used as performance metrics.

Target Identity Attacks. This set of experiments evaluated a scenario where perturbed images are presented in place of real candidate images during the exam registration process. The perturbed image would look similar to the real candidate image, but it would output the imposter or target identity representation.

In a real-world scenario, the counterfeiter would not know the facial recognition model that is used to authenticate supposed candidates. Therefore, the target identity attacks are evaluated for white-box and black-box facial recognition scenarios. In a white-box facial recognition scenario, the counterfeiter knows the facial recognition model used to authenticate candidates and generates perturbed images corresponding to the same facial recognition model. In a black-box facial recognition scenario, the counterfeiter does not know the facial recognition model used to authenticate candidates and, therefore, generates perturbed images corresponding to a different facial recognition model.

As mentioned above, 3,000 imposter pairs were considered when implementing the target identity attacks. One image in each pair was perturbed to obtain an identity representation similar to that of the other image (target identity) in the pair. To evaluate the performance, the distance between the target identity representation and the identity representation of the perturbed image was computed for each pair. In the ideal case, this distance should be zero for a successful attack.

Table 2 shows the mean distance scores for 3,000 imposter pairs before and after performing the target identify attacks. Note that good results are obtained for the white-box and black-box scenarios. For example, when perturbed images are generated for the VGGFace model and evaluated using the same model and the cosine distance metric, the mean distance is reduced by 0.34 ($= 0.42 - 0.08$). Similarly, when perturbed images are generated for the VGGFace model and evaluated using the ResNet50 model and the Euclidean metric, the mean distance score is reduced by 0.14 ($= 1.20 - 1.06$).

Figure 5 compares the imposter distance score distributions for 3,000 imposter pairs before and after target identity attacks in the white-box and black-box scenarios. Figure 5(a) shows the score distributions obtained using the VGGFace and ResNet50 models when the images were perturbed based on the ResNet50 model. Figure 5(b) shows the score distributions obtained using the VGGFace and ResNet50 models when the images were perturbed based on the VGGFace model.

Figure 5(a) and 5(b) consistently show that the distributions are shifted towards the left or to zero after the target identity attacks. This demonstrates that the target identity attacks are effective.

Figures 6 and 7 compare the genuine and imposter distance score distributions before and after identity target attacks in the white-box and black-box scenarios. The images in Figure 6 are perturbed based on the VGGFace model whereas the images in Figure 7 are perturbed based on the ResNet50 model.

Figures 6 and 7 consistently show that the imposter distance score distributions are shifted closer towards the genuine distance score distributions in the black-box scenario. Moreover, the overlaps between the genuine and imposter distance score distributions are increased. These results demonstrate that the target attacks are effective at fooling the facial recognition models.

Figure 8 shows three sets of images generated via morphing and via target identity attacks. The first and second columns in the figure show the images of two different people, denoted as identity A and identity B, respectively. The third column shows the images generated via morphing whereas the fourth column shows the images generated via target image attacks.

In the case of the morphed images, the visual appearances and the identities correspond to both A and B. However, in the case of the target identity attack images, the visual appearances correspond to A whereas the identities correspond to B. Clearly, the target identity attack images in the fourth column preserve the original A appearances to a greater degree than the morphed images in the third column. However, because their identities correspond to B, the target identity attack images could be used to successfully perpetrate exam fraud.

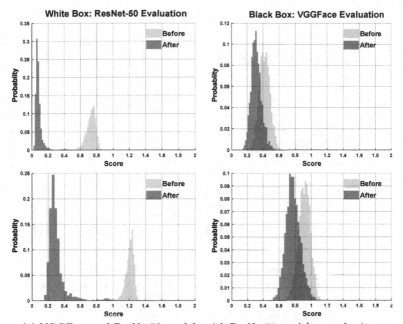

(a) VGGFace and ResNet50 models with ResNet50 model perturbations.

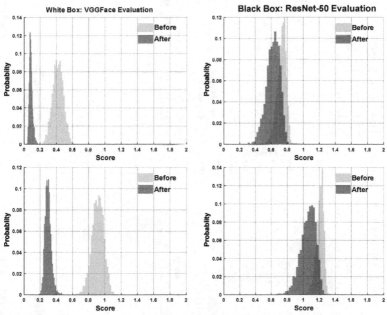

(b) VGGFace and ResNet50 models with VGGFace model perturbations.

Figure 5.   Comparison of impostor distance score distributions.

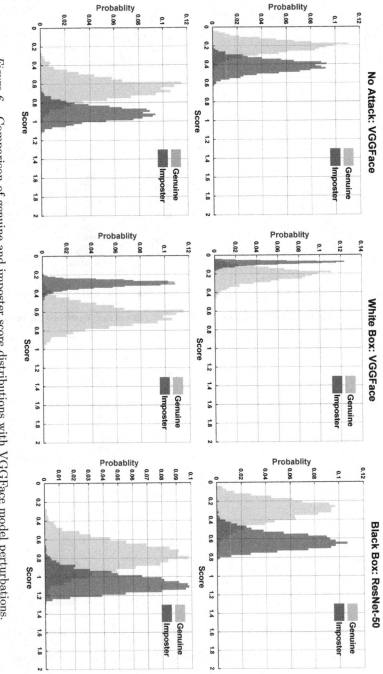

Figure 6. Comparison of genuine and imposter score distributions with VGGFace model perturbations.

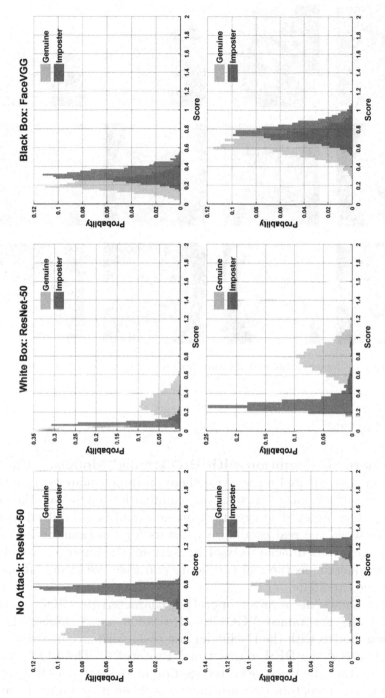

Figure 7. Comparison of genuine and imposter score distributions with ResNet50 model perturbations.

Identity A　　　　**Identity B**　　　　**Morphing**　　　　**Attack**

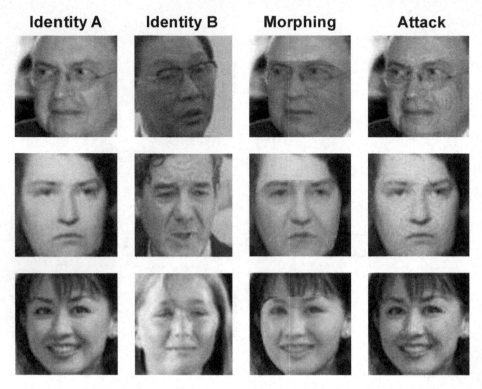

Figure 8. Images generated via morphing and target identity attacks.

Impersonator Recognition with Pre-Trained Models. This set of experiments evaluated a scenario where an impersonator uses a target identity attack image to take an examination on behalf the real candidate. The target identity attack image would be submitted to the authorities when the real candidate registers for the examination. By fooling the automated facial recognition system, the imposter would be able to masquerade as the real candidate and take the examination on behalf of the candidate.

Figure 9 shows the receiver operating characteristic (ROC) curves obtained using pre-trained VGGFace, ResNet50 and LCNN-29 facial recognition models with the Euclidean and cosine distance metrics. The experiments used the DFW dataset and Protocol 1. The ROC curves demonstrate that the three facial recognition models are not effective at identifying impersonators who use images generated by target identity attacks.

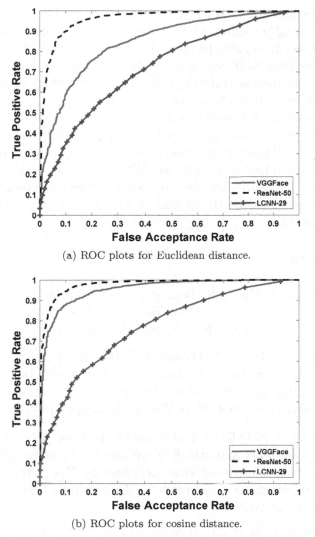

(a) ROC plots for Euclidean distance.

(b) ROC plots for cosine distance.

Figure 9. ROC plots for the ResNet50, VGGFace and LCNN-29 models.

5. Conclusions

Advancements in digital technology have significantly increased the number of cases involving the counterfeiting of exam identity documents. As a result, automated facial recognition systems are deployed at examination centers to match the registered facial images of candidates against the facial images of prospective examinees.

The novel identity target attack described in this chapter introduces perturbations in the facial image of the real candidate to create a manipulated image that looks just like the real candidate, but tricks an automated facial recognition system by outputting the identity features of the imposter who plans to take the exam on behalf of the candidate. Experiments using 3,000 image pairs from the Labeled Faces in the Wild (LFW) dataset demonstrate the effectiveness of target identity attacks in white-box as well as black-box scenarios.

Future research will focus on developing an algorithm that detects manipulated images and localizes the manipulated regions. Additionally, research will attempt to characterize the properties of manipulated images in the forensic context to identify the specific technique used for manipulation. This will help develop advanced facial authentication systems that are robust to attacks and provide forensically-sound evidence of manipulation.

References

[1] I. Batskos, A. Macarulla Rodriguez and Z. Geradts, Face morphing detection, *Proceedings of the Twentieth Irish Machine Vision and Image Processing Conference*, pp. 162–172, 2018.

[2] N. Damer, V. Boller, Y. Wainakh, F. Boutros, P. Terhorst, A. Braun and A. Kuijper, Detecting face morphing attacks by analyzing the directed distances of facial landmark shifts, *Proceedings of the German Conference on Pattern Recognition*, pp. 518–534, 2018.

[3] N. Damer, A. Saladie, A. Braun and A. Kuijper, MorGAN: Recognition vulnerability and attack detectability of face morphing attacks created by generative adversarial networks, *Proceedings of the Ninth IEEE International Conference on Biometrics Theory, Applications and Systems*, 2018.

[4] L. Debiasi, C. Rathgeb, U. Scherhag, A. Uhl and C. Busch, PRNU variance analysis for morphed face image detection, *Proceedings of the Ninth IEEE International Conference on Biometrics Theory, Applications and Systems*, 2018.

[5] M. Ferrara, R. Cappelli and D. Maltoni, On the feasibility of creating double-identity fingerprints, *IEEE Transactions on Information Forensics and Security*, vol. 12(4), pp. 892–900, 2017.

[6] G. Huang, M. Mattar, T. Berg and E. Learned-Miller, Labeled faces in the wild: A database for studying face recognition in unconstrained environments, presented at the *Workshop on Faces in Real-Life Images: Detection, Alignment and Recognition*, 2008.

[7] I. Korshunova, W. Shi, J. Dambre and L. Theis, Fast face-swap using convolutional neural networks, *Proceedings of the IEEE International Conference on Computer Vision*, pp. 3697–3705, 2017.

[8] A. Krizhevsky, I. Sutskever and G. Hinton, ImageNet classification with deep convolutional neural networks, *Proceedings of the Twenty-Sixth Annual Conference on Neural Information Processing Systems*, pp. 1106–1114, 2012.

[9] V. Kushwaha, M. Singh, R. Singh, M. Vatsa, N. Ratha and R. Chellappa, Disguised faces in the wild, *Proceedings of the IEEE Conference on Computer Vision and Pattern Recognition Workshops*, pp. 1–9, 2018.

[10] A. Makrushin, C. Kraetzer, T. Neubert and J. Dittmann, Generalized Benford's law for blind detection of morphed face images, *Proceedings of the Sixth ACM Workshop on Information Hiding and Multimedia Security*, pp. 49–54, 2018.

[11] A. Makrushin, T. Neubert and J. Dittmann, Automatic generation and detection of visually faultless facial morphs, *Proceedings of the Twelfth International Joint Conference on Computer Vision, Imaging and Computer Graphics Theory and Applications*, pp. 39–50, 2017.

[12] V. Mirjalili, S. Raschka and A. Ross, Gender privacy: An ensemble of semi adversarial networks for confounding arbitrary gender classifiers, *Proceedings of the Ninth IEEE International Conference on Biometrics Theory, Applications and Systems*, 2018.

[13] T. Neubert, C. Kraetzer and J. Dittmann, A face morphing detection concept with a frequency and spatial domain feature space for images on eMRTD, *Proceedings of the Seventh ACM Workshop on Information Hiding and Multimedia Security*, pp. 95–100, 2019.

[14] A. Othman and A. Ross, Privacy of facial soft biometrics: Suppressing gender but retaining identity, *Proceedings of the Computer Vision – European Conference on Computer Vision 2014 Workshops*, pp. 682–696, 2014.

[15] R. Raghavendra, K. Raja, S. Venkatesh and C. Busch, Transferable deep-CNN features for detecting digital and print-scanned morphed face images, *Proceedings of the IEEE Conference on Computer Vision and Pattern Recognition Workshops*, pp. 1822–1830, 2017.

[16] C. Rathgeb and C. Busch, On the feasibility of creating morphed iris codes, *Proceedings of the IEEE International Joint Conference on Biometrics*, pp. 152–157, 2017.

[17] U. Scherhag, D. Budhrani, M. Gomez-Barrero and C. Busch, Detecting morphed face images using facial landmarks, *Proceedings of the Eighth International Conference on Image and Signal Processing*, pp. 444–452, 2018.

[18] U. Scherhag, C. Rathgeb, J. Merkle, R. Breithaupt and C. Busch, Face recognition systems under morphing attacks: A survey, *IEEE Access*, vol. 7, pp. 23012–23026, 2019.

[19] C. Seibold, W. Samek, A. Hilsmann and P. Eisert, Detection of face morphing attacks by deep learning, *Proceedings of the International Workshop on Digital Watermarking*, pp. 107–120, 2017.

[20] K. Simonyan and A. Zisserman, Very Deep Convolutional Networks for Large-Scale Image Recognition, *arXiv*: 1409.1556v6, 2015.

[21] Staff Writer, 11 members of police exam cheating gang arrested in Jodhpur, *The Pink City Post*, July 12, 2018.

[22] L. Wandzik, G. Kaeding and R. Vicente-Garcia, Morphing detection using a general purpose face recognition system, *Proceedings of the Twenty-Sixth European Signal Processing Conference*, pp. 1012–1016, 2018.

[23] A. Yuhas, Chinese nationals charged with cheating by impersonation on US college tests, *The Guardian*, May 28, 2015.

[24] L. Zhang, F. Peng and M. Long, Face morphing detection using the Fourier spectrum of sensor pattern noise, *Proceedings of the IEEE International Conference on Multimedia and Expo*, 2018.

Chapter 14

ELECTRIC NETWORK FREQUENCY BASED AUDIO FORENSICS USING CONVOLUTIONAL NEURAL NETWORKS

Maoyu Mao, Zhongcheng Xiao, Xiangui Kang, Xiang Li and Liang Xiao

Abstract   Digital media forensics can exploit the electric network frequency of audio signals to detect tampering. However, current electric network based audio forensic schemes are limited by their inability to obtain concurrent electric network frequency reference datasets from power grids. In addition, most forensic algorithms do not provide high detection precision in adverse signal-to-noise conditions.

This chapter proposes an automated electric network frequency based audio forensic scheme that monitors abrupt mutations of tampered frames and discontinuities in the variations of electric network frequency features. Specifically, the scheme utilizes the multiple signal classification, Hilbert linear prediction and Welch algorithms to extract electric network frequency features from audio signals; the extracted features are passed to a convolutional neural network classifier to detect audio tampering. The negative effects of low signal-to-noise ratios on electric network frequency extraction are addressed by employing extra low-rank filtering that removes voice activity and noise interference. Simulation results demonstrate that the proposed scheme provides better audio tampering detection accuracy compared with a benchmark method, especially under adverse signal-to-noise conditions.

Keywords: Audio forensics, electric network frequency, neural networks

1.   Introduction

Audio editing software is often used by malicious actors to reduce the reliability of judicial evidence and defeat intellectual property protection. Audio tampering detection methods mostly rely on fingerprint information embedded in audio signals. Since fragile watermarks cannot assist in detecting private audio signal tampering [1], passive forensic schemes

© IFIP International Federation for Information Processing 2020
Published by Springer Nature Switzerland AG 2020
G. Peterson and S. Shenoi (Eds.): Advances in Digital Forensics XVI, IFIP AICT 589, pp. 253–270, 2020.
https://doi.org/10.1007/978-3-030-56223-6_14

based on extracted audio features can provide lightweight solutions. Researchers have developed detection methods based on local noise levels of audio signals [18] and voice activity detection [10]. The electric network frequency (ENF) of audio signals demonstrates that power grid features are applicable to digital media forensics [5]. Specifically, electric network frequency signals can be used to verify recording features such as time and location [7, 21], detect synchronization between audio and video data [20] and verify the authenticity of multimedia [14].

Electric network frequency based audio tampering detection techniques can verify if audio recordings have been edited at low computational cost. Ideally, the grid signal is a real sinusoid that fluctuates around its nominal value of 50 Hz or 60 Hz. Given that control mechanisms and power supply parameters are different in different parts of the world, electric network frequency signals display different fluctuations and peak frequency transformations. When signal-to-noise ratio (SNR) conditions are poor, disturbances near the electric network frequency component may be confused with the peak corresponding to the true electric network frequency [12]. Furthermore, due to legal restrictions, it is difficult to obtain concurrent reference datasets of power systems [7]. Additionally, many edit detection schemes based on electric network frequency variations adjust the classification thresholds manually. Although some automated tampering detection schemes do not rely on concurrent power reference datasets, new techniques are required to improve detection accuracy and reduce computational costs.

This chapter proposes an electric network frequency based audio forensic scheme that detects tampering. The scheme assumes a signal model containing the electric network frequency component, where the background noise is low enough to ensure that the electric network frequency signal is the energy-dominant signal around the nominal frequency. Audio tampering is detected without using concurrent reference electric network frequency signals from power networks. The scheme applies two-stage – low-rank and bandpass – filtering to purify electric network frequency signals in a narrow spectral vicinity and compensate for time delays in order to obtain accurate estimates of the real-time edit locations. Based on the sensitivity of electric network frequency features to phase discontinuity changes, variations in the electric network frequency based features extracted from the multiple signal classification, Hilbert linear prediction and Welch algorithms are combined as eigenvectors and input to an automatic classifier. A convolutional neural network (CNN) is employed in the audio tampering detection scheme to improve the generalization ability in practical situations. Simulation results demonstrate that the proposed audio tampering detection scheme has good accuracy and an expanded application scope.

2.   Related Work

Hua et al. [8] have discussed the limitations of electric network frequency based tampering detection systems and the challenges posed by noise and interference. Several electric network frequency extraction algorithms such as the short-time Fourier transform and time recursive iterative adaptive algorithms are incorporated in instantaneous frequency estimation techniques to achieve high-precision extraction by measuring the maximum energy or weighted energy recorded from the average frequencies of spectrograms [6].

A systematic assessment of parametric and non-parametric extraction techniques for electric network frequency signals has demonstrated that time-domain-based extraction algorithms are susceptible to frequency anomalies caused by sudden changes in noise or speech activity [11]. In addition, parametric algorithms such as the multiple signal classification and Welch algorithms can improve resolution frequency estimation of sinusoidal signals by using fewer data series than spectrogram-based extraction algorithms.

An electric network frequency extraction scheme proposed by Lin and Kang [12] applies robust principle component analysis to remove noise interference and purify the electric network frequency when signal-to-noise conditions are poor. It adopts the Hilbert linear prediction algorithm to capture the electric network frequency from fewer audio recordings in an efficient manner.

Nicolalde Rodriguez and Apolinario [16] have developed a digital audio authenticity evaluation scheme that detects electric network frequency phase transitions and leverages the spectral distance using an adaptive filter as a linear indicator. An electric network frequency based edit detection scheme for speech recordings designed by Esquef et al. [3] yields low equal error rate (EER) values by comparing electric network frequency variations around the nominal frequency with the upper limit of the normal variations observed in an unedited signal. Hua et al. [9] have analyzed the absolute error map between an electric network frequency database and test electric network frequency signals to perform timestamp verification and detect tampering via insertion, deletion and splicing attacks with image erosion.

Nicolaide Rodriguez et al. [17] have also developed an automated authenticity detection scheme for audio recordings via phase analysis of high-order electric network frequency harmonics. Reis et al. [19] have designed an adulteration detection scheme for audio recordings that integrates the kurtosis features of electric network frequency signals in rotational invariance techniques and Hilbert linear prediction in poor signal-to-noise conditions to autonomously classify audio recordings using a support vector machine. Although kurtosis extraction speeds up the classification, some characteristic information is lost.

Wang et al. [22] have developed a detection scheme that applies discrete Fourier transforms of audio signals to achieve instantaneous phase estimation using a support vector machine classifier. However, the accuracy of the scheme is unsatisfactory and the cost of using a support vector machine to evaluate the decision function is linearly related to the number of training samples. This results in high computational costs for large datasets.

Researchers have also applied convolutional neural networks to analyze audio recapture [13] and perform median filtering [2]. However, no research has applied convolutional neural networks to electric network frequency based audio tampering forensics.

3.   System Model

Figure 1 shows a schematic diagram of the proposed audio forensic scheme, which uses a convolutional neural network in conjunction with the multiple signal classification (MUSIC), Hilbert linear prediction and Welch algorithms.

The system initially reduces the sampling rate of an audio signal under test $x(m)$. Let ω_0 be the nominal electric network frequency. According to convention, the new sampling frequency f_s is adjusted to 20 times the nominal frequency ω_0. Therefore, the sampled signal $x_{ds}(n)$ where $0 < n \le m$ is obtained using a 1,000 Hz or 1,200 Hz sampling frequency.

The low-rank structure of the electric network frequency signal in the short-time Fourier transform (STFT) domain is leveraged to separate grid signals from interference by robust principal component analysis (RPCA). Let X_{ds} be the amplitude spectrum of the sampled signal $x_{ds}(n)$. Then, the robust principal component analysis objective is given by:

$$\min_{\hat{X}_C, X_E} \operatorname{rank}\left(\hat{X}_C\right) + \lambda \left\| X_E \right\|_0 \quad \text{s.t.} \quad \hat{X}_C + X_E = X_{ds} \tag{1}$$

where $\| \cdot \|_0$ is the L0-norm, $\lambda > 0$ is a parameter that trades off the low-rank part with the electric network frequency component $\hat{X}_C$, and X_E is the sparsity part containing the impulse noise and speech activity signal.

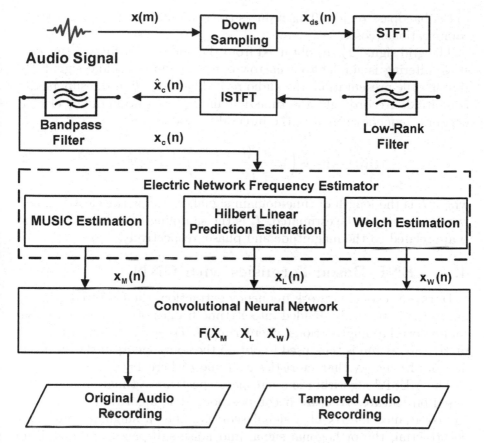

Figure 1. Proposed audio forensic scheme.

Due to the non-convex optimization objective, a relaxation is applied to Equation (1) according to [23]. Thus, the principal component analysis objective becomes:

$$\min_{\hat{X}_C, X_E} \left\| \hat{X}_C \right\|_* + \lambda \left\| X_E \right\|_1 \quad \text{s.t.} \quad \hat{X}_C + X_E = X_{ds} \qquad (2)$$

where $\| \cdot \|_*$ is a nuclear norm and $\| \cdot \|_1$ is the L1-norm.

Next, $\hat{X}_C$ is derived by the augmented Lagrange multiplier method [12] and the inverse short-time Fourier transform (ISTFT) is employed to determine the low-rank filtered signal sequence denoted by $\hat{x}_C(n)$.

Grid signals with electric network frequency components $x_C(n)$ are insulated from interference falling into the low-order space by filtering $\hat{x}_C(n)$. Instead of a finite impulse response filter, a fourth-order elliptic filter is adopted with a phase that is approximately linear and adjacent to the bandpass region. This reduces the computational complexity and computational costs.

The grid signal $x_C^k(n)$ obtained from the audio recording k after two-stage filtering is similar to a narrow-band pseudo-sinusoidal signal. To simplify the presentation, the audio recording index k in the superscript is omitted. Accordingly, the time-domain representation of the electric network frequency signal in the interval is modeled as:

$$x_C(n) = a \cos \left(2\pi \frac{x_F(n)}{f_s} n + \phi \right) \quad 1 \leq n \leq L \qquad (3)$$

where L is the length of time-domain signal, $x_F(n)$ is the electrical network frequency to be estimated, f_s is the sampling frequency and a and ϕ are related to the magnitude and phase, respectively.

4.   ENF-Based Forensics with CNN

During electrical network frequency extraction, the captured grid signal $x_C(n)$ is typically divided into Y time frames of fixed-length l containing overlapping portions where $Y \in \{L/l\}_{0 \leq l \leq L}$. A frequency estimation algorithm is then used to obtain the components of the electrical network frequency characteristics in frame i where $1 \leq i \leq Y$.

The MUSIC algorithm is a subspace spectrum estimation algorithm based on feature structure decomposition. The algorithm decomposes the covariance matrix of a signal sequence into a singular value. By constructing the orthogonal signal and noise subspaces, the algorithm provides spatial spectral functions that can be used to estimate electrical network frequency features. Since electrical network frequency signals contain one real sinusoid, two complex frequency sinusoids are embedded in the white noise P for electrical network frequency signals.

The algorithm first computes the $M \times N$ sample data matrix $\mathbf{A}$ based on the power grid signal $X_C^{(i)}$ of audio frame i:

$$\mathbf{A} = \left[\mathbf{a}_C(1) \ \mathbf{a}_C(2) \dots \mathbf{a}_C(N-1) \right]^T \qquad (4)$$

where $\mathbf{a}_C(n) = [x_C(n), x_C(n+1), \dots, x_C(n+M-1)]^T$, M is the order of the covariance matrix that is chosen to be larger than P and $M \in \left[\frac{N}{3}, \frac{2N}{3} \right]$ [6].

Next, the eigenvalue decomposition of the auto-covariance matrix $\mathbf{R} = \frac{1}{N} \mathbf{A}^H \mathbf{A}$ is computed. Since the signal and noise are independent, the covariance can be decomposed and the space comprising the eigenvectors corresponding to the large eigenvalues $(\mathbf{q}_1 \ \mathbf{q}_2 \dots \mathbf{q}_P)$ is the signal subspace **S**. Also, the space comprising the eigenvectors corresponding to the small eigenvalues $\left(\mathbf{q}_{P+1}\ \mathbf{q}_{P+2}\cdots\mathbf{q}_{P+M}\right)$ is the noise subspace $\mathbf{G}_n$.

The following assumptions are made for the complex form of the observation model described above:

- Different $x_C^{(i)}(n)$ signals are linearly independent of each other.

- The additive noise $u(n)$ is the complex noise with zero mean additive, uncorrelated and the same variance σ_u^2.

Given the orthogonality property of the white noise eigenvectors and signal steering vectors $\mathbf{v}\left(X_C^{(i)}\right)$, the signal steering vectors $\mathbf{v}\left(X_C^{(i)}\right)$ can be written in complex form as:

$$\mathbf{v}\left(X_C^{(i)}\right) = \left[1, e^{j2\pi X_C^{(i)}}, e^{j4\pi X_C^{(i)}}, \ldots, e^{j2(M-1)\pi X_C^{(i)}}\right]^H \tag{5}$$

where $j = \sqrt{-1}$ and $[\cdot]^H$ denotes the conjugate transposition.

The pseudo-spectral function P_{MU} is computed as:

$$P_{MU} = \frac{1}{\mathbf{v}^*\left(X_C^{(i)}\right)\mathbf{G}_n^i\mathbf{G}_n^{i*}\mathbf{v}\left(X_C^{(i)}\right)} \tag{6}$$

where $*$ is the element conjugate.

Ultimately, the estimated electrical network frequency X_{MU} is obtained by searching for the spectral peak of the spatial-spectral function P_{MU}. The MUSIC algorithm estimates a fixed parameter for each frame, which is the best electrical network frequency value in the least mean square sense for a given signal sequence.

The Hilbert linear prediction extraction algorithm is more sensitive to sharp phase changes than the MUSIC algorithm. However, the MUSIC algorithm is more robust to noise interference. According to Equation (3), the electrical network frequency value $\hat{h}_C(n)$ can be estimated by the transient phase change of the Hilbert transform from the real-valued estimate $x_C(n)$ as follows:

$$\hat{h}_C(n) = x_C(n) + jH\left\{x_C(n)\right\} \tag{7}$$

where $j = \sqrt{-1}$ and H is the Hilbert operator.

Since the analytical version of a pseudo-sinusoidal signal is equivalent to the real-valued signal with respect to $x_F(n)$, the linearly predictable property can be applied to the complex model. This yields:

$$\hat{h}_C(n) = ae^{\left(j2\pi\frac{x_F(n)}{f_s}n+\phi\right)} = \beta_1\hat{h}_C(n-1) \tag{8}$$

where $\beta_1 = e^{\left(j2\pi \frac{x_F(n)}{f_s}\right)}$ is the first-order prediction coefficient.

The signal entry $s(n) = x_F(n) + u(n)$ is then obtained by adding the additive complex noise $u(n)$.

Given the assumption that additive complex noise is always equivalent, the approximation $s(n) \approx \beta_1 s(n-1)$ is obtained according to Equation (8). Extending this equation to the entire audio recording yields: $\mathbf{S}_1 \approx \beta_1 \mathbf{S}_2$ where $\mathbf{S}_1 = [s(n-1), s(n-2), \ldots, s(n)]_{0 < n \leq m}$ and $\mathbf{S}_2$ is the sequence with one sample shift from $\mathbf{S}_1$.

Therefore, the crux of electrical network frequency estimation is to minimize the weighted linear prediction error in the minimum squared sense as follows:

$$\min J(\beta_1) = \mathbf{e}^T \mathbf{W} \mathbf{e} = (\mathbf{S}_2 - \beta_1 \mathbf{S}_1)^H \mathbf{W} (\mathbf{S}_2 - \beta_1 \mathbf{S}_1) \qquad (9)$$

where $\mathbf{W}$ is a symmetric weighting matrix, H is the conjugate transposition operator and $J(\beta_1)$ is the total cost function denoted by the weighted squared error $\mathbf{e}$.

The symmetric weighted matrix $\mathbf{W}$, which is obtained by Markov estimation, is given by:

$$\mathbf{W} = \begin{bmatrix} 1 + \|\beta_1\|^2 & -\beta_1 & 0 & 0 & \cdots & & 0 \\ -\beta_1^* & 1 + \|\beta_1\|^2 & -\beta_1 & 0 & \cdots & & 0 \\ \vdots & \vdots & \vdots & \vdots & & \vdots & \vdots \\ 0 & \cdots & 0 & -\beta_1^* & 1 + \|\beta_1\|^2 & & -\beta_1 \\ 0 & 0 & \vdots & 0 & & -\beta_1^* & 1 + \|\beta_1\|^2 \end{bmatrix}^{-1}$$

$$(10)$$

where $*$ and $[\cdot]^{-1}$ are the element conjugate and matrix inverse, respectively.

Upon setting the differential in Equation (9) to zero, the prediction coefficient β_1 is given by:

$$\beta_1 = \frac{\mathbf{S}_1{}^H \mathbf{W} \mathbf{S}_2}{\mathbf{S}_1{}^H \mathbf{W} \mathbf{S}_1} \qquad (11)$$

Equations (9) through (11) reveal that the computation of β_1 is an iterative process. Having obtained β_1, the Hilbert linear prediction of the electrical network frequency X_L is computed as:

$$X_L = f_s \frac{1}{2\pi} \angle(\beta_1) \qquad (12)$$

For consistency with other characteristics, X_L is divided into fragments and the maximum value of the absolute values is taken as the ith segment electrical network frequency estimate $X_L^{(i)}$.

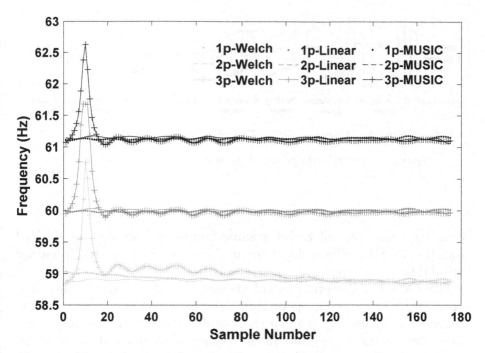

Figure 2. Electrical network frequency fingerprints in three recording fragments.

The Welch algorithm is an improved periodogram method. The algorithm reduces noise in the estimated power spectrum by enhancing the frequency resolution, yielding the largest maximum correlation coefficient around the nominal frequency compared with the MUSIC algorithm and other methods.

The Welch estimate is obtained from the power spectral density. The algorithm divides each audio recording into overlapped segments multiplied by a Hamming window. The frequency sample w, which corresponds to the maximum periodogram value, is extracted as the Welch-based electrical network frequency estimate denoted by $X_W^{(i)}$. Next, a quadratic interpolation is employed to fit the quadratic model of w. The Welch algorithm with a Hamming window improves the spectral distortion caused by the large-side lobe of the rectangular window, yielding an accurate electrical network frequency estimate X_W that is not affected by interference.

Figure 2 clearly shows the electrical network frequency based fingerprints used to verify the effectiveness of the proposed audio forensic scheme. The fingerprints are located in three recording fragments named $1p$, $2p$ and $3p$ at 60 Hz with slight offsetting for easy viewing. The three

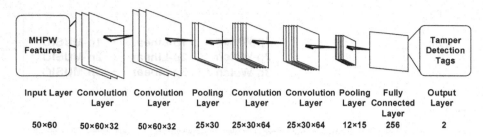

Input Layer	Convolution Layer	Convolution Layer	Pooling Layer	Convolution Layer	Convolution Layer	Pooling Layer	Fully Connected Layer	Output Layer
50×60	50×60×32	50×60×32	25×30	25×30×64	25×30×64	12×15	256	2

Figure 3. Network architecture of the proposed audio forensic scheme.

recording fragments, all with the same number of samples, are derived from the MUSIC, Hilbert linear prediction and Welch (MHPW) feature estimation algorithms.

The forensic fingerprints simultaneously display high stability and sensitivity to tampering operations. For example, the fingerprints in recording fragments $1p$ and $2p$ show stable pseudo-sinusoidal fluctuations whereas the fingerprints in the tampered fragment $3p$ show sensitive mutations.

Instead of manually determining the threshold, a novel deep learning approach is applied to identify tampered audio recordings. The electrical network frequency signals extracted by the three algorithms are directly modeled as features to avoid information loss when extracting the representative values of features.

Three-dimensional feature vectors $\mathbf{F} = \left[X_L^k, X_{MU}^k, X_W^k\right]_{0 < k \leq N}$ are obtained from the N audio recordings. When the lengths of the recordings in the audio dataset are different, the nominal frequency of $50\,\mathrm{Hz}$ or $60\,\mathrm{Hz}$ is applied to fill the feature vectors to the same length. The three feature channels with the same length constitute the input layer of the neural network structure.

Figure 3 shows the network architecture of the audio tampering detection scheme. The convolutional neural network model has four convolution layers, two pooling layers, one full connection layer and an input layer and output layer. Before processing the features, min-max normalization is used to amplify the differences and variation rules of the features. Next, given the overlaps of the adjacent electrical network frequency components, convolution is used to refine the energy changes in the electrical network frequency signals, which improves the detection accuracy. Finally, the tag distribution obtained by the convolutional neural network model is used to compute the detection performance metrics.

5.   Experiments and Results

This section describes the simulation experiments and the results obtained.

5.1   Experimental Setup

The experiments were performed on Matlab and Python 3.6 platforms with the scikit-learn package.

The electrical network frequency based features were extracted from two classical audio databases. The first was the Carioca 1 database [17], a telephone recording database of the public switched telephone network containing 16-bit mono waves at a 44.1 kHz sampling rate and coded by pulse code modulation with an electrical network frequency component around 60 Hz, The second was the Spanish Speech database [4] sampled at 16 kHz with a nominal electrical network frequency component around 50 Hz. The databases each contain 100 original voice audio recordings and 100 edited versions of the original voice audio recordings.

Simulations were performed to evaluate the performance of the audio forensic scheme with $N = 400$ audio recordings. Each recording was divided into time frames of length $l = 1$ second with an overlap of 0.5 seconds. In the simulations, 70% of the original audio recordings and tampered audio recordings were randomly chosen to train the convolutional neural network. The remaining 30% of all the recordings were randomly-chosen for the testing set. Distributing the data into training and testing datasets in this manner ensured that every portion of the data would be more representative. The data randomness had to be high due to the large number of parameters and strong learning ability of the convolutional neural network, and so that the random gradient descent optimization function did not get stuck in a local minimum.

Multiple evaluations were performed to achieve fair comparisons with the benchmark strategy proposed by Reis et al. [19]. The detection error tradeoff (DET) curves were obtained by plotting the false negative rate (FNR) versus false positive rate (FPR) curves for various thresholds [15]. In general, as the false positive rate increases to 100%, the false negative rate decreases, and vice versa. The equal error rate is the point at which the false negative rate and false positive rate are equal. The overall error rate (OER) is computed as the average of the false negative rate and false positive rate.

Table 1.   Overall error rates for combinations of fusion features.

Feature	Overall Error Rate
MUSIC	7.5%
Hilbert Linear Prediction	5.1%
Welch	6.3%
MUSIC + Hilbert Linear Prediction	6.3%
Hilbert Linear Prediction + Welch	4.4%
MUSIC + Welch	6.5%
MUSIC + Hilbert Linear Prediction + Welch (MHPW)	3.2%

5.2   Detection Performance

Table 1 shows the overall error rates for feature vectors obtained
by combining fusion features. Combining all three features (MUSIC,
Hilbert linear prediction and Welch (MHPW)) yields the lowest overall
error rate of 3.2% compared with using any one feature or any two features. When all three features are used together, the overall error rates
fall by 4.3%, 1.9% and 3.1%, respectively, from the overall error rates
when the MUSIC, Hilbert linear prediction and Welch algorithms are
used alone.

However, the overall error rates obtained for the mixed features extracted by two of the three algorithms may be suboptimal to those extracted by a single algorithm; this is due to the cancellation of the sharp
peak features of the two algorithms. For example, the overall error rate
for the fusion features extracted by the MUSIC and Welch algorithms
is reduced by 1.0% compared with the overall error rate of the features
extracted by the MUSIC algorithm alone. The proper choice of features
plays an important role in the accurate detection of audio tampering.

Table 2.   Overall error rates for various classifiers.

Classifier	Overall Error Rate
Neural Network	9.1%
Random Forest	9.1%
Decision Tree	7.3%
Logistic Regression	6.7%
Support Vector Machine	4.2%
Convolutional Neural Network	3.2%

Table 2 shows that the proposed scheme using the convolutional neural network with MUSIC, Hilbert linear prediction and Welch features

Table 3. Cross-domain evaluations of the audio databases.

Training Database	Testing Database	Overall Error Rate
Carioca 1	Spanish Speech	4.3%
Spanish Speech	Carioca 1	4.5%

has the lowest overall error rate compared with the other classifiers. For example, the overall error rate is 5.9% less than that obtained by the neural network scheme and is 1.0% less than that obtained by the support vector machine scheme. Additionally, the detection performance of the proposed scheme using the convolutional neural network with the MUSIC, Hilbert linear prediction and Welch features has an overall error rate that is 1.3% less than that obtained by the benchmark strategy with a support vector machine described in [19].

Table 3 shows the results of cross-domain evaluations when the Carioca 1 and Spanish Speech databases were used for training and testing, respectively, and vice versa. Using the combination of MUSIC, Hilbert linear prediction and Welch features trained with the Carioca 1 database yields slightly better prediction results (4.3%) compared with when the Spanish Speech database was used for training (4.5%). This could be because the extracted features of Caricoa 1 are more obvious, which renders the trained model more representative and the testing results more accurate.

However, the difference between the two overall error rates is small (0.2%), which may be due to the number of training sessions, number of iterations, final convergence and small differences in only one set of random values in the convolutional neural network. As observed above, a mixed training dataset yields better detection performance than using a single dataset for training. For example, the detection with the mixed (Carioca 1 and Spanish Speech) training dataset decreases the overall error rate by 1.3% compared with the single Carioca 1 training dataset and 1.1% compared with the single Spanish Speech dataset. The key insight is that the increased data diversity provided by mixed training increases the generality of the learned model, which improves the detection performance and reduces the overall error rate.

Figure 4 compares the detection performance of the proposed scheme using the convolutional neural network with MUSIC, Hilbert linear prediction and Welch features (CNN with MHPW) versus the detection performance of the benchmark strategy by Reis et al. [19]. The same Carioca 1 and Spanish Speech databases with $N = 400$ audio record-

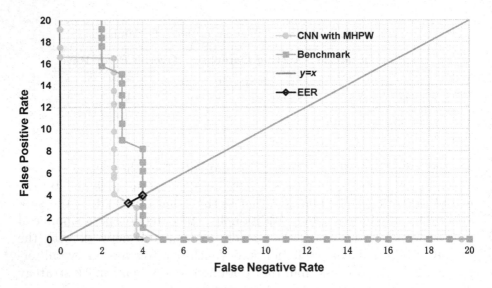

Figure 4. Comparison of detection performance.

ings and $l = 1$ second were used in the comparison. The DET curve of the proposed scheme (CNN with MHPW) is much closer to the y-axis (i.e., lower false negative rates) compared with the benchmark strategy. Moreover, the proposed scheme has an equal error rate of 3.3%, which is less than the 4% equal error rate of the benchmark strategy.

5.3   Results for Different SNR Conditions

This section evaluates the performance of the proposed audio forensic scheme under signal-to-noise ratios ranging from 5 dB to 30 dB. The speech activity detector of Esquef et al. [3] was used to separate the noise from speech signals in the Carioca 1 and Spanish Speech databases, following which various levels of additional background Gaussian noise were introduced. It is important to note that the results of this evaluation can be generalized to any audio recording.

Figure 5 shows the performance of the proposed audio forensic scheme (CNN with MHPW) under various signal-to-noise ratios. The equal error rates obtained for the datasets corrupted by Gaussian noise decrease with increasing signal-to-noise ratio because the classifier acquires more accurate electric network frequency information with less noise. The performance gap is much wider at lower signal-to-noise ratios, which validates the effectiveness of low-rank filtering for noise correction. For example, the proposed scheme decreases the equal error rate from 20.8% to 17.9% for the lowest signal-to-noise ratio of 5 dB. In fact, the proposed

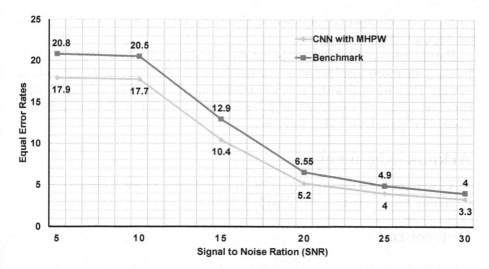

Figure 5. Performance of the audio forensic scheme under different SNR conditions.

scheme achieves optimal performance faster than the benchmark strategy with less signal information. Specifically, the equal error rate of the proposed scheme decreases from 17.9% at 5 dB to 4.0% at 25 dB whereas the benchmark strategy achieves the same equal error rate only at 30 dB. Moreover, despite showing a consistent performance trend, the proposed scheme is more effective than the benchmark strategy even for low signal-to-noise ratios. This demonstrates that the low-rank filtering incorporated in the proposed scheme improves the accuracy of detecting audio tampering, especially in poor signal-to-noise conditions.

6. Conclusions

The audio forensic scheme described in this chapter leverages a convolutional neural network classifier to evaluate electric network frequency features in audio signals to detect tampering without manual regulation or information about the concurrent reference frequency from the power grid. The experimental results demonstrate that the audio forensic scheme increases the accuracy of tamper detection and is better adapted to noisy environments than the benchmark strategy of Reis et al. [19]. For example, the proposed scheme reduces the overall error rate by 1.3% and increases the equal error rate by 0.7% compared with the benchmark strategy. Additionally, it increases the equal error rate up to 2.9% compared with the benchmark strategy under different signal-to-noise conditions. The tamper detection performance and robustness in noisy environments help ensure the reliability of audio evidence and protect intellectual property.

Future research will attempt to enhance detection accuracy and efficiency in more aggressive scenarios, and develop an online detection system that identifies the specific locations of audio tampering. Additionally, future research will explore the application of electric network frequency signals in video forensics.

Acknowledgement

This research was supported by the Natural Science Foundation of China under Grant nos. 61772571, U1536204, 61971366 and 61671396.

References

[1] M. Arnold, Audio watermarking: Features, applications and algorithms, *Proceedings of the IEEE International Conference on Multimedia and Exposition – Latest Advances in the Fast-Changing World of Multimedia*, vol. 2, pp. 1013–1016, 2000.

[2] J. Chen, X. Kang, Y. Liu and Z. Wang, Median filtering forensics based on convolutional neural networks, *IEEE Signal Processing Letters*, vol. 22(11), pp. 1849–1853, 2015.

[3] P. Esquef, J. Apolinario and L. Biscainho, Edit detection in speech recordings via instantaneous electric network frequency variations, *IEEE Transactions on Information Forensics and Security*, vol. 9(12), pp. 2314–2326, 2014.

[4] P. Esquef, J. Apolinario and L. Biscainho, Improved edit detection in speech via ENF patterns, *Proceedings of the IEEE International Workshop on Information Forensics and Security*, 2015.

[5] R. Garg, A. Varna, A. Hajj-Ahmad and M. Wu, "Seeing" ENF: Power-signature-based timestamps for digital multimedia via optical sensing and signal processing, *IEEE Transactions on Information Forensics and Security*, vol. 8(9), pp. 1417–1432, 2013.

[6] A. Hajj-Ahmad, R. Garg and M. Wu, Instantaneous frequency estimation and localization for ENF signals, *Proceedings of the Asia-Pacific Signal and Information Processing Association Annual Summit and Conference*, 2012.

[7] A. Hajj-Ahmad, R. Garg and M. Wu, ENF-based region-of-recording identification for media signals, *IEEE Transactions on Information Forensics and Security*, vol. 10(6), pp. 1125–1136, 2015.

[8] G. Hua, G. Bi and V. Thing, On practical issues of electric network frequency based audio forensics, *IEEE Access*, vol. 5, pp. 20640–20651, 2017.

[9] G. Hua, Y. Zhang, J. Goh and V. Thing, Audio authentication by exploring the absolute error map of ENF signals, *IEEE Transactions on Information Forensics and Security*, vol. 11(5), pp. 1003–1016, 2016.

[10] M. Imran, Z. Ali, S. Bakhsh and S. Akram, Blind detection of copy-move forgery in digital audio forensics, *IEEE Access*, vol. 5, pp. 12843–12855, 2017.

[11] G. Karantaidis and C. Kotropoulos, Assessing spectral estimation methods for electric network frequency extraction, *Proceedings of the Twenty-Second Pan-Hellenic Conference on Informatics*, pp. 202–207, 2018.

[12] X. Lin and X. Kang, Robust electric network frequency estimation with rank reduction and linear prediction, *ACM Transactions on Multimedia Computing, Communications and Applications*, vol. 14(4), article no. 84, 2018.

[13] X. Lin, J. Liu and X. Kang, Audio recapture detection with convolutional neural networks, *IEEE Transactions on Multimedia*, vol. 18(8), pp. 1480–1487, 2016.

[14] Y. Liu, Z. Yuan, P. Markham, R. Conners and Y. Liu, Application of power system frequency for digital audio authentication, *IEEE Transactions on Power Delivery*, vol. 27(4), pp. 1820–1828, 2012.

[15] A. Martin, G. Doddington, T. Kamm, M. Ordowski and M. Przybocki, The DET curve in assessments of detection task performance, *Proceedings of the Fifth European Conference on Speech Communication and Technology*, 1997.

[16] D. Nicolalde Rodriguez and J. Apolinario, Evaluating digital audio authenticity with spectral distances and ENF phase change, *Proceedings of the IEEE International Conference on Acoustics, Speech and Signal Processing*, pp. 1417–1420, 2009.

[17] D. Nicolaide Rodriguez, J. Apolinario and L. Biscainho, Audio authenticity: Detecting ENF discontinuity with high precision phase analysis, *IEEE Transactions on Information Forensics and Security*, vol. 5(3), pp. 534–543, 2010.

[18] X. Pan, X. Zhang and S. Lyu, Detecting splicing in digital audios using local noise level estimation, *Proceedings of the IEEE International Conference on Acoustics, Speech and Signal Processing*, pp. 1841–1844, 2012.

[19] P. Reis, J. da Costa, R. Miranda and G. Del Galdo, ESPRIT-Hilbert-based audio tampering detection with SVM classifier for forensic analysis via electrical network frequency, *IEEE Transactions on Information Forensics and Security*, vol. 12(4), pp. 853–864, 2016.

[20] H. Su, A. Hajj-Ahmad, M. Wu and D. Oard, Exploring the use of ENF for multimedia synchronization, *Proceedings of the IEEE International Conference on Acoustics, Speech and Signal Processing*, pp. 4613–4617, 2014.

[21] S. Vatansever, A. Dirik and N. Memon, Factors affecting ENF-based time-of-recording estimation for video, *Proceedings of the IEEE International Conference on Acoustics, Speech and Signal Processing*, pp. 2497–2501, 2019.

[22] Z. Wang, J. Wang, C. Zeng, Q. Min, Y. Tian and M. Zuo, Digital audio tampering detection based on ENF consistency, *Proceedings of the International Conference on Wavelet Analysis and Pattern Recognition*, pp. 209–214, 2018.

[23] Q. Zhao, D. Meng, Z. Xu, W. Zuo and L. Zhang, Robust principal component analysis with complex noise, *Proceedings of the Thirty-First International Conference on Machine Learning*, vol. II, pp. 55–63, 2014.

VII

NOVEL APPLICATIONS

Chapter 15

INSIDER THREAT DETECTION USING MULTI-AUTOENCODER FILTERING AND UNSUPERVISED LEARNING

Yichen Wei, Kam-Pui Chow and Siu-Ming Yiu

Abstract   Insider threat detection and investigation are major challenges in digital forensics. Unlike external attackers, insiders have privileges to access resources in their organizations and violations of normal behavior are difficult to detect.

This chapter describes an unsupervised deep learning framework for detecting insider threats by analyzing system log files. A typical deep neural network can capture normal behavior patterns, but not insider threat behavior patterns because of the presence of small, if any, amounts of insider threat data. For example, the autoencoder unsupervised deep learning model, which is widely used for anomaly detection, requires a dataset containing labeled normal data for training purposes and does not work well when the training dataset contains anomalies. In contrast, the framework proposed in this chapter leverages unsupervised multi-autoencoder filtering to remove anomalies from a training dataset and uses the resulting trained Gaussian mixture model to estimate the distributions of encoded and recognized normal data; data with lower probabilities is identified as insider threat data by the trained model. Experiments demonstrate that the multi-autoencoder-filtered unsupervised learning framework has superior detection performance compared with state-of-the-art baseline models.

Keywords: Insider threat detection, unsupervised deep learning, autoencoders

1.   Introduction

The insider threat continues to cause significant losses to governments, businesses, hospitals and educational institutions. Insiders are masqueraders, traitors [22] or unintentional violators whose behaviors are abnormal compared with their organizations' computer system conventions.

© IFIP International Federation for Information Processing 2020
Published by Springer Nature Switzerland AG 2020
G. Peterson and S. Shenoi (Eds.): Advances in Digital Forensics XVI, IFIP AICT 589, pp. 273–290, 2020.
https://doi.org/10.1007/978-3-030-56223-6_15

Malicious insiders are difficult to detect because they are located within their organizations and have privileges to access resources in their organizations.

Insider threat detection and investigation are challenging tasks in digital forensics. Malicious insiders may take actions such as inserting backdoors in internal systems to launch attacks later, installing keyloggers to gain credentials and steal sensitive information, even deleting traces of their unauthorized activities. According to the Breach Level Index [28], almost 214 sensitive data records are compromised every second in the world and around 40 percent of the compromises are due to insiders [20].

Digital forensics is *a posteriori* in nature – investigations are conducted after crimes were committed and the damage has been done. To address the insider threat, it is necessary to make *a priori* predictions with the help of deep learning methods that automatically detect anomalous user behavior and capture evidence of malicious activity.

This chapter presents a novel unsupervised deep learning insider threat investigation framework that can profile normal user behavior patterns and prevent data leakage. A synthetic insider threat dataset from the Software Engineering Institute at Carnegie Mellon University [26] is employed to evaluate the insider threat detection framework. The original log files in the dataset are pre-processed to extract daily system operation features and user metadata [29] that are used to distinguish insider threat activities from normal activities. Unfortunately, the dataset contains very limited, if any, insider threat data, which makes it difficult for traditional supervised deep learning models to learn insider threat behavior patterns.

The proposed framework employs a neoteric unsupervised deep learning model that is inspired by the basic autoencoder model [10]. The framework leverages unsupervised learning to solve the detection problem. It is based on the intuition that an autoencoder may not learn feature patterns well if it seldom or never observes insider threat behavior patterns; in other words, the reconstruction error of insider threat data would be large. Therefore, multiple autoencoders are cascaded to filter out data with large reconstruction errors as potential insider threat data, leaving the dataset with normal data. Following this, a Gaussian mixture model is employed to estimate the distribution of the recognized encoded normal data.

Experiments demonstrate that the proposed framework compares favorably with state-of-the-art unsupervised insider detection methods. Specifically, the framework increases the recall and area under the ROC curve (AUC) metrics by more than 19% and 23%, respectively.

2. Related Work

Insider threat detection has been studied widely by academia and industry. The Software Engineering Institute at Carnegie Mellon University has done considerable work on detecting insider threats. For example, researchers have inspected network traffic through the Squid proxy server [25], set up access control lists and signatures, and tagged documents to check if data leakage has occurred from within an organization. Splunk [27] has created mature security products for log management and anomaly detection.

In general, there are two broad insider threat detection solutions: (i) traffic inspection; and (ii) behavior profiling. Traffic inspection solutions examine network traffic content to check whether or not sensitive information leaks outward from an organization. Wei et al. [31, 32] have developed payload attribution techniques that trace data leaks. Another approach is to use steganography or watermarking to ensure that distributors of the marked files cannot deny their leakage [14].

While traffic inspection solutions perform *post mortem* detection of insider threats, behavior profiling solutions are useful for insider threat prediction. Le and Zincir-Heywood [15] have used a hidden Markov model to capture normal user behavior sequences; insider threat alarms are raised when normal sequence violations are observed. Graph-based anomaly detection methods have been used to discover insider threats [7]. Axelrad et al. [2] have developed a directed acyclic graph representation of a Bayesian network for insider threat detection. However, graph construction is costly and human experts are required to manually provide empirical estimates of probabilities.

Machine learning models [9, 15] such as self organizing maps [13] and C4.5 decision trees [19] have been applied to insider threat detection. While several well-designed supervised models have been used to detect anomalies [5], small numbers of insider threat records present in training datasets prevent supervised models from learning insider threat data patterns. Additionally, in real-world situations, labeled insider threat data is generally not available. As a result, unsupervised learning models should be applied to detect insider threats.

Popular unsupervised learning approaches include the k-means [17] and isolation forest [16] methods. One-class classification has also been used for anomaly detection (e.g., one-class kernel Fisher discriminant analysis [21] and one-class support vector machines [23]). However, these methods implicitly assume that all the training data is normal, which is not appropriate in practice. Thus, few, if any, insider threat detection techniques actually employ unsupervised deep learning.

Autoencoders [10] and variants such as denoising autoencoders [30] and variational autoencoders [12] have been used to detect anomalies. Although many anomaly detection applications claim that their models employ unsupervised learning, they still correspond to one-class classification models because they rely on *a priori* labeling to select only normal data for training. The state-of-the-art deep autoencoding Gaussian mixture model [33] also relies on labeled normal data for training, but its performance is sensitive to contamination by anomalies. In other words, the model is not well suited to insider threat detection without labeled data.

In the case of data leakage and intranet attacks, malicious insider activities tend to manifest themselves as anomalous behavior or abnormal network traffic content for the specific insider. For example, it is normal for a salesman to download price records from a remote sales department server and abnormal for a human resources specialist to do so, but the operation itself is normal in the enterprise system. In fact, insider threat behavior is very complex and it is infeasible to use traditional rule-based approaches and estimation theory for detection [3]. Moreover, collecting a large amount of labeled training data manually is difficult and time-consuming. The state-of-the-art unsupervised insider threat detection approach proposed by Tuor et al. [29] augments a basic deep neural network with long short-term memory to recognize insider threat data with high anomaly scores, but the recall rate is not high enough. In contrast, by relying on multiple autoencoders and true unsupervised learning, the proposed framework estimates the distribution of normal encoded data using a Gaussian mixture model and can identify insider threat data. Indeed, experiments demonstrate that the proposed multi-autoencoder-filtered unsupervised learning model has superior detection performance compared with state-of-the-art baseline models.

3.   Multi-Autoencoder Detection Framework

A basic autoencoder is a deep neural network with a symmetric structure (Figure 1). The network comprises two fully-connected-layer parts, encoder and decoder, that do not require supervisory labels. The objective of the network is to reconstruct the input in the output layer. In this feed-forward network, the encoder layers encode the input into the middle code layer, following which the decoder layers decode the code layer into the output. The basic loss function is defined as the reconstruction error between the input and output.

Traditionally, an autoencoder implements a non-linear reduction of high dimensional data [18]. Most unsupervised anomaly detection ap-

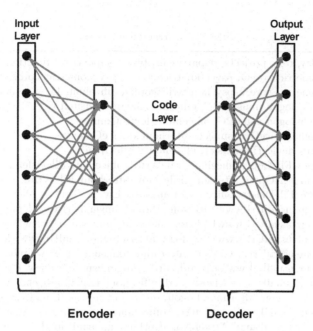

Figure 1. Basic autoencoder structure.

plications that use autoencoders require labeled normal data for training; their models are essentially semi-supervised because they assume that no anomalous data exists in their training sets (which is not realistic). This section presents a true unsupervised learning model that does not need labeled data at any time during its processing.

3.1   Problem Statement

Given a dataset of system logs about user operations without annotated labels, the objective is to detect potential insider threat activity within an organization. The assumption is that insider threat events are rare in system logs. The proposed framework is based on the idea that a deep neural network can learn the patterns of the majority normal data, but it would not reconstruct anomalous data patterns due to the paucity of insider threat data.

Feature aggregation should accommodate five insider threat scenarios [3]: (i) an employee logs in after working hours and uses removable devices to steal sensitive information; (ii) an employee suddenly visits job-hunting websites and emails large attachments to competitors; (iii) an employee masquerades as the employer to send email to employees and disrupt normal company operations; (iv) an employee logs into an-

Table 1.   Extracted features.

user, day, role, projects, department, team, supervisor, function, psychometricScoreO, psychometricScoreC, psychometricScoreE, psychometricScoreA, psychometricScoreN, officehour_logon_usualPC, afterhour_logon_unusualPC, officehour_logon_unusualPC, afterhour_logon_usualPC, officehour_deviceConnect, officehour_deviceDisConnect, afterhour_deviceConnect, afterhour_deviceDisconnect, officehour_ FileOpen, officehour_FileCopy, officehour_FileWrite, officehour_FileDelete, afterhour_FileOpen, afterhour_FileCopy, afterhour_FileWrite, afterhour_FileDelete, officehour_unusualUrl_wwwVisit, officehour_usualUrl_wwwVisit, officehour_ unusualUrl_wwwUpload, officehour_usualUrl_wwwUpload, officehour_unusualUrl_wwwDownload, officehour_usualUrl_wwwDownload, afterhour_unusualUrl_wwwVisit, afterhour_usualUrl_wwwVisit, afterhour_ unusualUrl_wwwUpload, afterhour_usualUrl_wwwUpload, afterhour_unusualUrl_wwwDownload, afterhour_usualUrl_wwwDownload, officehour_Logon, officehour_Logoff, afterhour_Logon, afterhour_Logoff, officehour_unusualEmail_AttachYes, officehour_usualEmail_AttachYes, officehour_unusualEmail_AttachNo, officehour_usualEmail_AttachNo, afterhour_unusualEmail_AttachYes, afterhour_usualEmail_AttachYes, afterhour_unusualEmail_AttachNo, afterhour_usualEmail_AttachNo

other employee's computer to find sensitive documents and emails the documents or stores them on a removable device; and (v) an employee suddenly uploads a large number of files to his/her mailbox.

In order to extract appropriate features to distinguish insider threat records from normal records, the log files containing device, email, file, network and login data are combined to aggregate the discriminating features of each record of each user for each day [29]. Event occurrences are recorded in the feature columns (e.g., how many times a user sent email messages with or without large attachments to an unusual third party after office hours in one day).

Table 1 shows the aggregated data and user metadata features after the deletion of meaningless columns. A value is deemed to be usual if it has appeared in more than 5% of the log records before the given log record.

3.2   Multi-Autoencoder Filtering

After extracting appropriate features from the log files, an aggregated feature matrix is constructed. Each row of the aggregated feature matrix corresponds to the operations done by a user during a day and each

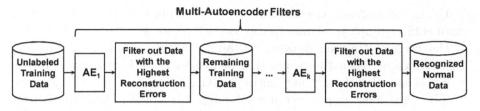

Figure 2. Multi-autoencoder filtering structure.

column represents the number of instances of a specific event or user metadata item. The feature matrix is randomly divided to produce the training and testing datasets.

In the following, the unlabeled training input and the corresponding output are denoted by $X = (x_i^{(j)})$ and $\hat{X} = (\hat{x}_i^{(j)})$, respectively, where $i = 1, \ldots, n; j = 1, \ldots, d; x_i^{(j)}, \hat{x}_i^{(j)} \in \mathbb{R}; n$ is the number of input records; and d is the dimension of the input and output matrices.

Figure 2 shows the multi-encoder filtering structure. The structure comprises k cascaded separately-trained autoencoders with the structure shown in Figure 1. The following steps are involved:

- **Step 1:** Train the first autoencoder (AE_1) using the entire training set.

- **Step 2:** Compute the reconstruction error $L(X, \hat{X})$ between the input X and output $\hat{X}$ according to the following equation:

$$f_i^{(j)} = \frac{\exp(\hat{x}_i^{(j)})}{\sum_{l=1}^{d} \exp(\hat{x}_i^{(l)})}, \quad L_i = -\sum_{j=1}^{d} x_i^{(j)} \cdot \log(f_i^{(j)}) \quad (1)$$

  where $L(X, \hat{X})$ is an n-dimensional vector whose i^{th} entry is denoted by L_i. Following this, filter out $r\%$ of the training set with the largest reconstruction errors.

- **Step 3:** Train the next autoencoder using the remaining training set. Repeat Step 2 until filtering has been done by all k autoencoders.

Assume that the proportion of the insider events in the entire training set is p_0. Then, the probability of randomly selecting an insider event record is p_0. Let c be a coefficient. Furthermore, let cp_0 be the probability of one autoencoder filtering out one item as an insider threat record. In other words, the ability of one autoencoder to filter insider threat data is c times better than random filtering.

Using the first autoencoder, the corresponding largest $r\%$ of training data is filtered out according to the reconstruction error metric $L(X, \hat{X})$. If the original training dataset contains n total records and s insider threat records, then the proportion of insider records remaining in the training set after the kth autoencoder (AE_k) is p_k.

The remaining proportion of insider threat records in the training set after the first autoencoder (also the same as the original insider threat record proportion before training the second autoencoder) is given by:

$$p_1 = \frac{np_0 - nrcp_0}{n(1 - r)} = \frac{1 - cr}{1 - r}p_0 \tag{2}$$

where $cr \leq 1$.

Mathematical induction yields the following expression:

$$p_k = (\frac{1 - cr}{1 - r})^k p_0 \tag{3}$$

In order to filter out all the insider threat records in the training set, the following condition must hold:

$$p_k n(1 - r)^k < 1 \quad \Rightarrow \quad (1 - cr)^k s < 1. \tag{4}$$

The multi-autoencoder filtering process yields data that is almost completely normal with a negligible number of insider threat records. The normal data is then encoded to its code layer representation for the kth autoencoder and the distribution of the recognized encoded normal records is estimated. This enables insider threat records to be identified when their encoded feature representations deviate from the distribution of recognized encoded normal records.

3.3   Insider Threat Prediction

After recognizing the compressed representation of pure normal data, the data is fitted to a Gaussian mixture model to estimate the distribution of normal encoded data.

Let $Z = (z_i^{(j)})$ be the compressed representation of the normal input to the code layer, where $i = 1, \ldots, m; j = 1 \ldots, d; z_i^{(j)} \in \mathbb{R}; m$ is the number of recognized normal records; and d is the dimension of the compression representation in the code layer. Then, the probability density function of the multivariate Gaussian mixture distribution parameterized by $\theta = \{(\theta_c = (\mu_c, \Sigma_c^2), \alpha_c)\}_{c=1}^{C}$ is given by:

$$P(z \mid \theta) = \sum_{c=1}^{C} \alpha_c \Phi(z \mid \theta_c) \tag{5}$$

where C is the number of Gaussian components, (μ_c, Σ_c^2) are the mean and covariance matrix of the cth Gaussian component, α_c is the probability that a sample belongs to the cth Gaussian component, and the probability density of the cth Gaussian component $\Phi(z \mid \theta_c)$ is given by:

$$\Phi(z \mid \theta_c) = \frac{1}{(2\pi)^{\frac{D}{2}}|\Sigma|^{\frac{1}{2}}} \exp\left(-\frac{(z-\mu)^T \Sigma^{-1}(z-\mu)}{2}\right) \tag{6}$$

Maximum likelihood estimation is employed to obtain the Gaussian mixture model parameters. Given a set of N samples $x_1, \ldots, x_N$ and assuming independent sampling, the likelihood $L(\theta)$ of a fixed parameter θ is given by:

$$L(\theta) = \prod_{j=1}^{m} P(z_j \mid \theta) \tag{7}$$

Hence, the log-likelihood $\log L(\theta)$ is given by:

$$\log L(\theta) = \sum_{j=1}^{m} \log P(z_j \mid \theta) \tag{8}$$

The expectation-maximization algorithm [6] is used to maximize the log-likelihood via the following iterative process:

- **Step 1:** Initialize the parameters $\theta = \{\mu_c, \Sigma_c^2, \alpha_c\}_{c=1}^{C}$.

- **Step 2:** Repeat Steps 3 and 4 in sequence to update θ until convergence.

- **Step 3:** Compute the probability γ_{jc} that sample j comes from the cth component as follows:

$$\gamma_{jc} = \frac{\alpha_c \Phi(z_j \mid \theta_c)}{\sum_{c=1}^{C} \alpha_c \Phi(z_j \mid \theta_c)}, \quad j = 1, \ldots, m; \quad c = 1, \ldots, C$$

- **Step 4:** Update the parameters:

$$\mu_c = \frac{\sum_j^m (\gamma_{jc} z_j)}{\sum_j^m \gamma_{jc}}, \quad c = 1, \ldots, C$$

$$\Sigma_c = \frac{\sum_j^m \gamma_{jc}(z_j - \mu_c)(z_j - \mu_c)^T}{\sum_j^m \gamma_{jc}}, \quad c = 1, \ldots, C$$

$$\alpha_c = \frac{\sum_j^m \gamma_{jc}}{C}, \quad c = 1, \ldots, C$$

Given a sample input x, it is compressed to z via multi-autoencoder filtering, after which the negative log probability density, $-\log P(z \mid \theta)$, is computed as its behavior score. All the samples with behavior scores larger than a threshold ε are predicted to be insider threat records. The threshold ε is set based on cross-validation.

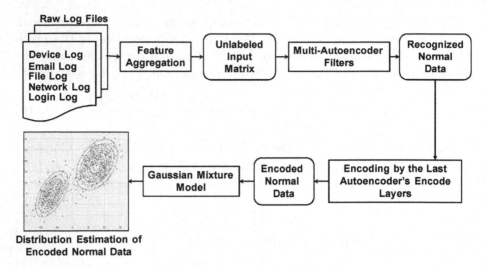

Figure 3. Framework workflow.

3.4 Framework Workflow

Figure 3 shows the overall framework workflow. A total of 53 features were aggregated from the log files of user login/logout activities, operations on devices, files, email and network connections, along with user metadata. The feature matrix was then used to train the multi-autoencoder filtering model in an unsupervised manner without labels. Each row in the matrix corresponded to user behavior on a given day. Multi-autoencoder filtering was used to recognize a portion of the normal data. Meanwhile, the code layer in the last autoencoder was treated as the appropriate low-dimensional representation of normal behavior profiling. Next, the compressed normal data was used to fit a Gaussian mixture model to estimate the distribution of normal encoded data. Records with behavior scores larger than the threshold were predicted to be insider threat records.

4. Framework Evaluation

This section presents the evaluation results obtained when applying the framework to the Insider Threat Dataset (r6.2) [26].

4.1 Multi-Autoencoder Filtering Performance

Figure 4 shows the theoretical minimum k values for different proportions $r = 10\%$, 20% and 30% for dropping insider threat items from the training set based on coefficient c (Equation (4)). The number of insider

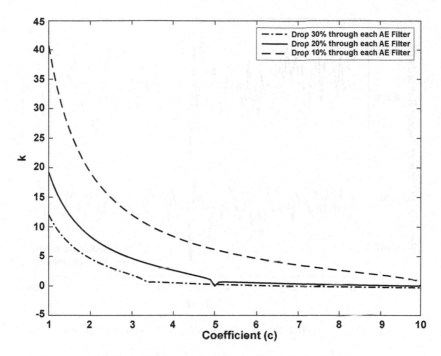

Figure 4. Minimum k values for eliminating all insider threat items.

records in the synthetic dataset after feature aggregation was $s = 73$ out of a total 1,391,247 records.

A key evaluation metric is the purification performance of autoencoder filtering versus that of random filtering. A coefficient c greater than one implies that autoencoder filtering of insider threat records is better than random filtering.

Figure 5 shows the percentages of insider threat records remaining in the training set after one round of autoencoder filtering and random filtering over 100 trials.

Figure 6 shows the percentages of insider threat records remaining in the training set after using five ($k = 5$) multi-autoencoder filters (MAFs) and after five random filtering rounds over 100 trials.

Table 2 shows the corresponding average remaining insider record percentages after multi-autoencoder and random filtering.

Figure 7 shows the filtering performance of five continuous autoencoder filters on the Insider Threat Dataset (r6.2) during a single trial. The graph reveals that the proportion of insider threat records remaining in the training set continuously decreases from autoencoder to autoencoder.

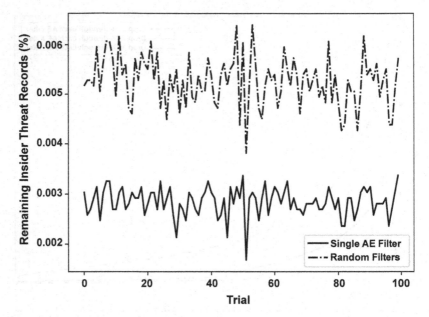

Figure 5.   Insider threat records after one round of filtering.

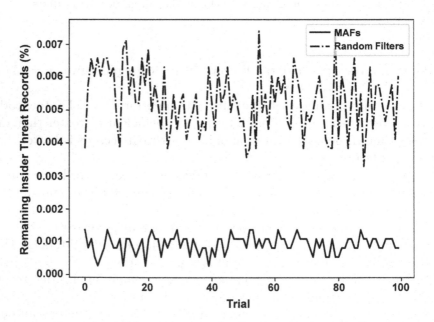

Figure 6.   Insider threat records after five rounds of filtering.

Table 2.   Average percentages of remaining insider threat records after filtering.

Filtering Technique	Remaining Insider Threat Records	
	One Round	Five Rounds
Autoencoder Filtering	0.0028301982%	0.0009267764%
Random Filtering	0.0052504669%	0.0052508192%

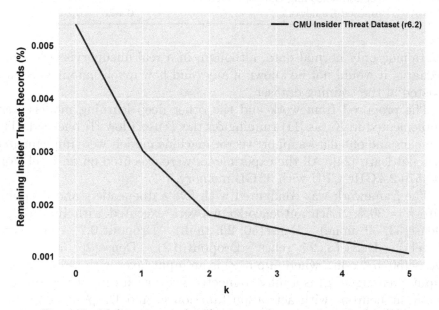

Figure 7.   Multi-autoencoder filtering performance in a single trial.

4.2   Comparison Against Baseline Methods

This section compares the performance of the proposed framework against state-of-the-art baseline models, specifically, the k-means, one-class support vector machine, unsupervised deep neural network [29], one-class autoencoder [8] and deep autoencoding Gaussian mixture [33] models using the Insider Threat Dataset (r6.2).

Applying feature extraction to the dataset yielded 53 dimensions of 1,391,247 instances that included only 73 insider threat records. The dataset was randomly split into a training set, cross-validation set and testing set with percentages of 80%, 10% and 10%, respectively. Note that the one-class classification models (i.e., one-class support vector machine, one-class autoencoder and deep autoencoding Gaussian mixture models) were semi-supervised over the entire anomaly detection process. The implicit assumption was that they had a high-quality training set

Table 3.	Comparison of the proposed framework against five baseline models.

Method	Recall	AUC
k-means model	0	NA
One-class support vector machine model	0.733	0.405
Unsupervised deep neural network model	0.556	0.625
One-class autoencoder model	0.364	0.589
Deep autoencoding Gaussian mixture model	0.476	0.692
Proposed framework	**0.923**	**0.925**

containing only normal data, although, in a real unsupervised learning scenario, it would not be known if any (and how much) anomalous data existed in the training dataset.

The proposed framework and the other deep learning models were implemented in Keras [11] running on the TensorFlow [1] backend. The k-means and one-class support vector machine models were implemented in scikit-learn [24]. All the experiments were executed on an Intel Core i5-3570 2.4 GHz CPU with 32 GB memory.

The framework was configured with five autoencoders and dropping rate $r = 20\%$. Each autoencoder network executed with Input(53) – Dense(53, 50, none) – Dense(50, 25, tanh) – Dropout(0.2) – Dense(25, 8, relu) – Dense(8, 25, relu) – Dropout(0.2) – Dense(25, 50, tanh) – Dense(50, 53, relu), where Input(x) is an input layer with x-dimensional input, Dense(i, o, g) is a fully connected layer with i input neurons and o output neurons with activation function g, and Dropout(d) denotes a drop out of d% of neurons to avoid overfitting. All the autoencoders were compiled by a stochastic gradient descent optimizer with a learning rate of 1×10^{-4}, training epoch number of 500 and batch size of 1,024.

In insider threat detection scenarios, due to the property that malicious insiders are rare and just one overlooked incident could cause considerable damage, the recall metric is more significant than other metrics. In other words, it is critical to detect the insider threat even if the number of false alarms are increased. At the same time, a good solution would reduce the number of false alarms to the extent possible while maintaining a high recall value. Because recall (also called the true positive rate) and the false positive rate constitute a tradeoff, the area under the ROC curve (AUC) is also used as a metric. Note that the horizontal and vertical axes of the ROC curve correspond to the false positive rate and true positive rate (recall), respectively.

Table 3 compares the performance of the proposed framework against the five baseline models. The proposed framework clearly outperforms all the baseline models. Indeed, the proposed framework has recall and

AUC scores that are more than 19% and 23% higher, respectively, than the best scores of the other five models.

5. Conclusions

The proposed unsupervised deep learning framework for insider threat detection is an advancement over other unsupervised deep learning models that require a training dataset containing labeled normal data and do not work well when the training dataset includes anomalous (i.e., insider threat) data. The framework leverages automated multi-autoencoder filtering to eliminate anomalies and then estimates the distributions of encoded and recognized normal data using a Gaussian mixture model. Data with negative log probability density values larger than a threshold are identified as insider threat data. Experiments demonstrate that the multi-autoencoder-filtered unsupervised learning framework has much better recall and AUC scores compared with five state-of-the-art insider threat detection models.

The framework is founded on the notion that an autoencoder can reconstruct the majority normal data, but cannot reconstruct rare insider threat data satisfactorily. Due to the difficulty of detecting insider threat data using a deep neural network without supervisory labels, the only option is to filter out potentially anomalous data with larger reconstruction errors. However, this approach filters out portions of normal data, which reduces the amount of normal data for estimating the multivariate Gaussian mixture model distribution, contributing to an elevated false positive rate [4]. Future research will modify the framework to decrease the false positive rate.

The current version of the framework is designed for static data. Future research will extend the framework to detect anomalies in sequential and spatial data. Since the encoded non-linear representation of the input is automatically generated by multi-autoencoder filtering, the research will treat concatenated log files as inputs and use natural language processing methods to solve the anomaly detection problem.

References

[1] M. Abadi, P. Barham, J. Chen, Z. Chen, A. Davis, J. Dean, M. Devin, S. Ghemawat, G. Irving, M. Isard, M. Kudlur, J. Levenberg, R. Monga, S. Moore, D. Murray, B. Steiner, P. Tucker, V. Vasudevan, P. Warden, M. Wicke, Y. Yu and X. Zheng, TensorFlow: A system for large-scale machine learning, *Proceedings of the Twelfth USENIX Symposium on Operating Systems Design and Implementation*, pp. 265–283, 2016.

[2] E. Axelrad, P. Sticha, O. Brdiczka and J. Shen, A Bayesian network model for predicting insider threats, *Proceedings of the IEEE Security and Privacy Workshops*, pp. 82–89, 2013.

[3] S. Axelsson, A Preliminary Attempt to Apply Detection and Estimation Theory to Intrusion Detection, Technical Report, Department of Computer Engineering, Chalmers University of Technology, Goteborg, Sweden, 2000.

[4] S. Axelsson, The base-rate fallacy and the difficulty of intrusion detection, *ACM Transactions on Information and System Security*, vol. 3(3), pp. 186–205, 2000.

[5] V. Chandola, A. Banerjee and V. Kumar, Anomaly detection: A survey, *ACM Computing Surveys*, vol. 41(3), article no. 15, 2009.

[6] A. Dempster, N. Laird and D. Rubin, Maximum likelihood from incomplete data via the EM algorithm, *Journal of the Royal Statistical Society: Series B (Methodological)*, vol. 39(1), pp. 1–38, 1977.

[7] W. Eberle and L. Holder, Applying graph-based anomaly detection approaches to the discovery of insider threats, *Proceedings of the IEEE International Conference on Intelligence and Security Informatics*, pp. 206–208, 2009.

[8] D. Ellison, Fraud detection using autoencoders in Keras with a TensorFlow backend, *Oracle AI and Data Science Blog*, August 9, 2018.

[9] G. Gavai, K. Sricharan, D. Gunning, J. Hanley, M. Singhal and R. Rolleston, Supervised and unsupervised methods to detect insider threats from enterprise social and online activity data, *Journal of Wireless Mobile Networks, Ubiquitous Computing and Dependable Applications*, vol. 6(4), pp. 47–63, 2015.

[10] G. Hinton and R. Salakhutdinov, Reducing the dimensionality of data with neural networks, *Science*, vol. 313(5786), pp. 504–507, 2006.

[11] Keras, Keras API Reference (`keras.io/api`), 2020.

[12] D. Kingma and M. Welling, Auto-Encoding Variational Bayes, *arXiv:* 1312.6114v10, 2014.

[13] T. Kohonen, Self-organized formation of topologically correct feature maps, *Biological Cybernetics*, vol. 43(1), pp. 59–69, 1982.

[14] A. Kumar and K. Pooja, Steganography – A data hiding technique, *International Journal of Computer Applications*, vol. 9(7), pp. 19–23, 2010.

[15] D. Le and A. Zincir-Heywood, Evaluating insider threat detection workflow using supervised and unsupervised learning, *Proceedings of the IEEE Security and Privacy Workshops*, pp. 270–275, 2018.

[16] F. Liu, K. Ting and Z. Zhou, Isolation forest, *Proceedings of the Eighth IEEE International Conference on Data Mining*, pp. 413–422, 2008.

[17] J. MacQueen, Some methods for classification and analysis of multivariate observations, *Proceedings of the Fifth Berkeley Symposium on Mathematical Statistics and Probability*, vol. 1, pp. 281–297, 1967.

[18] K. Pearson, On lines and planes of closest fit to systems of points in space, *The London, Edinburgh and Dublin Philosophical Magazine and Journal of Science*, vol. 2(11), pp. 559–572, 1901.

[19] J. Quinlan, *C4.5: Programs for Machine Learning*, Morgan Kaufmann, Burlington, Massachusetts, 2014.

[20] T. Rashid, I. Agrafiotis and J. Nurse, A new take on detecting insider threats: Exploring the use of hidden Markov models, *Proceedings of the Eighth ACM International Workshop on Managing Insider Security Threats*, pp. 47–56, 2016.

[21] V. Roth, Kernel Fisher discriminants for outlier detection, *Neural Computation*, vol. 18(4), pp. 942–960, 2006.

[22] M. Salem, S. Hershkop and S. Stolfo, A survey of insider attack detection research, in *Insider Attack and Cyber Security*, S. Stolfo, S. Bellovin, A. Keromytis, S. Hershkop, S. Smith and S. Sinclair (Eds.), Springer, Boston, Massachusetts, pp. 69–90, 2008.

[23] B. Scholkopf, R. Williamson, A. Smola, J. Shawe-Taylor and J. Platt, Support vector method for novelty detection, *Proceedings of the Twelfth International Conference on Neural Information Processing Systems*, pp. 582–588, 1999.

[24] scikit-learn, Machine learning in Python (`scikit-learn.org`), 2019.

[25] G. Silowash, T. Lewellen, J. Burns and D. Costa, Detecting and Preventing Data Exfiltration Through Encrypted Web Sessions via Traffic Inspection, Technical Note, CMU/SEI-2013-TN-012, Software Engineering Institute, Carnegie Mellon University, Pittsburgh, Pennsylvania, 2013.

[26] Software Engineering Institute, Insider Threat Test Dataset, Carnegie Mellon University, Pittsburgh, Pennsylvania (`resources.sei.cmu.edu/library/asset-view.cfm?assetid=508099`), 2016.

[27] Splunk Technology, Splunk, San Francisco, California (`www.splunk.com`), 2020.

[28] Thales Digital Identity and Security, Breached records more than doubled in H1 2018, reveals Breach Level Index, *Thales Digital Identity and Security Blog*, October 23, 2018.

[29] A. Tuor, S. Kaplan, B. Hutchinson, N. Nichols and S. Robinson, Deep learning for unsupervised insider threat detection in structured cybersecurity data streams, presented at the *Thirty-First AAAI Conference on Artificial Intelligence Workshop on AI and OR for Socal Good*, 2017.

[30] P. Vincent, H. Larochelle, I. Lajoie, Y. Bengio and P. Manzagol, Stacked denoising autoencoders: Learning useful representations in a deep network with a local denoising criterion, *Journal of Machine Learning Research*, vol. 11, pp. 3371–3408, 2010.

[31] Y. Wei, F. Xu, X. Chen, Y. Pu, J. Shi and S. Qing, Winnowing double structure for wildcard query in payload attribution, *Proceedings of the Seventeenth International Conference on Information Security*, pp. 454–464, 2014.

[32] Y. Wei, F. Xu, X. Chen, J. Shi and S. Qing, Winnowing multihashing structure with wildcard query, *Proceedings of the Asia-Pacific Conference on Web Technologies and Applications*, pp. 265–281, 2014.

[33] B. Zong, Q. Song, M. Min, W. Cheng, C. Lumezanu, D. Cho and H. Chen, Deep autoencoding Gaussian mixture model for unsupervised anomaly detection, poster presented at the *Sixth International Conference on Learning Representations*, 2018.

Chapter 16

DETECTING LOCAL MACHINE DATA LEAKAGE IN REAL TIME

Jingcheng Liu, Yaping Zhang, Yuze Li, Yongheng Jia, Yao Chen and Jin Cao

Abstract   Data privacy leaks are becoming a serious problem. A large percentage of privacy leaks are due to inadvertent user errors. Most data leak detection solutions do not have privacy-preserving functionality. Moreover, due to the third-party delivery of data in the cloud, it is not possible to guarantee real-time leak detection.

This chapter proposes a local-side data leakage detection method that uses a suffix array. The method also employs encryption for data protection. The method is compared with mature data leak detection algorithms to demonstrate its effectiveness in real time and that the additional data protection overhead is acceptable.

Keywords: Real-time data leak detection, suffix array, data privacy

1.   Introduction

The mobile Internet has brought great convenience to modern society. However, massive amounts of data are now transmitted over the Internet, which renders the task of securing sensitive private data extremely important.

Detecting and stopping privacy leaks are important components of data security. Private data leaks have three main causes. The first and most common is leakage during transmission, where a user directly transmits unencrypted or weakly encrypted data over the Internet. HTTPS-based encryption is a common solution to data leakage during transmission. The second is data leakage caused by local malware or malicious users. Since the stolen private data is typically encrypted before transmission, the leakage cannot be detected by examining the transmitted data. Therefore, these data leaks are detected by monitoring for abnor-

© IFIP International Federation for Information Processing 2020
Published by Springer Nature Switzerland AG 2020
G. Peterson and S. Shenoi (Eds.): Advances in Digital Forensics XVI, IFIP AICT 589, pp. 291–308, 2020.
https://doi.org/10.1007/978-3-030-56223-6_16

mal transmission behaviors. The third cause is inadvertent data leakage due to user error or incorrect operations. Examples include erroneously sending internal email to external entities and uploading sensitive data to social networking sites. Inadvertent data leaks are difficult to detect because they are caused by ordinary users who perform normal operations.

Several researchers have focused on detecting and preventing private data leaks by users. If the private data is identified in advance, it is feasible to perform simple plaintext matching or deep packet inspection of outbound traffic. Strict data access policies should be implemented on the host, sensitive data should be watermarked and anomalies in outbound data flows should be detected and investigated. However, these methods consume significant resources and the private data could itself be acquired by malware that compromises the matching process [5].

This research focuses on local-side data leakage detection in real time while protecting the private data. In the proposed data leakage detection workflow, the user first selects the private data and provides it to the detection system. The system compares the outbound data flows from the user against the private data in real time to detect potential leaks. The system immediately alerts the user to the potential leaks and can stop the outbound data flows.

The proposed data leakage method employs algorithms that secure and detect private data in outbound flows while minimizing time and space consumption. In particular, it employs byte stream encryption to secure the private data used for matching as well as the outbound flows themselves. Also, it employs a suffix array technique for local-side leakage detection of encrypted flows in real time. The computational time and memory footprint are optimized for real-time leakage detection. Despite providing data security as an additional feature, the overall performance of the proposed method is comparable with the performance of the classical Knuth-Morris-Pratt and finite automaton string matching algorithms.

2. Related Work

Early data leakage detection was mainly performed on the host side [6, 9]. Several researchers have proposed deep packet inspection of outbound flows to detect data leakage [15, 19]. The approaches leverage efficient string matching algorithms such as finite automaton, heuristic and filtering based algorithms [8, 10, 16]. Finite automaton based algorithms perform matching in linear time, but this comes with large memory requirements in the worst case. The heuristic and filtering based algorithms use less memory, but they are vulnerable to targeted data attacks that cause surges in the matching time.

Researchers have also proposed methods such as MapReduce, fuzzy fingerprinting and verifiable search for data leakage detection [3, 11, 14, 20]. However, the time and space requirements can be prohibitive and the methods do not protect private data.

The advent of cloud computing enables third parties to provide data leak detection services [1, 13, 17, 18]. However, outsourcing this service can result in secondary leaks of private data from the third parties themselves. It is also important to note that third parties are high-value targets for attackers because they handle private data from numerous clients. When third parties cannot be trusted completely, additional pre-processing and post-processing are required to prevent secondary data leaks. Moreover, it is not possible for third parties to guarantee leakage detection in real time.

3.   String Matching with a Suffix Array

This section describes string matching using a suffix array. In the following, a text string submitted by a user is denoted as S and its length is n. The pattern string (private data) to be matched is denoted as T and its length is m. The number of strings involved in multi-pattern matching is k.

The suffix array algorithm has strong stability and versatility properties. In the worst case, it can maintain processing efficiency and consume little computational time due to special circumstances underlying its design. Although it takes a long time to pre-process text strings, the complexity of a single match is only $O(m + log\,n)$ after pre-processing. This is better than string matching, which has a general complexity of $O(m + n)$. The performance can be improved further with multi-pattern matching if the relative relationships between strings to be matched are known. Additionally, the matching of a suffix array using binary search facilitates the use of encryption to maintain data security.

3.1   Suffix Array

A suffix array [12] is commonly used for string processing. At the core of a suffix array is a series of complex pre-processing procedures. By pre-processing a series of target strings and making full use of the relationships between the suffixes of a target string, information about the target string can be obtained. The pre-processing of target strings can be performed in $O(n)$ time and a single search can be performed in $O(m + log\,n)$ time.

Algorithm 1: String matching using a suffix array.

Data:
T: Pattern string to be matched.
SA: Suffix array of the text string.
Result:
True or *False*: Matching result.

$a \leftarrow 0, b \leftarrow n - 1$
while $b - a > 1$ **do**
   $c \leftarrow (a + b)/2$
   if *Compare(SA[c], T > 0)* **then**
    | $a = c$
   else
    | $b = c$
   end
   return *Compare(SA[b], T = 0)*
end

A string of length n has n suffixes of different lengths (i.e., substrings from the ith character of the string to the nth character). The process of string matching is expressed as follows:

$$\alpha = \rho | \beta \tag{1}$$

where α and β are two different suffixes, ρ is the string to be matched and | is a connective operation on strings. After the strings are matched, there must be two suffixes, α and β, that satisfy Equation (1). Furthermore, if the string to be matched ρ is a substring of the text string S, there will be at least one suffix of S that makes ρ become its prefix.

The process of string matching using a suffix array involves examining the applicability of Equation (1) to the text string. Suppose that the n suffixes have been sorted, then a suffix array SA is obtained by storing the starting positions of the ith small suffixes, where i ranges from 1 to n.

Algorithm 1 specifies the process of string matching using a suffix array.

In order to match a string, binary search can be used to identify the suffixes that have been sorted at least once. The range of the search can be halved with each comparison of the matched string and a suffix. Thus, a single search is performed in $O(m \log n)$ time.

The relationships between suffixes can be leveraged to enhance search efficiency. Let $LCP[i]$ denote the longest common prefix of two suffixes beginning with $SA[i-1]$ and $SA[i]$. Then, the following relationship exists between the pth and $p-1^{th}$ suffixes of the input text T:

Algorithm 2: Creating a longest common prefix array.

Data:
S: Text string.
SA: Suffix array of the text string.
Result:
LCP: Longest common prefix array of the text string.

$j \leftarrow 0,\ k \leftarrow 0$
for $i = 0 \rightarrow n - 1$ **do**
  | $Rank[SA[i]] \leftarrow i$
end
for $i = 0 \rightarrow n - 2$ **do**
  if $k > 0$ **then**
    | $k \leftarrow k - 1$
  end
  $j \leftarrow SA[Rank[i] - 1]$
  while $S[i + k] = S[j + k]$ **do**
    | $k \leftarrow k + 1$
  end
  $LCP[Rank[i]] \leftarrow k$
end
  return LCP

$$LCP[p] \geq LCP[p-1] - 1 \qquad (2)$$

This property can be used to obtain the LCP array in $O(n)$ time [7].

Algorithm 2 specifies the process of creating the LCP array. In the algorithm, the $Rank$ array and suffix array SA are inverses of each other, i.e., $Rank[i]$ represents the order of the suffix that starts with the ith character in all the suffixes.

Having created the LCP array, it is necessary to revisit the search process with the pattern string. If the comparison is only performed with the ith small suffix, it would be compared with the jth small suffix. Let $LCP(i,j)$ denote the longest common prefix of the two suffixes, then $LCP(i,j)$ corresponds to the minimum value in $LCP[i+1], \ldots, LCP[j]$. If the value of $LCP(i,j)$ could be obtained, then unnecessary matches during the search would be eliminated. Since the LCP has been created, the problem of obtaining $LCP(i,j)$ reduces to a problem with the range of the minimum query, which can be realized in $O(1)$ time after pre-processing, where the pre-processing complexity is $O(n \log n)$. Thus, the time complexity of a single search is reduced to $O(m + \log n)$.

Algorithm 3 specifies the single search process with the longest common prefix array LCP. Note that the $FastLCP$ function in the algorithm computes the value of $LCP(i,j)$ for the ith and j^{th} small suffixes in $O(1)$ time.

Algorithm 3: Searching with a longest common prefix array.

Data:
T: Pattern string to be matched.
SA: Suffix array of the text string.
LCP: Longest common prefix array of the text string.
Result:
True or *False*: Matching result.

$last \leftarrow 0$
$a \leftarrow 0, b \leftarrow n - 1$
while $b - a > 1$ **do**
  $c \leftarrow (a + b)/2$
  if $Compare(FastLCP(last, c), SA[c], T > 0)$ **then**
  $\quad | \quad a = c$
  else
  $\quad | \quad b = c$
  end
  $\quad last \leftarrow c$
end
return $Compare(FastLCP(last, c), SA[c], T = 0)$

The final task is to obtain the suffix array SA. Since the n suffixes are parts of the original text string, considerable space is required to store the suffixes when employing the regular $O(n \log n)$ sorting method. Therefore, the algorithm proposed by Manber and Myers [12] is employed to quickly sort the suffix array.

Figure 1 illustrates the algorithm for creating the suffix array SA. Assume that the text string is **aabaaaab**. First, the n substrings of length one are sorted. This sort corresponds to the size relationship between the characters, which means that the rank of **a** is one and the rank of **b** is two.

Next, each substring is merged with its subsequent substrings to double its length. The rank of the substring is also equivalent to that of the two substrings, which is an n-ary two-digit number. Note that the last substring cannot be merged with other substrings, which is equivalent to the emergence of an empty string with rank zero. The new rank value is then obtained. Following this, the rank value of each suffix and the suffix array SA are obtained by repeating the process $\log n$ times. Thus, the complexity of the entire algorithm is $O(n \log n)$.

3.2   Multi-Pattern Matching

The following three issues must be considered to implement real-time data leakage detection while ensuring data security:

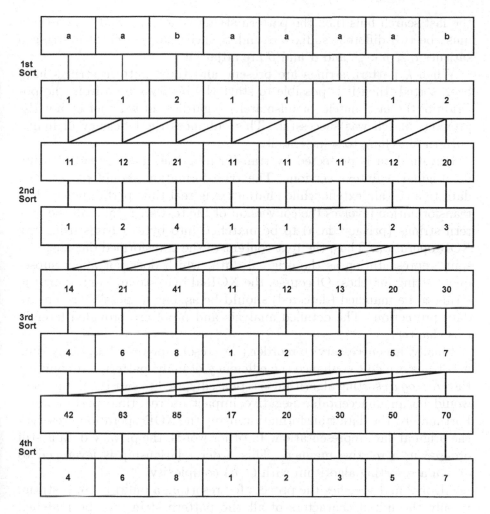

Figure 1. Creating a suffix array.

- The efficiency of the suffix array algorithm should be enhanced when performing multi-pattern matching.

- The data security method that protects private data should not negatively impact data leakage detection.

- Improvements should be incorporated that shorten the search time to ensure good real-time performance.

When a suffix array is used to search for a single string, if the last search succeeds (i.e., the pattern string is matched), then there must be two different suffixes α and β such that Equation (1) holds. However, if the last search fails (i.e., the pattern string is not matched), then there must be two different suffixes α and β such that the pattern string ρ satisfies $\alpha < \rho < \beta$, and α and β are adjacent.

When k pattern strings are present and these pattern strings have been sorted, then it is possible to start the binary search from the position of the last match (or mismatch) regardless of whether or not the previous match was successful. This enhances the efficiency of multi-pattern matching to some extent.

Private data is protected by transforming the data instead of using its original plaintext version. The transformation should protect the data to a certain extent while guaranteeing real-time performance. The transformation involves the conversion of the text string and all the pattern strings (privacy data) to be matched into byte streams using the XOR operation. Thus, the text content of the transformed data has the same representation as the original data, which does not affect subsequent string matches. Of course, the XORed byte stream containing the string to be matched (detected) should be as long as possible to ensure data protection. The detailed analysis and proof are provided later in this chapter.

Finally, it is necessary to reorder (i.e., resort) private data every time it is transformed to enhance the efficiency of multi-pattern matching. If the $O(n \log n)$ sorting algorithm is repeatedly used to sort the data, there would be an unacceptable negative impact on real-time performance. Fortunately, the data transformation using the XOR operation preserves the original data representation. In other words, the privacy data is still ordered in a relative manner. This order relationship is leveraged to design a resorting algorithm with $O(n)$ complexity.

Algorithm 4 specifies the process for resorting a multi-pattern string. If only the initial characters of all the pattern strings to be matched are considered, then after the XOR operation, the pattern strings with the same initial characters would be concentrated in the same continuous interval after reordering. Since there are only 256 possibilities for a single byte, the starting position of the interval and length of the interval for each possibility must be recorded, and the 256 intervals are reordered so that the initial characters of all the strings are already ordered. Next, the second characters are considered until all the pattern strings are reordered. This process is repeated for each subsequent character of each string. Since there is only one traversal, the total time complexity is $O(n)$.

Algorithm 4: Resorting a multi-pattern string.

Data:
Multi: Pattern string to be resorted.
l: Left border of the resorted range.
r: Right border of the resorted range.
pos: Pending position.
deep: Deep character to be compared.
Result:
Resort: Resorted array.

Resort(*Multi*, *l*, *r*, *pos*, *deep*)
if *l* = *r* then
 | *Resort*[*pos*] ← *Multi*[*l*]
 | return
end
for *i* = 0 → 255 do
 | *cnt*[*i*] ← 0 *pos*1[*i*] ← −1
end
for *i* = *l* → *r* do
 | if *Multi*[*i*].*length* = *deep* then
 | | *Resort*[*pos*] ← *Multi*[*i*]
 | | *pos* ← *pos* + 1
 | | *continue*
 | end
 | *k* ← *Multi*[*i*][*deep*]
 | if *pos*1[*k*] = −1 then
 | | *pos*1[*k*] ← *i*
 | end
end
cnt[*k*] ← *cnt*[*k*] + 1
for *i* = 0 → 255 do
 | if *cnt*[*i*] > 0 then
 | | Resort(*Multi*, *pos*1[*i*], *pos*1[*i*] + *cnt*[*i*] − 1, *pos*, *deep* + 1)
 | end
 | *pos* ← *pos* + *cnt*[*i*]
end
return

---

4.   Implementation and Evaluation

The experimental evaluation used a typical laptop computer with four 2.50 GHz CPUs and 12 GB RAM. All the algorithms were implemented in Java.

The performance of each stage of the overall algorithm was assessed by recording its execution time. The Java system method `nanoTime()` was employed to obtain execution times accurately to the nanosecond level. Although the `currentTimeMillis()` method could have been used in theory, it is based on the real time, which means that it does

Table 1. Comparison of execution times.

Text String Length (bytes)	Proposed Method (ns)	KMP (ns)	Finite Automaton (ns)
1,000	161,992	108,457	104,658
2,000	229,878	215,487	174,521
5,000	377,953	522,648	324,758
10,000	750,369	1,054,925	491,358
50,000	4,658,695	5,427,345	2,478,547
10,0000	12,309,142	10,873,483	4,657,857

not provide nanosecond accuracy. The Classmexer instrument agent was used to obtain the memory requirements. These two metrics enable the evaluation of the overall algorithm – whether or not the algorithm meets the real-time standard and whether or not the memory usage is within an acceptable range to meet the real-time standard.

The Enron Email Corpus [2] was employed in the experimental evaluation; email headers as well as email bodies were used in the evaluation. Email is one of the main communication modes and email leaks occur frequently. Therefore, using email data in the evaluation makes for an excellent real-world data leakage scenario. The Chromosome04 gene dataset was also used to evaluate algorithm performance and some extreme cases.

4.1   Comparison with Other Methods

The proposed method incorporates some additional steps to the string matching algorithm in order to implement data protection. Obviously, these steps impact the performance of the overall algorithm.

The first set of experiments was conducted to evaluate if the proposed method meets the real-time standard. The proposed method was evaluated on the local side against two classical string matching algorithms, Knuth-Morris-Pratt (KMP) and finite automaton. All the algorithms were implemented in Java and the Chromosome04 gene dataset was used to evaluate their performance (execution times). Multiple experiments were conducted by selecting text strings of different lengths and fixing the number of pattern strings k and length m for multi-pattern matching to 100 bytes.

Table 1 shows the experimental results. The results reveal that the proposed method has slightly longer execution times than the two traditional algorithms, but this is expected because of the additional steps and the consequent higher time complexity. Nevertheless, the time overhead is within the acceptable range given that data security is also maintained.

4.2 Enron Email Corpus Experiments

Two sets of experiments were performed using the Enron Email Corpus. One involved single string matching without encryption and the other involved multi-pattern matching with encryption and resorting. Each set of experiments involved matches of all the email in the corpus. In the case of single string matching, the matching string length was set to 10 bytes. In the case of multi-pattern matching, 100 strings of length 10 bytes were matched. All the strings to be matched were random substrings selected from the original strings.

Figure 2 shows the results for single string matching without encryption. Figures 2(a), 2(b) and 2(c) show the setup (pre-processing) times, search times and storage requirements, respectively, for various text string lengths. To simplify the presentation, the experimental results obtained for text string lengths in 500-byte intervals were averaged. In the figures, the maximum, minimum, mean + standard deviation and mean − standard deviation for each interval are displayed in the form of candlestick plots. Intervals with less than five data points were excluded to ensure data validity and eliminate interference by external factors.

The experimental results reveal that the pre-processing time and storage requirements of the proposed method grow at the rate of $n\,log\,n$ with the length of the string to be matched. With regard to the search times, it should be noted that the lengths of strings to be matched were fixed at 10 bytes and the lengths of the text strings ranged from zero to 200,000 bytes. Thus, the expected time complexity of $m + log\,n$ is seen in Figure 2(b). Additionally, when n approaches 200,000 bytes, the pre-processing time plus the search time is still less than 0.1 s. Thus, leak detection of text without encryption meets the real-time standard.

The second set of experiments increased the number of strings to be matched to simulate real-world scenarios and encrypted all the data to ensure security. The efficient resorting algorithm described above was employed after the data was encrypted.

Figures 3 and 4 show the results for multi-pattern matching with encryption and resorting. Figures 3(a), 3(b) and 3(c) show the setup (pre-processing) times, search times and encryption times, respectively, for various text string lengths. Figures 4(a) and 4(b) show the resorting times and storage requirements, respectively, for various text string lengths.

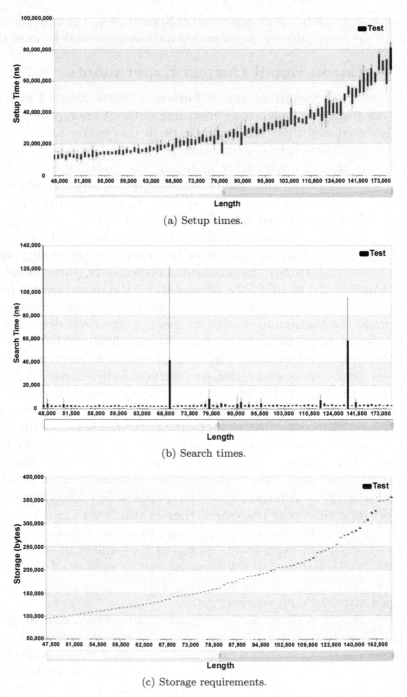

(a) Setup times.

(b) Search times.

(c) Storage requirements.

Figure 2. Results for single string matching without encryption.

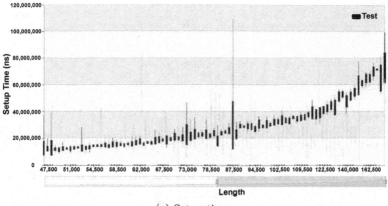

(a) Setup times.

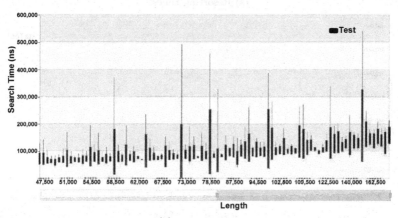

(b) Search times.

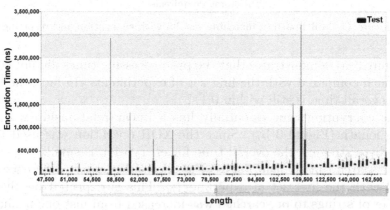

(c) Encryption times.

Figure 3. Results for multi-pattern matching with encryption and resorting.

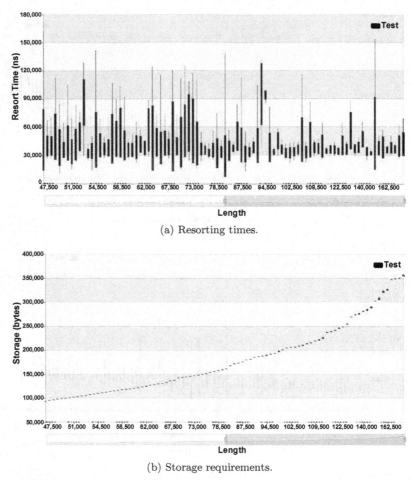

(a) Resorting times.

(b) Storage requirements.

Figure 4. Multi-pattern matching results with encryption and resorting.

Figure 3(a) demonstrates that the pre-processing times did not change too much compared with the first set of experiments. In fact, the maximum overall time is still within 0.1 s.

The encryption time essentially has a linear relationship with text string length (Figure 3(b)). Since the XOR operation was used to encrypt byte streams, the overall time for encryption is small.

The search time plot in Figure 3(c) shows the largest difference compared with the first set of experiments. This is expected because the number of strings to be searched was increased from just one in the first set of experiments to 100, and the corresponding $O(log\,n)$ time complexity is reflected in the results. However, it is important to note that the overall search time does not grow rapidly, and is still negligible compared with the time required for pre-processing.

Figure 4(a) shows that the resorting time and space requirements are significant. This is expected because resorting is a recursive procedure with large overhead. The resorting time plot does not reflect the theoretical linear relationship with string length. Nevertheless, the maximum time requirement of 10^{-4} s is within the acceptable range.

The results of the two sets of experiments reveal that the time overhead increased as a result of implementing data security. However, the time overhead has little impact on real-time performance. In fact, the overhead is acceptable given the data security requirement.

With regard to the memory overhead in Figure 4(b), it is important to note that only the recursive resorting procedure has significant memory usage. Fortunately, since the maximum resorting time is just 10^{-4} s, the increased memory is required for a miniscule duration and, therefore, does not impact local resources in a significant manner.

5. Discussion and Analysis

Gog and Ohlebusch [4] have demonstrated that it is possible to reduce the time complexity of the suffix array and longest common prefix array computations. However, it was decided not to implement the enhancements in the proposed model for three reasons:

- **Data Security:** Data security is an important goal of the proposed method for outbound data leakage detection. The encryption technique, while providing protection, should ensure that the transformed data can be resorted efficiently. Thus, the proposed method opted to create the suffix array and longest common prefix array as discussed above.

- **Real-Time Performance:** While the time complexity is the principal consideration for real-time data leakage detection, the memory consumption is also an important issue. Recursion, which requires significant runtime memory, is restricted to the resorting stage to minimize the runtime memory consumption and enable users to perform their normal computing tasks while the real-time leakage detection system is operational.

- **Real-World Scenarios:** For individual users, the normal outbound text data throughput is on the order of 100,000 bytes/s. Thus, algorithms with $O(n \log n)$ or $O(n)$ time complexity have little effect on the overall execution time. Therefore, the proposed method opted to use an algorithm with $O(n \log n)$ time complexity to create the longest common prefix array.

Table 2. Time and space complexity of the four stages.

Stage	Time Complexity	Space Complexity
Pre-Processing	$n \log n$	$n \log n$
Searching	$m + \log n$	1
Encryption	n	n
Resorting	n	n

Table 2 shows the time and space complexity of the four stages in the proposed method for real-time leakage detection with data security. Since the byte stream length used in the XOR operation is one byte, there are 256 possibilities for a transformed string. Thus, local malware would be able to obtain the original string after a maximum of 256 attempts. When the byte stream length is increased to two bytes, the maximum number of attempts required would be 65,536. When the strings are long enough, it would be practically impossible for local malware to obtain the original strings. The resorting algorithm also makes it more difficult for local malware to monitor the data transformations. Indeed, the proposed method achieves data security by making it computationally infeasible for local malware to defeat the protection mechanism.

6. Conclusions

Data privacy leaks are a serious problem, especially inadvertent data leaks caused by user error or incorrect operations. Inadvertent data leaks are difficult to detect because they are caused by ordinary users who perform normal operations.

The novel data leakage method presented in this chapter employs algorithms that secure and detect private data in outbound flows while minimizing time and space consumption. It leverages byte stream encryption for data protection and a suffix array technique for local-side leakage detection of encrypted flows in real time. The computational time and memory footprint are optimized for real-time data security and data leakage detection. Despite providing data security as an additional feature, experiments demonstrate that the overall performance of the proposed method is comparable with that of the classical Knuth-Morris-Pratt and finite automaton string matching algorithms.

The proposed method requires users to identify private data in advance, which is undoubtedly a time-consuming task. Moreover, users may not be able to mark all their sensitive data because of a lack of understanding about their data. Additionally, the volume and types of private data are constantly increasing. Future research will attempt to use machine learning techniques to automate the task of identifying private data.

References

[1] S. Ananthi, M. Sendil and S. Karthik, Privacy preserving keyword search over encrypted cloud data, in *Advances in Computing and Communications*, A. Abraham, J. Lloret Mauri, J. Buford and S. Thampi (Eds.), Springer, Berlin Heidelberg, Germany, pp. 480–487, 2011.

[2] CALO Project, Enron Email Dataset, SRI International, Menlo Park, California (`www.cs.cmu.edu/~./enron`), 2015.

[3] F. Chen, D. Wang, R. Li, J. Chen, Z. Ming, A. Liu, H. Duan, C. Wang and J. Qin, Secure hashing based verifiable pattern matching, *IEEE Transactions on Information Forensics and Security*, vol. 13(11), pp. 2677–2690, 2018.

[4] S. Gog and E. Ohlebusch, Fast and lightweight LCP-array construction algorithms, *Proceedings of the Meeting on Algorithm Engineering and Experiments*, pp. 25–34, 2011.

[5] S. Jha, L. Kruger and V. Shmatikov, Towards practical privacy for genomic computation, *Proceedings of the IEEE Symposium on Security and Privacy*, pp. 216–230, 2008.

[6] C. Kalyan and K. Chandrasekaran, Information leak detection in financial email using mail pattern analysis under partial information, *Proceedings of the Seventh WSEAS International Conference on Applied Informatics and Communications*, vol. 7, pp. 104–109, 2007.

[7] T. Kasai, G. Lee, H. Arimura, S. Arikawa and K. Park, Linear-time longest-common-prefix computation in suffix arrays and its applications, *Proceedings of the Twelfth Annual Symposium on Combinatorial Pattern Matching*, pp. 181–192, 2001.

[8] H. Kim, H. Hong, H. Kim and S. Kang, Memory-efficient parallel string matching for intrusion detection systems, *IEEE Communications Letters*, vol. 13(12), pp. 1004–1006, 2009.

[9] K. Li, Z. Zhong and L. Ramaswamy, Privacy-aware collaborative spam filtering, *IEEE Transactions on Parallel and Distributed Systems*, vol. 20(5), pp. 725–739, 2009.

[10] P. Lin, Y. Lin, Y. Lai and T. Lee, Using string matching for deep packet inspection, *IEEE Computer*, vol. 41(4), pp. 23–28, 2008.

[11] F. Liu, X. Shu, D. Yao and A. Butt, Privacy-preserving scanning of big content for sensitive data exposure with MapReduce, *Proceedings of the Fifth ACM Conference on Data and Application Security and Privacy*, pp. 195–206, 2015.

[12] U. Manber and G. Myers, Suffix arrays: A new method for on-line string searches, *SIAM Journal on Computing*, vol. 22(5), pp. 935–948, 1993.

[13] Y. Shi, Z. Jiang and K. Zhang, Policy-based customized privacy preserving mechanism for SaaS applications, *Proceedings of the Eighth International Conference on Grid and Pervasive Computing and Collocated Workshops*, pp. 491–500, 2013.

[14] X. Shu, D. Yao and E. Bertino, Privacy-preserving detection of sensitive data exposure, *IEEE Transactions on Information Forensics and Security*, vol. 10(5), pp. 1092–1103, 2015.

[15] X. Shu, J. Zhang, D. Yao and W. Feng, Rapid and parallel content screening for detecting transformed data exposure, *Proceedings of the IEEE Conference on Computer Communications Workshops*, pp. 191–196, 2015.

[16] X. Shu, J. Zhang, D. Yao and W. Feng, Fast detection of transformed data leaks, *IEEE Transactions on Information Forensics and Security*, vol. 11(3), pp. 528–542, 2016.

[17] B. Wang, S. Yu, W. Lou and Y. Hou, Privacy-preserving multi-keyword fuzzy search over encrypted data in the cloud, *Proceedings of the IEEE Conference on Computer Communications*, pp. 2112–2120, 2014.

[18] D. Wang, X. Jia, C. Wang, K. Yang, S. Fu and M. Xu, Generalized pattern matching string search on encrypted data in cloud systems, *Proceedings of the IEEE Conference on Computer Communications*, pp. 2101–2109, 2015.

[19] H. Wang, K. Tseng and J. Pan, Deep packet inspection with bit-reduced DFA for cloud systems, *Proceedings of the International Conference on Computing, Measurement, Control and Sensor Networks*, pp. 221–224, 2012.

[20] J. Zhou, Z. Cao and X. Dong, PPOPM: More efficient privacy preserving outsourced pattern matching, *Proceedings of the Twenty-First European Symposium on Research in Computer Security*, part I, pp. 135–153, 2016.

Printed in the United States
by Baker & Taylor Publisher Services

Printed in the United States
by Baker & Taylor Publisher Services